Abductions in the
American Revolution

Abductions in the American Revolution

Attempts to Kidnap George Washington, Benedict Arnold and Other Military and Civilian Leaders

CHRISTIAN McBURNEY

McFarland & Company, Inc., Publishers
Jefferson, North Carolina

LIBRARY OF CONGRESS CATALOGUING-IN-PUBLICATION DATA

Names: McBurney, Christian M.
Title: Abductions in the American Revolution : attempts to kidnap George Washington, Benedict Arnold and other military and civilian leaders / Christian M. McBurney.
Description: Jefferson, North Carolina : McFarland & Company, Inc., Publishers, 2016. | Includes bibliographical references and index.
Identifiers: LCCN 2016011864 | ISBN 9781476663647 (softcover : alkaline paper) ∞
Subjects: LCSH: United States—History—Revolution, 1775–1783—Prisoners and prisons. | Political kidnapping—United States—History—18th century. | Washington, George, 1732–1799. | Arnold, Benedict, 1741–1801. | United States—History—Revolution, 1775–1783—Secret service. | United States—History—Revolution, 1775–1783—Campaigns.
Classification: LCC E281 .M43 2016 | DDC 973.3/85—dc23
LC record available at https://lccn.loc.gov/2016011864

BRITISH LIBRARY CATALOGUING DATA ARE AVAILABLE

ISBN (print) 978-1-4766-6364-7
ISBN (ebook) 978-1-4766-2429-7

© 2016 Christian McBurney. All rights reserved

No part of this book may be reproduced or transmitted in any form or by any means, electronic or mechanical, including photocopying or recording, or by any information storage and retrieval system, without permission in writing from the publisher.

On the cover: detail from engraving *Lieutenant Moody, James Moody freeing Robert Maxwell from the Sussex County Court House jail in New Jersey in 1780* by Robert Pollard, 1785 (reproduced by permission of the Society of the Cincinnati, Washington, D.C.)

Printed in the United States of America

McFarland & Company, Inc., Publishers
Box 611, Jefferson, North Carolina 28640
www.mcfarlandpub.com

Table of Contents

Acknowledgments — vii
Preface — 1

I. The Fighting Begins (April 1775 to June 1776) — 7
    From Lexington and Concord to Mount Vernon — 7
    Was There a Plot to Kidnap King George III? — 11
    The Tory Plot to Kidnap Washington in New York City — 14

II. The Fall of New York City and New Jersey (July 1776 to March 1778) — 20
    Signers of the Declaration of Independence — 20
    John Fell in the Provost — 27
    The Capture of Major General Charles Lee — 33
    Richard Witham Stockton, the Land Pilot — 43
    The Retaliatory Capture of Major General Richard Prescott — 48
    George Washington Supports Kidnapping Attempt Against British Headquarters in New York City — 57

III. The Fall of Philadelphia (September 1777 to April 1778) — 61
    Delaware's Chief Executive Is Abducted from His House — 61
    Congress Responds to Tory Kidnappings — 63
    John Paul Jones Strikes Fear in Great Britain — 69

IV. The War in the North (January 1778 to February 1781) — 72
    Multiple Attempts to Kidnap Governor William Livingston of New Jersey — 72
    Retaliatory Kidnappings: The Cases of Connecticut's General Silliman and Long Island's Judge Jones — 80
    Raid Across the Frozen Hudson River: The Attempt to Kidnap Washington at Morristown — 82
    Washington Attempts to Kidnap the Traitor Benedict Arnold in New York City — 96

Washington's Second Attempt Against the British Commander-in-Chief in New York City	103
The Abduction and Dramatic Escape of General Peleg Wadsworth in Maine	108
V. The War in the South (January 1781 to August 1781)	**112**
"This greatest of all traitors": Attempts to Kidnap Arnold in Virginia	112
Banastre Tarleton Almost Bags Thomas Jefferson	117
When the Kidnapper Becomes the Hunted: The Case of Benjamin Cleveland	124
The Execution of Isaac Hayne	127
VI. British Secret Service Operations in Upstate New York and Vermont (July 1781 to June 1782)	**134**
The British Attempt to Capture Major General Philip Schuyler at Albany	134
The Great Kidnap Caper of 1781 Falls Apart	142
Thomas Johnson: British Agent or Double Agent?	145
VII. Yorktown and Beyond (September 1781 to September 1783)	**149**
David Fanning Captures North Carolina's Governor	149
Murder in North Carolina and Georgia	153
Washington Plans to Abduct a Future King of Great Britain from New York City	157
Living with the Risk of Kidnappings	166
Appendix A: Letter from Colonel James Abeel Summarizing Information Regarding the Raid Intended to Capture Washington in February 1780	169
Appendix B: Colonel Matthias Ogden's Plans for Capturing Prince William Henry in New York City in March 1782	171
Chapter Notes	173
Bibliography	203
Index	213

Acknowledgments

I would like to thank all of the outstanding librarians and archivists who assisted me in researching this book, particularly those at the Daughters of the American Revolution Library, Society of the Cincinnati Library, Library of Congress, and David Library of the American Revolution. The Society of the Cincinnati Library was particularly helpful in making several images available from its fine collection, including the splendid image for the book cover.

I would like to extend my gratitude to a number of individuals who provided helpful information to me regarding particular kidnapping attempts: Eric Olsen, ranger and historian at Morristown National Historical Park (attempt on George Washington in February 1780 and attempts on William Livingston); Chris Hay of British Columbia, Canada (substantial material on Richard Witham Stockton, as well as on the Battle of Bennett's Island; Chris is the fifth great grandson of Richard Witham Stockton); Dennis Conrad at the Early History Branch of the Naval History & Heritage Command (Nathanael Greene); Bruce Venter, President of America's History, LLC (Alexander McDougall); and Kim Burdick, founder and Chair of the American Revolutionary Round Table of Delaware (John McKinly). Nicholas Henderson did another great job for me researching the Henry Clinton Papers at the William L. Clements Library at the University of Michigan.

I am very grateful to those who read drafts of my manuscript or portions of it. William Welsch, President and founder of the American Revolutionary War Roundtable of Richmond, read a late draft. Dennis Conrad at the Early History Branch of the Naval History & Heritage Command reviewed a short, early draft. Todd Braisted of the On-Line Institute for Advanced Loyalist Studies (at www.royalprovincial.com) provided comments on the chapter on the attempt on Washington at Morristown. I am very thankful to my neighbor, Bert Caudron, for his terrific proofreading of several drafts and galleys of the book. This is the fourth book of mine that he has proofread, and I am lucky for his thoughtful comments. Nonetheless, any mistakes that remain in this book are my own.

When using original sources I have, when possible, cited to publications. For the convenience of the modern reader, I have corrected spelling, grammar and punctuation in quoted material. Please check the bibliography for the full citations to published and unpublished sources referred to in the footnotes. I have used the terms "Patriot," "Whig" and "Rebel" (this last term was used by the British) interchangeably to identify supporters of the American independence movement, and I have used the terms "Loyalist" and "Tory" interchangeably to identify opponents of the American independence movement.

I again thank my (British) wife, Margaret, for her support of this book.

Preface

In my recent book, *Kidnapping the Enemy: The Special Operations to Capture Generals Charles Lee and Richard Prescott* (Westholme, 2014), I focused on two of the outstanding special operations of the Revolutionary War. The first was the stunning capture of Major General Charles Lee, second-in-command in the Continental army, by Lieutenant Colonel William Harcourt and a party of British dragoons in December 1776. The second was the bold kidnapping of Major General Richard Prescott, the commander of British troops in Newport, Rhode Island, by state troops led by Lieutenant Colonel William Barton. Barton seized Prescott so the Americans would have a British officer of the same rank to exchange for Lee.

This book summarizes those two special operations but also goes further in describing many other Revolutionary War special operations to kidnap high-ranking military officers and government officials.

The term "kidnap" is generally defined as to carry off or abduct by force, especially for use as a prisoner or to extract ransom.[1] This book will use the term to mean seizing an enemy leader after making plans to do so. Typically, the attempt was made at night at the enemy leader's sleeping quarters, but not always. In the Revolutionary War, the main reason for abducting a military or civilian leader was to remove the person from the war on the side of the enemy. A captive general cannot lead his troops in battle and a captive governor cannot govern his state. The imprisoned leader could also be used in exchange for a captive of the same rank held by the enemy.

The term "special operation" has a broader meaning today, and was not used during the Revolutionary War. Then, such operations frequently took the form of attempted kidnappings of enemy officers and civilian leaders by undertaking raids in enemy territory. Many were tried but they were difficult to pull off. First, raiders had to be confident that the target was where he was reported to be on the day of the attempt. Thus, excellent intelligence—and luck—was crucial. Second, if the target was somehow alerted to the danger, he could easily

2 Preface

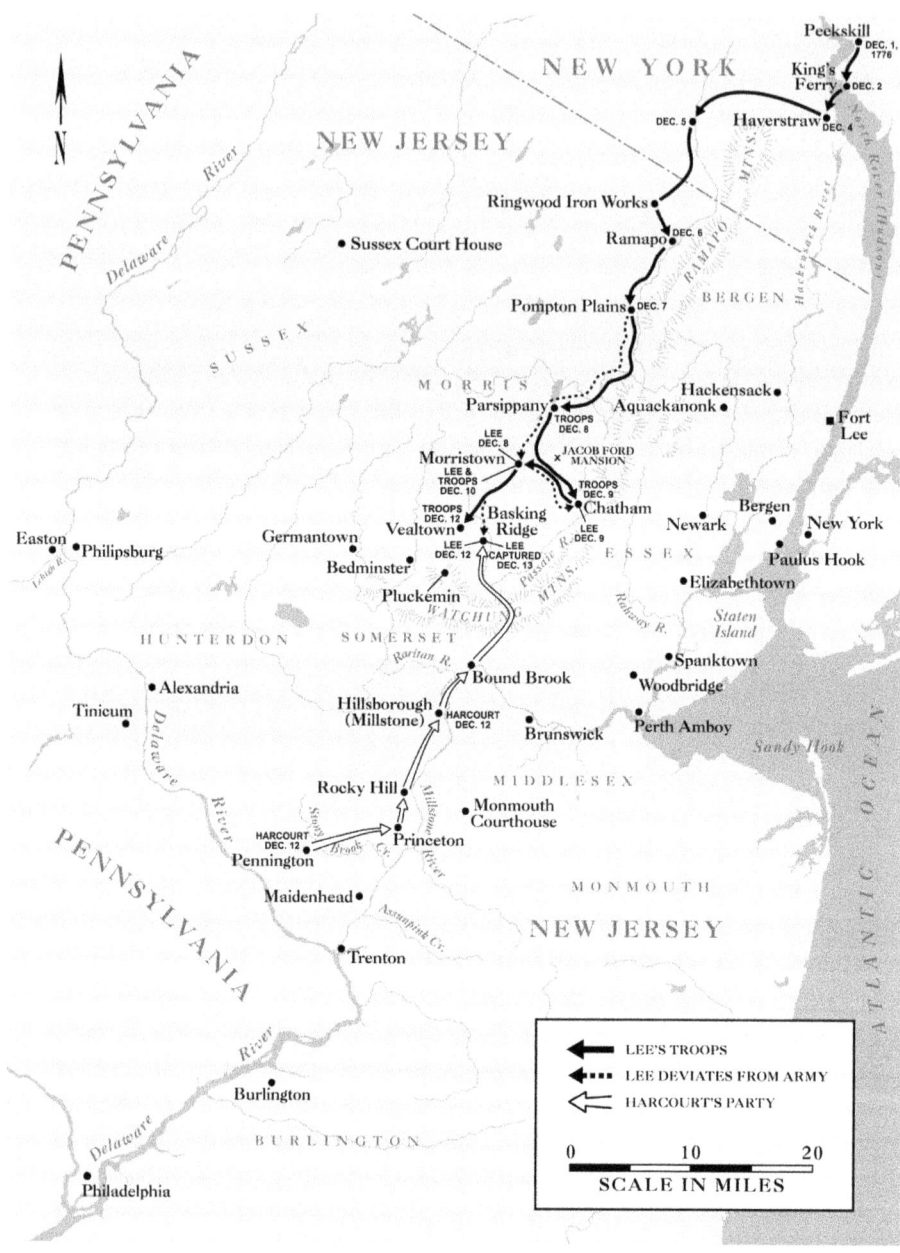

Map showing New Jersey and New York City, where many kidnapping attempts during the Revolutionary War occurred. The arrows show the routes of Charles Lee and William Harcourt, meeting at Basking Ridge (McBurney, *Kidnapping the Enemy*; reproduction by permission of Westholme Publishing).

evade capture by staying elsewhere, or by slipping away at the last minute. This could leave the raiders in a precarious spot, in enemy territory. Raiders therefore relied on secrecy and speed. Finally, even if the raiders captured their man they then had to bring him out safely, sometimes through an aroused countryside—no easy task.

The focus of this book will be on attempts to kidnap military leaders of the rank of lieutenant colonel and above, and civilian leaders who served as governors of colonies or states (as well as one young man who was third in line to the Royal Crown). Occasionally, attempts to kidnap lower-level military officers and government officials will be mentioned, but there is by no means any effort to mention or discuss all such kidnapping attempts. There were probably more than a thousand of them during the war.

The Roman historian Tacitus once wrote, "The principal office of history I take to be this: to prevent virtuous actions from being forgotten."[2] Was kidnapping an enemy leader from his sleeping quarters virtuous? Army officers on both sides thought so. In their minds, if it helped to win and shorten the war, it was justified.

None of the officers on either side intentionally planned to kidnap an enemy's leading figure for the purpose of killing him. Indeed, no major military or government leader mentioned in this book was assassinated. Capturing an opposing general or governor was itself a sufficient prize. The Revolutionary War occurred at a time when "gentlemen" typically treated each other with honor and respect. For example, a captured British army or Continental army officer, after signing a parole promising not to escape, was typically permitted during daylight hours to roam freely in the town or city where he was held. Thus, during the day, captive Continental army officers could be seen strolling the streets of British-held New York City and, in turn, captive British army officers walked around Whig-held Boston.

Washington himself applauded and supported kidnapping efforts undertaken by the American army. Referring to a bid to capture British commander-in-chief Henry Clinton at his headquarters in New York City in 1778, he wrote, "I think it one of the … most desirable and honorable things imaginable taking him prisoner…."[3] In addition to two attempts against Clinton, Washington supported plans to carry off from Manhattan Island the traitor Benedict Arnold, and even a future king of Great Britain. Continental navy hero John Paul Jones tried to kidnap a British earl in Great Britain itself, in order to exchange him for American sailors rotting in British prisons.

Viewing society organized as a hierarchy, with aristocrats and gentlemen at the top of the pyramid, the British tended to believe that great men led and controlled events and to ignore seeing the American independence movement as broad-based and popular. Thus, the British officer corps believed the problems of the rebellion could be resolved by removing influential Americans from circulation. Accordingly, British plots were hatched to kidnap the American commander-in-chief at his Morristown, New Jersey, headquarters; the influential Whig governor of New Jersey, William Livingston; the chief executive of the state of Delaware, John McKinly; and Major General Philip Schuyler at his Albany, New York, residence. The British almost nabbed Thomas Jefferson at his beloved Monticello (and, in turn, Jefferson plotted to kidnap Benedict Arnold).

Loyalists generally viewed the world the same as the British. New York City Loyalists thus plotted to kidnap (or, it was rumored, assassinate) General Washington in 1776. Tory raiders carried off numerous enemy leaders, including Richard Stockton, a signer of the Declaration of Independence, and Connecticut militia general Gold Selleck Silliman. Later in the war a kidnapping war broke out among Long Island, New York, Loyalists and Connecticut Patriots, and Loyalists and Patriots in the South. Most of these attempts against top leaders failed, but a few succeeded spectacularly or came within a whisker of succeeding. An example in the former category was David Fanning's raid that targeted and captured North Carolina's Whig governor, Thomas Burke.

Patriots controlled the institutions of state government in most parts of the former thirteen colonies. Thus, they did not always need to resort to kidnapping in order to remove a Tory leader. They could use a sheriff to issue a warrant to a local Tory, require the Tory to be tried and convicted in a county court, and have the Tory sentenced to, and thrown in, a local county jail. This was done, for example, by New Jersey authorities against the last royal governor of New Jersey and staunch Loyalist William Franklin, the son of Benjamin Franklin. By contrast, opposing militant Tories, such as James Moody, Abraham Van Buskirk, and David Fanning, typically needed to seek protection in a British-controlled area and use it as a base for attempting to kidnap Patriot leaders.

Those military and civilian leaders who were successfully kidnapped faced alarming risks to their reputations. Inevitably, suspicions would arise in certain quarters that the victim had allowed himself to be captured. More ominously, suspicions would often arise that during captivity the kidnapping victim had been turned to the enemy's side. This happened to a signer of the Declaration of Independence, Richard Stockton of New Jersey, as well as to Governor John McKinly of Delaware, Brigadier General Andrew Williamson of North Carolina, and Lieutenant Colonel Thomas Johnson of Vermont. In three of these cases, the suspicions were warranted. (The fourth, Johnson, was probably a double-agent supporting the Whig cause.) Furthermore, one other kidnapping victim, Governor Thomas Burke of North Carolina, arguably violated his parole agreement, which effectively ended his promising political career.

Kidnapped victims could become so demoralized that they would retire from service. This happened with Massachusetts militia generals Peleg Wadsworth and Charles Cushing, each of whom was kidnapped in separate incidents in Maine.

The kidnapper also undertook great risks, for if he was caught, he could be hanged. Several kidnappers were, in fact, caught and hanged during the war, including Colonel Isaac Hayne, Captain William Riddle and William Hammet.

Whig leaders such as General George Washington and New Jersey Governor William Livingston typically went to considerable lengths and sacrifice to avoid putting themselves in a position where they were vulnerable to being kidnapped. In taking such precautions, they performed a substantial service to the Patriot cause. Several military and civilian leaders who were captured in special operations, including Major Generals Charles Lee and Richard Prescott, performed a disservice to their cause by not keeping a proper guard to protect them from kidnapping attempts.

For military and civilian leaders on both sides, the stress and strains of living with the risk of being kidnapped was yet another sacrifice these men undertook as part of their struggle to win the cause for which they fought.

In the recent wars in Iraq and Afghanistan, American forces learned to excel at special operations to extract enemy leaders from their safe havens. These special operations expanded to kidnapping even ordinary enemy soldiers on an unprecedented, even daily basis, to successful effect. From the kidnapping attempts described in this book, it can be seen that the tactic of attempting to kidnap enemy military and civilian leaders has deep antecedents that go back to the American Revolutionary War.

I

The Fighting Begins (April 1775 to June 1776)

From Lexington and Concord to Mount Vernon

In Massachusetts, leading Whig revolutionaries became alarmed by the prospect of being captured and imprisoned by the British army even before the first shots were fired at Lexington and Concord on that fateful day of April 19, 1775. When alerted by the innkeeper to marching British regulars approaching the front of the Black Horse Tavern in Menotomy (present-day Arlington), three members of the Massachusetts Committee of Safety—Jeremiah Lee, Azor Orne and Elbridge Gerry—fearing arrest, fled out the back door. They hid outside in the damp cold in their nightshirts, in the stubble of a fallow cornfield, until the long line of soldiers moved on toward Lexington. In Lexington, after being warned by Paul Revere that the British column wanted to seize them, John Hancock and Samuel Adams escaped with only minutes to spare ahead of the arriving Redcoats.[1] When the two Whig leaders arrived in Woburn, and were preparing to enjoy a meal of salmon, a Lexington man burst into the house where they were staying, shouting wildly, "The Regulars are coming!" Hancock and Adams ran into the Woburn woods and hid.[2]

In fact, Governor-General Thomas Gage never issued any written orders to arrest Hancock, Adams, or any other Whig leaders. While he was instructed to do so by his superiors in London, and he had been informed by a Loyalist spy that Hancock and Adams were then staying at Lexington, Gage did not want to engage in such provocative conduct. Rather, he chose the more conservative goal of seizing gunpowder and other military supplies at Concord.[3] Tragically, Jeremiah Lee shortly thereafter caught a bad cold, probably from being exposed for more than an hour to the cold weather wearing only his nightshirt, and died the next month.[4] If he had stayed in the Black Horse Tavern, he probably would have avoided becoming deathly ill.

After the Battle of Lexington and Concord, and the Battle of Bunker Hill in June of 1775, New England militiamen and "alarm" men set siege to Boston. They were not strong enough to push past British defenses surrounding the port city, but they were numerous enough to prevent the British in Boston from attacking them. A stalemate ensued. Newly appointed by the Continental Congress to serve as commander-in-chief of the Continental army, George Washington arrived outside Boston shortly after the fierce fighting at Bunker Hill had ended. Washington was accompanied by his third-in-command (soon to be second-in-command), a transplanted Englishman with republican beliefs, Major General Charles Lee. While General Thomas Gage sat trapped in Boston, the September 5, 1775, edition of the Newburyport's *Essex Journal* contained the following jest: "Ah! Tommy, see that wakeful guards you keep, lest you yourself be kidnapped while they sleep!"

In August 1775, George Washington was informed of rumors by Alexandria, Virginia, men that his wife, Martha, might be a kidnapping target for John Murray, fourth Earl of Dunmore, the last royal governor of Virginia. At the time, Dunmore commanded a flotilla of British warships operating off Norfolk, within striking distance of Washington's beloved Mount Vernon home.[5] Dunmore's vessels were small enough to slip north up the Potomac River on just such a mission. Prior to the war, Washington had often socialized with Dunmore in Williamsburg, and had successfully lobbied him to issue land grants. Shocked, Washington wrote to his cousin, Lund Washington, who looked after his business affairs at Mount Vernon. "I can hardly think that Lord Dunmore can act so low and unmanly a part as to think of seizing Mrs. Washington by way of revenge upon me," he remarked. Nevertheless, the worried husband requested that Lund make available a "place of safety" for "her and my papers."[6] Although no kidnapping attempt was actually ever made (and there is no firm evidence one was ever contemplated), it was clear to the commander-in-chief that kidnapping was a weapon that could be used not only against his army but even against his family.

Washington was not the only Virginia Whig leader worried about his wife falling into the clutches of Lord Dunmore. A concerned Thomas Jefferson, while a delegate to the Continental Congress in Philadelphia, warned his wife, Martha, then travelling in Virginia with their daughter Patsy, "to keep yourselves at a distance from the alarms of Lord Dunmore."[7]

News of Dunmore's purported plans swept through Boston, and soon a new play was advertised, in which "Lord Kidnapper" had an important role.[8] Reading between the lines, it seems clear that Lord Kidnapper was intended to be Lord Dunmore.

Once news of the Battles of Lexington and Concord and Bunker Hill reached the eleven royal governors of the thirteen colonies (Connecticut and Rhode Island did not have them), they knew that they could be the targets of kidnapping attempts. Most eventually fled to the safety of a British warship.

In North Carolina, even before the Battle of Lexington and Concord, the colony's royal governor, Josiah Martin, feared for his safety. At a session of the General Assembly held at New Bern that opened on April 4, 1775, the delegates refused obedience to Martin and the King, and even expelled a delegate for speaking in favor of royal authority. Not feeling safe and narrowly avoiding arrest, Martin rode with his wife to Wilmington, where British warships were stationed off shore.[9] Martin later travelled "incognito" with his family to Fort Johnston on the Cape Fear River, arriving in early June.[10] Here, after sending his family to the safety of Long Island, New York, Martin made some efforts to gather military supplies and Loyalist support. On July 15, 1775, Robert Howe led 500 militiamen from Brunswick Town on a raid with the intent of burning nearby Fort Johnston, and he may also have had in mind seizing Martin. But by then Martin was safe on board another nearby British warship and had ordered the abandonment of the dilapidated Fort Johnston.[11]

In Georgia, as Whigs began to consolidate their power following the Battle of Bunker Hill, royal governor James Wright, despite his fifteen years as a well-liked governor, wrote, "I begin to think a King's governor has little or no business here." Already dominating the Privy Council, in July Patriots seized control of the provincial militia and a few months later, the courts. Patriots resorted to violence as well, particularly if a suspected Tory failed to subscribe to an oath supporting the Continental Congress. In August in the town of Augusta, Thomas Brown refused to subscribe to the test oath, with the result that a Patriot fractured his skull with the butt of a musket and other Patriots tortured him "with unparalleled barbarity" by tying him to a tree and lighting a fire under his feet.[12]

Governor Wright tried to retain royal control by relying on the arrival of British warships. On the night of January 18, 1776, he summoned Whig leaders Joseph Clay and Dr. Noble Wimberly Jones to his home—on the corner of modern-day Telfair Square in Savannah—to discuss the Royal Navy ships off the coast near Tybee Island. He informed them that the commander of the small squadron of five British warships, led by the 28-gun H.M.S. *Syren*, had been instructed to treat those found to be in arms "as in a state of rebellion" and, if possible, "destroy their towns and property." But the governor promised that if the ships were allowed safe anchor and permitted to provision themselves at market prices, he would "endeavor to settle" affairs with the British officers in order "to prevent their doing any injury to this town."[13]

After leaving the governor, Clay and Jones rushed to Tondee's Tavern, just a few blocks away at the northwest corner of Broughton and Whitaker streets, and informed the Georgia Council of Safety, which was dominated by Patriots. Its members decided the time had come to order the arrest of Governor Wright, as well as three Provincial Council members, on the ground that they were a dangerous threat to the liberty of the people.[14]

Major Joseph Habersham, the twenty-four-year-old son of the governor's recently deceased best friend, was given the task of following the Privy Council's order to apprehend Governor Wright. Habersham and a small party accompanying him made their way to the Wright's mansion, about a half-mile away, and then stormed into the dining room of the governor's house, where Wright was meeting with a host of state officials. Placing his arm on Governor Wright's shoulder, as his guests scattered in all directions, Habersham declared, "Sir James, you are my prisoner."[15]

A few hours later, the Council of Safety allowed Wright to be confined to his mansion for a few days before granting him parole upon the conditions that he remain in his home and not correspond "with any of the officers or others on board the ships of war now at Tybee [Island], without the permission of this Board." But fearing worse treatment, the harassed deposed governor decided to break his parole and escape from his home. In the early morning of February 12, Wright snuck out of the back door of his house, and with his family and several members of his Privy Council, was rowed to the safety of the British armed vessel *Scarborough*.[16] Upon Wright's arrival at about 9 a.m., Captain Andrew Barkley of the *Scarborough* ordered his gunners to fire a fifteen-gun salute, which was answered by a fifteen-gun salute from the nearby H.M.S. *Raven*, all of which must have startled

King George III purportedly was the target of a kidnapping attempt. From a painting by Benjamin West, ca. 1778 (National Archives).

Savannah's residents.[17] Referring to the breaking of his parole, Henry Laurens of South Carolina wrote the Georgia Provincial Congress, "We blush for Governor Wright's perfidy."[18]

William Franklin was the only son of Whig leader Benjamin Franklin, but he was also the last royal governor of New Jersey and an inveterate Tory. He was finally ordered to be arrested by the New Jersey Provincial Congress on June 15, 1776. Nine days later, with the approval of the Continental Congress, Franklin was made a prisoner and sent to several Connecticut towns. After violating his parole, he spent some time closely confined in manacles. He was not finally freed until October of 1778, when he was exchanged for Governor John McKinly of Delaware.[19]

None of these kidnapping efforts involved careful planned operations in enemy territory, with the imprimatur of the commander-in-chief or other high-ranking general. That would come later in the war.

Was There a Plot to Kidnap King George III?

Londoners read about these captures and kidnappings in the many newspapers that were published in their city, but soon perused articles containing charges of a spectacular plot to kidnap their king, George III. On October 23, 1775, Stephen Sayre, an American long resident in London, was interrupted at breakfast at his fashionable house in Oxford Street, placed under arrest on a charge of high treason, and locked up in the Tower of London.

Sayre's arrest was based on evidence given by Frank Richardson, a Pennsylvanian who was a lieutenant in the First Regiment of Foot Guards in London. Richardson, an acquaintance of Sayre's, happened to run into Sayre a few days earlier at the Pennsylvania Coffee House, a favorite hangout of Americans in London. Richardson claimed that Sayre had taken him into a private room where he proposed to Richardson that he should assist in a plan to kidnap George III as he made his way in his coach to the opening of Parliament on October 26 and incarcerate him in the Tower. A London mob would distract his guards and make the capture of the king possible. Sayre's plan was not to kill the royal personage, but force him to return to his native German dominions in Hanover. Next, John Wilkes, the current Lord Mayor of London and a known opponent of the Crown, would gather politicians to address the future of monarchy in Britain and to resolve the conflict with America. Richardson further alleged that Sayre had informed him that some £1,500 had already been distributed to soldiers who policed the city, in order to buy their support. Now, according to Richardson, Sayre wanted his help to prevent his Guards regiment from crushing the plot and to bribe the Tower garrison to cooperate. What gave the lieutenant even more reason to believe that a plot existed was that in subsequently discussing the matter with a fellow officer of the Guards, Captain Nicholas Nugent, the latter revealed that he too had also been approached by someone like Sayre about a similar plot.[20]

Stephen Sayre, a merchant from New York, was a close confidante of John Wilkes, who was renown on both sides of the Atlantic for promoting the cause of liberty and opposing despotism prior to the American Revolution. When Madame de Pompadour, the mistress of King Louis XV of France, once asked Wilkes how far freedom of the press extended in England, he was said to have replied, "I do not know. I am trying to find out." In the early 1760s, in his *North Briton* periodical, Wilkes made scandalous allegations accusing King George III's mother of having an affair with then Prime Minister Earl of Bute, claiming that the Archbishop of Canterbury committed buggery, and accusing the Bishop of Gloucester's wife of being a professional prostitute. An outraged George III called him "that devil Wilkes." When Wilkes in issue number 45 of *The North Briton* labeled Cabinet ministers "tools of despotism and corruption" and implied that the king's speech to Parliament contained false information, Crown authorities imprisoned Wilkes and prosecuted him, but unsuccessfully. Then came a parade of Wilkes being elected to the House of Commons and being prevented from taking his seat, which only increased his popularity among Whigs both in American and England.[21]

For the Earl of Rochford, the government official who had ordered Sayre's arrest and confinement, the alleged plot came at a sensitive time. Two months prior to the arrest, George III had issued a Proclamation of Rebellion, which declared that not only were the American colonies in rebellion, but also warned that the "rebellion hath been much promoted and encouraged by the traitorous correspondence, counsels and comfort of diverse wicked and desperate persons within this realm," meaning Great Britain. When he referred to "aiding and abetting," the king probably had most in mind John Wilkes and his circle. Not only had Wilkes supported the American Revolution, comparing it to England's Glorious Revolution of 1688, he had included among his supporters in London Whig elites from America, such as William and Arthur Lee of Virginia and Sayre himself. At the time, the king had announced the sending of troops to America, and there was some concern that a London mob could rise in protest.[22]

Wilkes often had the support of London mobs, which could sometimes turn violent in a flash. When Parliament passed legislation permitting the naturalization of Jews in 1753, howling mobs took to the streets until the law was repealed shortly thereafter. In the 1760s, the height of Wilkes's power, crowds flocked onto the streets, marched, cheered, badgered the support of bystanders, and intimidated opponents. Fear of popery sparked the infamous Gordon Riots in 1780, leaving London at the mercy of "King Mob" for more than a week. Some £100,000 of damage was inflicted by mobs, until the army was brought to restore order, at the cost of some 290 lives. So the British cabinet understandably worried about mobs rising to oppose a potential war against fellow English-speaking Americans, which meant higher taxes, press gangs for Royal Navy ships, and potentially involuntary drafts into the army.

Three days after Sayre's arrest, the opening of Parliament came and went without incident, with King George III under a heavier guard than usual. Other than Richardson's testimony, no further direct evidence of the plot was uncovered. Captain Nugent was brought in for questioning, but he refused to identify who had contacted him and insisted that the meeting had nothing to do with what Richardson had reported. Taken before Lord Chief Justice William de Grey, Sayre admitted meeting Richardson at the Pennsylvania Coffee House but denied that any "treasonable" conversation had taken place. Hamstrung by weak laws permitting the jailing of those accused of treason, just six days after Sayre was arrested, de Grey ordered his release and for the charges against him to be dropped. Sayre was a free man.[23]

Sayre's arrest and release soon became a *cause célèbre* in Whig circles both in America and Britain. After all, the plot seemed too absurd to be believed. "We have been for a week past in perpetual laughter about the late dreadful plot," crowed one of Wilkes's supporters. London newspapers turned their attention to the story, with one claiming that Sayre's arrest was "the subject of ridicule in every coffee house in town." The newspapers also accused the government of heavy-handed behavior, with one exclaiming that Sayre's arrest was an example of "French law" and showing that the present cabinet was "capable of violent, arbitrary, and unjust executions of power, as if the Tower of London were actually the Bastille." In America, the *New England Chronicle* portrayed Sayre as a virtuous Roman hero.[24]

What really happened? Even to this day, it is not clear. While Lieutenant Richardson's credibility was somewhat suspect based on his reputation for engaging in scandalous affairs with married women, it seems unlikely that he invented the story of the kidnapping plot from whole cloth. He had no apparent reason for wanting Sayre charged with, and executed for, treason. In his testimony before Chief Justice William de Grey, Sayre explained that "it was all a jest in the first place, that he had a mind to try Richardson in the next place, that it was idle conversation and he meant nothing in the world by it."[25] Thus, Sayre in effect admitted that he had told Richardson about a plot to kidnap King George III. On the other hand, no evidence has surfaced indicating that a conspiracy to kidnap the king existed. If a plot did exist, one would expect that eventually one or more persons with knowledge of it, perhaps the many soldiers who were supposedly bribed, would have revealed details of its existence.

One British historian, James Lander, has convincingly argued that the Sayre affair was a deliberate hoax perpetrated by John Wilkes and his cronies designed to provoke the government into heavy-handed action and test its recent Proclamation of Rebellion. In the weeks following the proclamation, Wilkes had practically dared the government to arrest his supporters, so that the proclamation could be challenged in court as a violation of constitutional rights. According to Lander:

> The trick, of course, was to limit the evidence, providing enough to encourage some zealous official to act upon the Proclamation by arresting someone "found carrying on correspondence with, or in any manner or degree aiding or abetting the persons now in open arms and rebellion," but providing too little evidence for a genuine prosecution under the 1696 Treason Trials Act, which required two sworn witnesses to the same overt act or to separate overt acts of the same treason. To perform this trick, Wilkes resorted to "hoax" evidence, which at first glance appeared corroborative but, upon investigation, proved useless for a formal prosecution.[26]

Julie Flavell, author of *When London was Capital of America*, called Lander's argument "persuasive" and pointed out that during the Napoleonic Wars, "another former Wilkes supporter, the Reverend John Horne Tooke ... deliberately tricked authorities into arresting him for treason by leaving a false trail of evidence. Tooke, like Sayre, was locked in the Tower. Ultimately, the government looked both foolish and heavy-handed when the evidence collapsed."[27]

Playing a dangerous game, Stephen Sayre was eventually forced to leave London. He sued Lord Rochford for false arrest and won, but was awarded a relatively small sum which, on a legal technicality, he never received. With his reputation under a cloud, a bank he had operated failed and in 1777 he was imprisoned briefly for debt. He left for Paris to serve as secretary to Arthur Lee, then a diplomat for the Continental Congress, but the two men had a bitter quarrel and the erratic Lee fired him. Traipsing around the capitals of Europe, even though he was short of cash, Sayre in 1783 finally returned to New York, after being absent for seventeen years. In his mid-fifties, he married a wealthy Jamaican heiress and was able to live comfortably for the remainder of his days.[28]

The Tory Plot to Kidnap Washington in New York City

Naturally, Loyalists in America would have most liked to have kidnapped the commander-in-chief of the Continental army, George Washington. It

General George Washington, commander-in-chief of the Continental army. From a painting by Cogniet, 1836 (Library of Congress).

appears that there were at least two nascent Loyalist plans to do so, but nothing serious was ever attempted.

New York City would become in the war the center for plotting kidnappings, and the military leaders who occupied it would be the targets of abduction plots. These efforts started in October 1775, when Major General Charles Lee urged a New York Whig leader to try to seize and make a hostage the deposed governor of New York and committed Loyalist, William Tryon. Lee later recommended that the captain of the British warship then stationed in New York Harbor and threatening to bombard the city be warned that if he fired his ship's cannon, it would result in a "funeral pyre" for Governor Tryon.[29] Lee's plan was not adopted, but the Americans continued to hold New York City for the rest of 1775 and the first part of 1776.

Even General Washington could see that former Governor Tryon was up to something. Aboard the 74-gun warship HMS *Duchess-of-Gordon* anchored in New York Harbor, Tryon was active in meeting with Loyalists arriving and departing in small boats. What Tryon was scheming, Washington did not know. The commander-in-chief complained in a letter to the President of the Continental Congress, John Hancock, on June 10, "The encouragements given by Governor Tryon to the disaffected, which are circulated no one can tell how; the movements of this kind of people, which are more easy to perceive than to describe."[30]

During the spring and summer of 1776, Tryon and David Mathews, appointed by Tryon as New York City's mayor in February 1776, conspired to kidnap Washington. After the war, Mathews included in his claim for compensation as a Loyalist before the Royal Commission in London the following: "He had formed a plan for the taking of Mr. Washington and his guard prisoners, but which was not effected by an unfortunate discovery that was made."[31]

Mathews was probably referring to Thomas Hickey and Michael Lynch, two former members of Washington's Life Guard. In prison for passing counterfeit money, they had bragged to their cellmate, Isaac Ketchum, about a plan for Continental soldiers to desert and then seize and secure the bridge at Kingsbridge at the northern tip of Manhattan Island for the British. In an effort to save his own skin, Ketchum reported the information to Whig authorities. Further investigation revealed thirteen more supposed conspirators, including Mayor Mathews. On June 21, the local Committee of Safety requested Washington to arrest Mayor Mathews and the general agreed. General Nathanael Greene was then ordered to take the mayor into custody at exactly 1:00 a.m. the following morning, a mission that was accomplished by a detachment of Continental soldiers "who surrounded his house and seized his person precisely" at the designated time.[32] Washington also sent Captain Caleb Gibbs and a detachment of trusted members of his Life Guard to arrest the other conspirators.[33]

Under interrogation by the Committee of Safety, Mathews admitted that he had met with Tryon aboard the *Duchess-of-Gordon* anchored in New York Harbor, having received permission from General Israel Putnam to meet with the former governor at his floating headquarters. Quite unexpectedly, according to Mathews, Tryon had sought his assistance in paying local gunsmith Gilbert Forbes for bringing guns to the ship. When Forbes was then brought in for interrogation, the gunsmith conceded he had been assisting Tryon, explaining that he had aided in gathering intelligence in preparation for the arrival of the British army at New York City.[34] Wisely, Mathews did not mention anything about a plot to kidnap Washington.

The next day, June 23, the Committee of Safety interrogated "William Cooper, soldier," and William Savage, who stated that they knew a man named John Clayford who was intimate with a New Jersey woman named Mary Gibbons, also called Judith. The two men told of conversations in which they participated that dealt with the party abducting General Washington and how Judith had agreed to cooperate with them. But after discussing the plot more, they deemed it was too risky. On this the Committee decided to recess for three days to allow them to confer with Washington, stating, "It would be but justice to the General, as he is some way affected by the last witnesses to apprize him of it, and consult with him."[35] About this time, it was reported, "Yesterday, the General's housekeeper was taken up; it is said she is concerned."[36] Was this the mysterious Mary Gibbons, alias Judith, or someone else? Was her discovery what Mathews referred to as ruining his plan to abduct Washington?

Thomas Hickey was a privileged member of Washington's Life Guard, which Washington had established in March of 1776 at Cambridge, Massachusetts. The unit's purpose was to provide personal security for Washington, as well as handle and protect the baggage of his headquarters and the money and official papers of the Continental army. Their unique uniforms consisted of "a blue coat with white facings; white waistcoat and breeches; black stock and black half-gaiters, and a round hat, with blue and white feathers." In addition, a special flag was created, made of white silk and bearing an image of a guardsman holding a horse while receiving "a flag from Genius of Liberty, who is personified as a woman leaning upon the Union shield" and with the Life Guard's motto "Conquer or Die" emblazoned across the top.[37]

Thomas Hickey, still in jail, was an Irish immigrant who had deserted from the British army a few years previously. He had been living in Wethersfield, Connecticut, and had served in the elite Knowlton's Rangers outfit. It was said that he was well received by Washington, gaining his confidence and was considered "a favorite."[38]

On June 26, Continental officers were lenient with the others charged, who were either released or served short jail terms, but they made an example of Hickey. The deserter was charged with "sedition and mutiny, and also of holding a treacherous correspondence with the enemy."[39] Four witnesses established to the satisfaction of the court-martial board that Hickey had recruited members of Washington's Life Guard to aid the British and had received money to the end. In testifying in his defense, Hickey claimed that he had "engaged in the scheme at first for the sake of cheating the Tories, and getting some money from them" and that he had allowed his name to be sent to Tryon so that "if the enemy should arrive and defeat the Army here, and he should be taken prisoner, he might be safe."[40] Hickey's argument made no impression and he was in short order found guilty and sentenced "to suffer *death*."[41]

Neither the evidence disclosed in the court-martial nor Ketchum's testimony specifically mentioned kidnapping or otherwise harming Washington. Nonetheless, word quickly spread that the commander-in-chief had been targeted for assassination. Solomon Drowne, a Rhode Island surgeon working for Washington's main army, revealed as much in a June 24 letter. "A most infernal plot has lately been discovered here, which, had it been put into execution, would have made America tremble, and been as fatal a stroke to us, this Country, as Gun Powder Treason would to England, had it succeeded," he wrote. "The hellish conspirators were a number of Tories (the Mayor of the City among them) and three of General Washington's Life Guards. The plan was to kill Generals Washington and Putnam, and as many other commanding officers as possible."[42]

News of the plot against Washington provoked city mobs to tar and feather some Tories. Others were subjected to the torture of "riding the rail," a cruel punishment whereby a man was forced atop a sharp fence rail held on the shoulders of two men and paraded in the streets.[43]

Washington had to approve or reject Hickey's conviction and death sentence. Perhaps concerned that rumors of a plot against him might be seen as coloring his objectivity, the commanding general on June 27 submitted the matter to a council of officers consisting of himself and Generals William Heath, Joseph Spencer, Nathanael Greene, Lord Stirling, and Thomas Mifflin, and Colonel Charles Scott. The council unanimously advised to approve the sentence and order it the next day. Washington then issued the order approving the sentence for Hickey to "be hanged tomorrow at eleven o'clock."[44]

On June 28 Thomas Hickey was brought to his place of execution, according to a New York newspaper, "near the Bowery Lane, in the presence of near 20,000 spectators," including four brigades of the Continental army.[45] According to an eyewitness, after wiping tears from his eyes, Hickey gave an ominous warning to General Nathanael Greene, that "unless General Greene was very cautious, the design would *as yet* be executed on him."[46] After Hickey was hanged,

Lieutenant Joseph Hodgkins of the 12th Continental Regiment wrote, "I wish twenty more were served the same."[47] Hickey was the first American soldier ever executed for treasonous conduct.[48]

It appears William Eustis, a surgeon in the American army in New York City, and Solomon Drowne, the Rhode Island physician, must have heard the same rumor or shared it with each other. Eustis wrote of "the discovery of the greatest and vilest attempt ever made against our country. I mean the *plot*, the infernal *plot* which has been contrived by our worst enemies, and which was on the verge of execution." Eustis continued, "The mayor of New York with a number of villains who were possessed of fortunes, and who formerly ranked with gentlemen, had impiously dared an undertaking … to have murdered (with trembling I say it) the best man on earth: General Washington was to have been the first of their unheard of SACRIFICE. Our magazines which, as you know, are not capacious, were to have been blown up; every general officer and every other who was active in serving his country in the field was to have been assassinated; our cannon were to be spiked up." Eustis attended Thomas Hickey's hanging: "We are hanging them as fast as we can. I have just now returned from the execution from one of the General's Guard. He was the first to have been tried. Yesterday at 11 o'clock he received his sentence and today at 11 o'clock he was hung in the presence of the whole army."[49]

While there was a Loyalist conspiracy in New York City backed by Tryon and Mathews, there is no evidence supporting the claim that assassination was intended. Based on Mathews's post-war statement, it appears that a plan to kidnap Washington was contemplated, but it also appears that it had not gone much beyond the state of considering it.

In a June 28 letter, Washington mentioned Hickey's impending hanging and that the conspiracy had "been traced up to Governor Tryon and the Mayor," but he did not discuss that the plotting involved either kidnapping or assassinating him.[50] In his biography of the commanding general, Ron Chernow wrote of this letter that "Washington didn't want to exaggerate the plot, which might have been demoralizing."[51]

In his orders issued to his troops following Hickey's execution, oddly, Washington drew the lesson that his soldiers should "avoid lewd women, who, by the dying confession of this poor criminal, first led him into practices which ended in an untimely and ignominious death."[52] This could be an obtuse reference by Washington that a woman was involved in plotting against him.

II

The Fall of New York City and New Jersey (July 1776 to March 1778)

Signers of the Declaration of Independence

After occupying New York City, the British army rolled through New Jersey and seized Long Island, New York, in late 1776. Loyalists, able to call on nearby British soldiers, now had the chance to even scores. It was not a good place and time for signers of the Declaration of Independence.

It is difficult to imagine now, but when delegates to the Continental Congress strode up to affix their names on the Declaration, it was with some trepidation. While waiting to sign, Benjamin Harrison, a Virginia planter and a large man, told the diminutive delegate from Massachusetts, Elbridge Gerry, "I will have a great advantage over you, Mr. Gerry, when we are all hung for what we are now doing. From the size and weight of my body I shall die in a few minutes, but from the lightness of your body you will dance in the air an hour or two before you are dead."[1] Many years later, Pennsylvania's Dr. Benjamin Rush remembered the solemnness of the proceedings in a letter he wrote to John Adams of Massachusetts: "Do you recollect the pensive and awful silence which pervaded the house when we were called up, one after another, to the table of the president of Congress to subscribe what was believed by many at the time to be our own death warrants?"[2]

Richard Stockton of New Jersey was the only signer taken prisoner specifically because of his status as a signatory to the Declaration. The son of a wealthy landowner, he was born in 1730 at Morven, the family estate and his lifelong home, at Princeton, New Jersey. He graduated from the College of New Jersey, later named Princeton University, and then practiced law, becoming one of New Jersey's best attorneys. He was later appointed to the Royal Council of

New Jersey and as a justice to the New Jersey Supreme Court. With Benjamin Rush of Philadelphia, who later would marry Stockton's daughter Julia, Stockton sailed to Scotland in 1766 and the two men successfully recruited the Reverend John Witherspoon to become the first president of the college. Witherspoon would become a strong Whig and play an important role in the lives of many Patriots, including James Madison and Aaron Burr.

As the Revolutionary movement grew, Stockton associated with the Whig cause, although he was a moderate and dreaded the prospect of war. After he was elected to the Continental Congress on June 22, 1776, and had his credentials presented to Congress six days later, he voted for independence and signed the Declaration. Reverend Witherspoon also signed the Declaration, which led to celebrations in Princeton centered at the college's main building. "Nassau Hall," the *Philadelphia Evening Post* reported, "was grandly illuminated, and independency proclaimed under a triple volley of musketry."[3] When Stockton lost his bid for the governorship of New Jersey to William Livingston in a close and bitter vote by the state's legislature, he remained in Congress.

In late September of 1776, Stockton and fellow delegate George Clymer left Philadelphia to inspect American troops at Fort Ticonderoga and other parts of the Northern Department in upper New York State. After filing helpful reports and recommendations with Congress on November 27,[4] Stockton hurried home, worried about the ongoing British invasion of New Jersey. He removed his family from his beloved Morven to Federal Hall, the country estate of John Covenhoven at Hopewell in Monmouth County. As this county was known for harboring some strong Tories, Stockton would have done better to flee across the Delaware River to Pennsylvania, as did many of his neighbors.

On December 2, Stockton submitted a claim to Congress for his travel expenses.[5] Perhaps that very night, militant Loyalists who had discovered he was staying at Hopewell, seized him as well as Covenhoven. It appears that Stockton's captors were not simply local Tory civilians, as most histories of the event suggest, but instead were from the New Jersey Volunteers, a Loyalist brigade in the British army.[6] The man who informed the soldiers of the location of Stockton was a local, Cyrenus Van Mater. According to one letter writer from Philadelphia on December 30, Stockton's captors "treated him with the greatest barbarity, driving him, on foot, through rivers and creeks, with the greatest precipitation, to Amboy, where we hear he lies dangerously ill."[7] Even prominent Loyalist William Smith recorded in his journal that Stockton's captors had "apprehended and forced [him] away naked to Amboy, in a most distressed condition."[8]

The New Jersey Volunteer captors turned Stockton over to the British, who reportedly imprisoned him under harsh conditions at Perth Amboy, New Jersey. Transferred to New York City, he was imprisoned in the infamous Provost Jail like a common criminal. He reportedly was put in irons, kept without food for twenty-four hours, and then given only the coarsest fare.[9] Dr. Benjamin Rush, a fellow signer, wrote to Richard Henry Lee on December 30, "I have heard from good authority that my much honored father-in-law, who is now a prisoner with General Howe, suffers many indignities and hardships from the enemy, from which not only his rank, but his being a man, ought to exempt him."[10]

On November 30, General Howe had issued a proclamation offering a "full pardon" to anyone who, within sixty days, swore an oath of loyalty to the king. Within a month of his captivity, Stockton apparently signed a declaration of allegiance to the king, giving his word of honor that he would not oppose the Crown. It is not known if Stockton cracked under the pressure of imprisonment or honestly believed that the country should return to Crown rule.

The following document, discovered only recently by Loyalist historian Todd Braisted, indicates the extent to which Stockton had been pardoned by the two British commanders, Lord Richard Howe and General William Howe:

> Lord and General Howe having granted a full pardon to Richard Stockton, Esq., by which he is entitled to all his property, and he having informed that his horse, bridle and saddle were taken from the ferry by some of the people under your command, you will upon receipt of this restore the same horse and such other of his effects as shall come within your department to the said Mr. Stockton at the house of John Covenhoven in Monmouth. I am sir yours, etc.
> James Webster
> Lt. Col. 33d Regt.
> Perth Amboy
> December 29, 1776
> To Col. Elisha Lawrence of the New Jersey Volunteers[11]

Lieutenant Colonel James Webster's use of the term "full pardon" strongly indicates that Stockton had sworn an oath of loyalty to King George III.

Congress finally passed a resolution to file a formal remonstrance with General Howe about the conditions of Stockton's confinement on January 3, 1777, complaining that the signer had "been ignominiously thrown into a common goal [jail] and there detained."[12] Three days later John Hancock, President of the Congress, wrote to General Washington that while negotiating with the British over military prisoners he should "make enquiry whether the report which Congress have heard of Mr. Stockton's being confined in a common jail by the enemy, has any truth in it, or not."[13] But by then Stockton, after having spent only about one month in captivity, was on his way home or may have arrived there already. It appears General Howe allowed the signer to be released and did not wait for him to be exchanged (most histories incorrectly state that he was exchanged). Lord Richard Howe and General William Howe typically allowed gentlemen civilians who had sought the Crown's protection to be granted their paroles and permitted to return to their homes.[14]

II. The Fall of New York City and New Jersey 23

Ironically, Stockton had relatives and friends who showed deep concern about the terrible treatment of American prisoners held in New York City. John Witherspoon, Stockton's Princeton friend, penned an influential Congressional report detailing British atrocities in the war in New Jersey and New York, including treating prisoners "with the greatest barbarity."[15] Stockton married Annis Boudinot, sister of Elias Boudinot, who, after training for the law at Stockton's office, married one of Stockton's sisters. During the Revolutionary War, Boudinot held the important position of Commissary of Prisoners for the Continental Congress and did his best to make the lives of American prisoners held by the British bearable. He was assisted in this effort by former New York merchant Lewis Pintard, who married another of Stockton's sisters.[16] Boudinot also served as president of the Continental Congress in 1782 and 1783.

When he returned to Morven, Stockton was in poor health. He found that his home had been occupied by some dragoons under Lieutenant Colonel William Harcourt, the captor of Major General Charles Lee, and that they had plundered some of his furniture and other possessions. Perhaps with some exaggeration, Stockton's son-in-law, Dr. Benjamin Rush, wrote that "the whole of Mr. Stockton's furniture, apparel, and even valuable writings have been burnt. All his cattle, horses, hogs, sheep, grain, and forage have been carried away by them. His losses cannot amount to less than £5,000."[17] Elias Boudinot, an important New Jersey Patriot and brother-in-law to Stockton, later reported that Harcourt's dragoons had taken away bonds, notes and other personal property worth about £4,000 to £5,000.[18]

Back in Congress, a rumor began to circulate that Stockton had claimed the King's protection. On December 23, 1776, Congressional delegate Elbridge Gerry wrote to James Warren in Massachusetts, "Judge Stockton of the Jerseys who was also a member of Congress has sued for pardon. I wish every timid Whig or pretended Whig in America would pursue the same plan, as their weak & ineffectual system of politics has been the cause of every misfortune that we have suffered."[19] On February 8, Congressional delegate Abraham Clark wrote to signer John Hart that New Jersey was seeking a replacement for Stockton in Congress because "Mr. Stockton by his late procedure cannot act" (meaning he could not serve in Congress and oppose the Crown without violating his recent oath).[20] The next day, Hancock informed Robert Treat Paine, "Stockton it is said, & truly, has received General Howe's protection."[21] On February 15, the New Jersey legislature received the judge's formal resignation as delegate to the Continental Congress.

Writing about the period just after Stockton's return to Princeton, the Reverend John Witherspoon on March 17 wrote, "Judge Stockton is not very well in health & much spoken against for his conduct. He signed Howe's declaration & also gave his word of honor that he would not meddle in the least in American affairs during the war."[22] The fact that his first cousin, Richard Witham Stockton, was a known Tory who had helped to capture Major General Charles Lee, likely did not help matters for the signer.

Because he had spent time behind enemy lines, or perhaps due to the rumors of his taking the Crown's protection, on December 22, 1777, Stockton was called before the New Jersey Council of Safety, then meeting at nearby Princeton, and requested to sign an oath of allegiance to the Continental Congress, "which he took and subscribed the same, and was thereupon dismissed."[23] Stockton did not turn in any papers related to his oath of allegiance to the Crown, as was required.

Judge William Smith of New York, a strong Loyalist with an intellectual bent, kept tabs on Stockton and his journal entries suggest that Stockton harbored some Loyalist views. In July of 1779, Stockton asked Miss E. Livingston to inform Judge Smith that "he dare no longer appear as counsel for the persecuted Loyalists, that they [the Whigs] threaten to mob him, and he finds a tyranny in the Country instead of liberty and law."[24] This reference likely refers to Stock-

Statue of Richard Stockton at National Statuary Hall in the U.S. Capitol (Architect of the Capitol).

ton's representing Loyalists whose property was ordered to be confiscated by the state. His son-in-law, Benjamin Rush, alluded to this episode when he remembered Stockton as a man who was "sincerely devoted to the liberties of his country" but who "loved law and order, and once offended his constituents by opposing the seizure of private property in an illegal manner by an officer of the army."[25]

According to Dr. Rush, it took almost two years after his release from his captivity for Stockton to regain his health, but he did recover.[26] As indicated in the above paragraph, he had recovered enough by 1779 to begin practicing law again. Two years later Stockton died at Princeton at just the age of 50 on February 28, 1781, of a cancer in his neck, after suffering from cancer for more than a year.[27]

Stockton was the only signer to sign an oath of allegiance to the Crown. It appears that that Stockton was neither a Loyalist nor a committed Patriot, and that after his capture, he decided to remain neutral and not to be actively favoring either side of the war.

Stockton had voluntarily signed the Declaration of Independence and prior to his capture had worked diligently for the Patriot cause in Congress. Had he not been captured, he would have likely never had his patriotism questioned. But once captured, it appears that he was not so strongly attached to the Whig cause that he was willing to suffer discomfort in jail and risk death from a disease caught in confinement. In this limited sense, Stockton sacrificed for the American cause; but he was no hero either. However, he may have faced harsher treatment than other gentlemen captives since he was a signer.

By the 1820s, as explained by historian J. L. Bell, Stockton's family had created a myth about Stockton's patriotism, which many Revolutionary War historians have bought into. The myth is that British treatment of the signer was so cruel that he became ill in captivity and died of the illness before the war ended.[28] In 1888 the State of New Jersey even selected Stockton as one of two New Jersey heroes to have their statues placed in The National Statuary Hall Collection in the U.S. Capitol in Washington, D.C. The on-line description accompanying Stockton's statue indicates that those who selected Stockton were not privy to all of the facts: "Shortly after he signed the Declaration of Independence, he was taken prisoner by the British. Although he remained in prison for only a month, his health was broken. He became an invalid and died at Princeton on February 28, 1781."[29] While this item and several histories claim that Stockton never regained his health after his captivity, this claim is not accurate.

A state, if approved by its governor and legislature, is permitted to request the Architect of the Capitol to withdraw one of the state's two statues in the

National Statuary Hall Collection and accept a new one.[30] The state of New Jersey should consider replacing Stockton's statue.

The man who informed the New Jersey Volunteers of Stockton's location at Hopewell back in December of 1776 did not fare well. The July 8, 1778, edition of *The New Jersey Gazette* reported that at a trial at the Monmouth County court house, a jury convicted Cyrenus Van Mater of "giving information to the enemy, and thereby being the cause of their taking the Hon. Richard Stockton, Esq. and John Covenhoven, Esq. in the month of December, 1776." Van Mater was sentenced to pay £300 and spend six months in jail. But according to the *Gazette*, during the campaign that ended in the Battle of Monmouth Courthouse in early July of 1778, Van Mater was released from his imprisonment by the British army and "after having piloted them through his own neighborhood, went off with them to New York, leaving a large real and personal estate behind him, which we presume will be forfeited for his crimes."

With New Jersey being overrun by the British army in December of 1776, the state was not a safe place for any signer of the Declaration of Independence. John Hart of Hunterdon County, then about 70 years old and the only Baptist to sign the Declaration, was described by Benjamin Rush as a "plain, honest, well meaning Jersey farmer, with but little education but with good sense enough to discover and pursue the true interests of his country." Hart had earned the trust of his neighbors and had been elected several times to the New Jersey Assembly and had served as the Speaker of the House before the legislature disbanded on December 2 in the face of General Charles Cornwallis's invasion. As British and Hessian troops swept through the area around Hopewell, the same town in which Stockton had been seized earlier, Hart fled to the woods, hiding for a short time in caves and in the Sourwood Mountains. While troops plundered his farm, they did not entirely destroy his house.[31]

Francis Lewis, a Continental Congress delegate representing New York from 1774 to 1779, after accumulating wealth as a New York City merchant, had purchased a country estate at Whitestone on Long Island. Due to the influence of Tories in New York, Lewis was instructed not to vote for independence on July 1 or July 2. But, patriotic as he was, he signed the Declaration of Independence on August 2. Following the Battle of Long Island on August 27, 1776, Long Island was held by the British for the remainder of the war. Shortly thereafter, while Lewis was still in Philadelphia serving in Congress, his Whitestone house was burned and his farm destroyed, amounting to a loss of some £12,000, on orders of Lieutenant Colonel Samuel Birch of the 17th Light Dragoons. His wife was also taken prisoner and held for eight months before being exchanged for the wives of British officials captured by the Americans.[32] Her health reportedly was, however, ruined while in captivity, and she died in 1779.

The grief-stricken Lewis immediately left Congress, but continued to serve on the Board of Admiralty until 1781. He died in 1802 and was buried in an unmarked grave in the yard at Trinity Church in New York City.[33]

John Fell in the Provost

Once General Howe's armies secured northern New Jersey, Long Island, New York, and pockets around New York City, militant Tories engaged in a campaign of kidnappings of state and local Whig civilian leaders. After their targets were abducted, they were typically hustled to one of the military jails quickly established in New York City, where an awful fate awaited many of them.

John Fell, a successful merchant and staunch supporter of the American cause who lived near Paramus, New Jersey, was one prominent victim. A judge of the court of common pleas in Bergen County from 1766 to 1774 and from 1776 to 1786, Fell became a member of the provincial congress in 1775 and a member of the New Jersey Council (equivalent to a senate) in the first state legislature in 1776, where he served as an important advisor to Governor William Livingston. In his various official capacities, Judge Fell had occasion to cause local Tories to be jailed, threatened, or otherwise punished.

On the night of April 22, 1777, a band of twenty-five Tory raiders came to Fell's house (still standing at Allendale) and bundled the judge to Bergen Point and then to New York City.[34] Stephen Kemble, the deputy adjutant general of the British army at New York, reported in his journal for April 23–24, the "bringing in a great Tory Hunter, John Fell, by some people from near Tappan."[35]

Governor Livingston even wrote to General Washington about this particular kidnapping, complaining that Fell "was lately taken out of his own bed in Bergen County by the Tories and carried a prisoner to New York." Livingston urged Washington to work for his exchange, in light of his "public utility as a very valuable member of our legislative and incorruptible attachment to the cause of American liberty" and in light of "the delicacy of his constitution and advanced years" (Fell was then 56 years old).[36] The New Jersey governor also penned a diatribe to the New Jersey legislature, stating that the British had "lately adopted the base and unmanly practice of encouraging" New Jersey Tories "to kidnap the members of our legislature" and specifically described how a band of militant Loyalists from Bergen County had "surprised in his bed, and with brutal violence hurried to New York, the honorable John Fell, Esq., an aged and venerable member of the Legislative Council of this State, and there delivered him into the hands of the British tormenters."[37]

The leader of the Tory band that abducted Fell was Lieutenant Colonel Abraham Van Buskirk from Teaneck, the leading Loyalist of Bergen County. In 1775 Buskirk had served with Fell on the Bergen County Committee of Correspondence and in the Provincial Congress Safety. Buskirk, a physician, had even been appointed surgeon of the Bergen County militia in February 1776.[38] But once General Howe controlled New York and parts of New Jersey, Buskirk enlisted as an officer in the New Jersey Volunteers, one of the largest Loyalist outfits of the war, and commanded its fourth battalion.[39]

The night Fell was seized, he was brought to Bergen Point, a new British post next to another one at Paulus Hook. The following story is often repeated when local historians discussed the kidnapping. Upon seeing Fell, the lieutenant colonel said, "Times are altered since we last met." "So I perceive," Judge Fell answered dryly. Buskirk continued, "Well, you are a prisoner and going over to New York, where you will be presented to General [James] Robertson, with whom I have the honor to be acquainted. I will give you a letter of introduction to him." Fell thanked him and accepted the letter, which he afterward presented to General Robertson when the two met in New York City. Fell and Robertson were acquainted, having worked together during the French and Indian War. Opening the letter, Robertson read to himself, "John Fell is a notorious Rebel and rascal" and that he should be treated as such. Handing the letter back to Fell, Robertson told the judge, "My old friend, John Fell, you must be a very altered man and a very great rascal indeed if you can equal this Colonel Buskirk."[40]

Once Fell arrived at the New York City building that would be his prison, it would be no laughing matter. Ever since Howe's victories at the Battle of Long Island and the capture of Fort Washington, hordes of American captives had been herded into empty New York sugar houses, churches, and other public buildings, or onto prison ships off of Brooklyn. Given little or rotten food lacking in nutrition, the starved prisoners quickly weakened, and became vulnerable to disease. They were further subjected to foul water, overcrowding, and scant clothing, blankets, and firewood in the brutally cold winter months. They began to die by the cartload.

Historian Edwin Burrows, who studied the plight of American prisoners in New York City during the Revolutionary War, concluded that the death rate in its prisons was an astounding 50 to 70 percent. Burrows persuasively rejected arguments that while Americans may have suffered in British prisons, the British were blameless. Burrows did not claim that the British *intended* the deaths of so many captives, as many Americans argued during the war. Instead, he concluded that the deaths were the result of "something well beyond the usual brutalities and misfortunes of war—a lethal convergence, as it were, of obstinacy, condescension, corruption, mendacity, and indifference. Although the British did not deliberately kill American prisoners in New York, they might as well have done."[41]

American officers, at least those in the Continental army who were recognized by British military authorities as officers, fared better than common privates, sailors and other non-officers. An officer, it was thought, was a gentleman, a man of taste and breeding above ordinary folk. Based on vestiges of knighthood from the Middle Ages, it was believed that a gentleman could be trusted to keep his promise not to escape before being exchanged. Thus, officers could be paroled within a town, allowed to stroll around the town in the daytime, and stay in cleaner and less-crowded housing with other officers.

British officers, however, laughed at the pretensions of American militia officers, whom they could not distinguish from rank-and-file soldiers, and often ended up treating them as ordinary privates. The case of Colonel Ethan Allen, the Vermont militia officer who led the successful assault on Fort Ticonderoga but later was captured in Canada, became infamous, as a result of his awful treatment in various British jails.[42] Captured privateer captains who had wreaked havoc on British commercial and military supply vessels were considered nothing less than pirates. Such men were simply thrown into prisons along with common sailors. Whig political leaders, such as John Fell, were not treated as "gentlemen" officers, but were instead also thrown into common jails.

John Fell, Ethan Allen and other prominent prisoners, many of them victims of kidnapping by Loyalists, were mostly brought to the Provost, a large stone building that had served for many years as New York City's municipal jail. It was run by two vile and insensitive men, Captain William Cunningham and Sergeant O'Keefe. Lewis Pintard, Richard Stockton's brother-in-law who served as an agent for American prisoners held in New York City jails, compiled a list of grievances of the appalling conditions in the Provost, which he submitted to British general Daniel Jones on September 26, 1777:

> Close confined in jail without distinction of rank or character, amongst felons (a number of whom are under sentence of death), without their friends suffered to speak to them, even through the grates. On the scanty allowance of 2 lbs. hard biscuit and 2 lbs. raw pork per man per week, without fuel to dress it. Frequently supplied with water from a pump where all kinds of filth is thrown that can render it obnoxious and unwholesome (the effects of which are too often felt) when good water is as easily obtained. Denied the benefit of a hospital, not allowed to send for medicine, nor even a doctor permitted to visit them when in greatest distress. Married men and others who lay at the point of death refused to have their wives or relations admitted to see them, and for attempting it often beat from prison. Commissioned officers and other persons of character, without a cause, thrown into a loathsome dungeon, insulted in a gross manner, and vilely abused by a Provost Marshal [Captain Cunningham], who is allowed to be one of the basest characters in the British army, and whose power is so unlimited that he has caned an officer on a trivial occasion, and frequently beats the sick privates when [they were] unable to stand.[43]

Not surprisingly, the petition had no effect except to irritate Sergeant Keith, who punished the prisoners by locking the doors to their rooms.[44]

John Pintard assisted his uncle, Lewis Pintard, in attempting to relieve the wants of American captives. He recalled some specifics about the Provost regarding the area in the jail where Whig military and civilian leaders were held:

> The Provost was destined for the more notorious Rebels, civil, naval and military.... The northeast chamber, turning to the left on the second floor, was appropriated to officers and characters of superior rank and distinction, and was called Congress Hall. So closely were they packed that when they lay down at night to rest, when their bones ached on the hard oak planks and they wished to turn, it was altogether by word of command—"*right, left,*" being so wedged and compact so as to form almost a solid mass of human bodies. In the daytime, the packs and blankets of the prisoners were suspended from the walls, every precaution being used to keep the rooms ventilated and the walls and floors clean, to prevent jail fever.... Among other characters there were at the same time, the famous Colonel Ethan Allen and Judge Fell, of Bergen County, New Jersey. When Captain Cunningham entertained the young British officers accustomed to command the provost guard, by dint of curtailing the prisoners' rations, exchanging good for bad provisions, and other embezzlements practiced on John Bull, the captain, his deputy, and indeed all commissaries generally, were enabled to fare sumptuously. In the drunken orgies that usually terminated his dinners, the captain would order the Rebel prisoners to turn out and parade for the amusement of his guests, pointing them out, "This is the damned rebel, Colonel Ethan Allen, that a rebel judge, an Englishman," etc....[45]

Fell was soon joined by other notables kidnapped by Loyalists. Captain Wynant van Zandt, a neighbor of Fell's in Bergen County and an officer in the New Jersey militia, was seized by New Jersey Volunteers on April 26 (probably again by Buskirk's men) and deposited in the Provost. Jacobus Blauvelt, also of Bergen County, was abducted and sent to the Provost, where he would not leave alive. Long Island Tories bagged the Reverend Joshua Hart, a 300-pound Presbyterian minister from Smithtown, who was famous for sermons ranting against the Crown. He arrived at the Provost on May 27, along with a Colonel Smith from Long Island. Cornelius and Peter Van Tassel of Westchester County, New York, were seized by British regulars on the night of November 18, probably because Peter was a prominent member of a local committee of safety that dealt with recalcitrant Tories. Their Tarrytown houses were burned to the ground and the two men were reportedly roped to the tails of their horses and dragged down to the Provost on November 24, where they stayed for some three years.[46]

An important reason for why militant Loyalists often resorted to clandestine kidnappings was that they had no alternative to remove enemy leaders: political institutions and the courts of the states were invariably controlled by Whigs. Patriots, by contrast, could use the criminal court system to issue official warrants to arrest Tories for the crimes of treason against the state or failing to sign an oath pledging allegiance to the Continental Congress, have them convicted in courts, and have them sentenced to be confined in government jails. Indeed, this even occurred in connection with the cases of John Fell and Captain Van Zandt. Two prominent Tories, James Parker and Walter Rutherford, after having been required to appear before the Morris County court and then refusing to take an oath before the court, on August 15 were ordered to appear to face charges of disaffection. After being jailed for a day on August 20, they were released on condition that they remain within a mile of the court house. The Council of Safety then instructed Elias Boudinot to try to exchange Fell and Van Zandt for Parker and Rutherford.[47] On November 21, the Council of Safety ordered the Sheriff of Morris County to confine the two Tories in "a private room nearest the Court House for a space of three weeks."[48] But this effort at retaliation, using the machinery of New Jersey's government, did not work and only served to irritate General James Robertson. Meanwhile, Fell, Van Zandt, and others remained confined in New York City.

John Fell kept a daily record of the insults, indignities and other conditions of life in the Provost. Here are a few entries in his journal:

> May 20. Lewis Pintard came per order of Elias Boudinot to offer me money; refused admittance.
> ...
> May 30. Not allowed to fetch good water.
> ...
> June 3. Captain Van Zandt sent to dungeon for resenting Capt. Cunningham's abusing and insulting me.
> ...
> June 10. Prisoners very sickly.
> ...
> June 13. Melancholy scene, women refused speaking to their sick husbands, and treated cruelly by sentries.
> ...
> June 23. Mr. Haight died.
> ...
> June 26. Justice Moore died & carried out.
> ...
> Aug. 12. Serg. Keith took all the pens and ink out of each room, and forbid the use of any on pain of dungeon.
> ...
> Aug. 14. Jacobus Blauvelt died in morning—buried at noon.
> ...
> Sept. 4. Horrid scenes of whipping.
> ...
> Oct. 6. G. Miller died of small pox—p.m. buried.
> ...
> Oct. 14. Sergeant Keith sent Lt. Mercer and Nathaniel Fitz Randolph to the dungeon for complaining their room had not water sufficient.
> ...

> Nov. 16. Jail exceedingly disagreeable—many miserable & shocking objects nearly starved with cold & hunger—miserable prospect before us.
> ...
> Nov. 24. 6 tailors brought here from the prison ship ... they say the people on board very sickly—300 sent on board reduced to 100.
> ...
> Dec. 8. Maj. Gen. Robertson with Mayor [David Mathews] came to Provost to examine p[risoners]. I was called & examined, & requested my parole. Gen. [Roberston] said I had made base use of indulgence granted me in letting my daughter come to see me and by ordering Mr. Parker and Mr. Rutherford confined.
> ...
> Dec. 16. Sent message to Mr. Pintard for wood. Cold & exceedingly out of wood.[49]

When John Fell became very ill during his confinement in late December, Colonel Allen sent a petition to General James Robertson, requesting that Fell be released from the Provost for health reasons. Robertson permitted Fell to be moved to the house of a friend in the city, where he recuperated.

Fell's fate at this time almost took an unfortunate turn. In September 1777, New Jersey militia had captured a party of Tories who were on their way to join the British army at Staten Island before they were intercepted and seized. Two of the captured men, Lieutenant John Iliff of the New Jersey Volunteers and John Mee, a British soldier out recruiting for the same Tory regiment, as examples were hanged for the crime of treason at Morristown on December 2, 1777. One of the Morristown guards, Israel Abner, wrote in his pension application many years later: "Two officers ... who had recruited a company for the enemy, were tried at Morristown, condemned and hanged by Sheriff Alexander Carmichael. The privates of the [company] were condemned but were pardoned on condition of enlistment in the American Army." Governor William Livingston, recognizing that merely "adhering" to the enemy fell with the state's treason law, not too convincingly also argued that Iliff and Mee could have instead been hanged as spies.[50] General Robertson wrote to Livingston, that even though the executions of Iliff and Mee constituted "murder" in his view, he was still willing to release an ill John Fell from the Provost.[51] In response, Livingston wrote of the "cries of murder" from American prisoners "who are constantly perishing in the gaols of New York, which the governor described as "the coolest and most deliberate kind of murder."[52] Still, Fell was lucky that Robertson chose not to retaliate against him for the harsh treatments of Iliff and Mee.

Fell was finally paroled by his captors and allowed to return to New Jersey in January 1778, and he was formally exchanged the following May. While Fell had not been kidnapped when he was a member of the Continental Congress, he did subsequently become a Congressional delegate from New Jersey after his release from prison. Fell served as a delegate to the Continental Congress from 1778 to 1780 and again as a member of the New Jersey legislative Council from

1782 to 1783. His diary of the Continental Congress's proceedings remains one of the best sources of information about Congress during the time of his service in Philadelphia.

Abraham Van Buskirk himself avoided a kidnapping attempt. A New York newspaper reported that on December 5, 1777, "a party of Rebels, consisting of some officers and twelve men, proceeding on an enterprise to seize the person of Mr. Van Buskirk, at Bergen Point" had their plans foiled when troops from nearby Paulus Hook fired at them.[53] Buskirk survived the war, but on a ship bound for Nova Scotia in 1783, he died at the age of thirty-three.[54]

The Capture of Major General Charles Lee

Charles Lee was probably the most remarkable personality of the American Revolution on either side. He was brilliant but eccentric, and well educated and well-schooled in military matters, but bitingly sarcastic with his superiors.[55]

Charles Lee was an Englishman who was largely ignored by his mother and his father was usually absent on duty as an officer in the British army. His father did train and educate Lee to become an officer in the British army, and Lee took to it.

Lee was not an attractive man. He was thin and had a large nose—an American friend called him Naso. Lee loved dogs, which, while common today, was then seen as eccentric. Once when he was asked by a genteel young woman if he was fond of dogs, Lee retorted, "Yes, madam, I love dogs, but I detest bitches."[56]

Lee's first military experience was in North America, during the French and Indian War. He showed courage by being wounded in a charge at the failed British siege of Fort Ticonderoga in 1758. But he was also incredibly insulting to his superior generals. He called Major General James Abercrombie a "stupid blunderer" and "our booby-in-chief." Lee was, needless to say, not making friends in the British establishment. In some circles, he was known as "Mad Lee."[57]

After a successful stint leading dragoons in Portugal, Lee had been promoted to lieutenant colonel. But with the downsizing of the army after the war, he was put on half-pay and temporarily retired. Lee decided to become a soldier of fortune. He served in high positions in Poland, gaining valuable experience. On one trip back to England, he reportedly insulted King George III in person after the king supposedly broke his promise to promote Lee.

Lee began to make it clear in his letters home that he was against the British monarchy and favored republican government. He decided to move to America in 1773. "Liberty I adore," he explained, and "where she lives, that is

Charles Lee in England about 1770. This caricature was "allowed by all who knew General Lee to be the only successful delineation either of his countenance or his person." The dog may be Lee's Pomeranian, Spado. From a drawing by Barham Rushbrooke (reproduction by permission of the Society of the Cincinnati, Washington, D.C.).

my country."[58] With his impressive military background, he was immediately hailed as a Patriot leader. He wrote a popular pamphlet arguing that, should the contest with Britain end in war, American militiamen, with their experience handling guns, motivation to fight for their liberty, and sheer numbers, could defeat professional British regulars.

With the coming of war after Lexington and Concord, the Continental Congress chose its leading generals. The former colonel from Virginia, George Washington, not surprisingly, was named commander-in-chief of the Continental Army. Lee desperately wanted to be second in command. However, John Adams persuaded Congress that since most of the army then outside Boston was from New England, Massachusetts's Artemis Ward should be the second in command. Lee was selected as the third highest ranking general. An outraged Lee's response was typical—overly harsh but accurate. He described the Harvard-educated Ward as "a fat old gentleman who had been a popular church warden, but had no acquaintance whatever with military affairs."[59] After a few months, Ward both suffered from health problems and realized he was in over his head, and retired, leaving Lee as second-in-command.

By November 1776, the Continental army was in dire straits. Washington had tried to defend New York City, but had failed miserably. At the Battle of Long Island on August 27, the British commander-in-chief, William Howe, crushed Washington's army. Howe then easily maneuvered to capture New York City. Washington fortified Fort Washington, the Continental army's last bastion on Manhattan Island, but on November 17, Howe's troops overran the fort, resulting in 50 American soldiers killed and more than 2,800 captured. A few days later Fort Lee, named after Charles Lee and on the New Jersey side of the Hudson River, fell to a British force led by General Earl Cornwallis. While the relative few American defenders abandoned the fort in time to avoid becoming captives, they left behind tremendous stashes of sorely needed military supplies and foodstuffs. All told, these were some of the worst disasters of the war for the Americans.

At this time, Lee lost confidence in Washington as commander-in-chief. Lee had not been part of the loss at the Battle of Long Island, and he had advised against reinforcing Fort Washington prior to its fall. Washington was not yet the mythical figure he would become. Lee appears to have made the decision that he deserved to replace Washington as commander-in-chief of the American army.

After the fall of Fort Lee, Cornwallis commanded a powerful British column that chased the remnants of Washington's army out of New Jersey. Outnumbered with only about 3,000 soldiers remaining, Washington desperately needed help. Washington's subordinate, Nathanael Greene, wrote, "When we left Brunswick, we had not 3,000 men, a very pitiful army to trust the liberties of America upon."⁶⁰ Lee at the time commanded 4,000 troops at White Plains, New York. Washington asked, but did not order, Lee to march his forces to join him across the Delaware River in Pennsylvania. But during what was probably the most dangerous time for the existence of Washington's army, Lee dithered and delayed. While he was too smart to leave an obvious paper trail, it appears that Lee wanted to maintain an independent command for as long as possible. That was his path to glory. And if Washington's army was crushed by Cornwallis, as seemed probable at the time, Lee might vault to the top command of the Continental army.

Lee received the first request from Washington to join him on November 22, but most of his regiments did not start marching until November 28, and they did not all cross the Hudson River at King's Ferry, New York, until December 4. And when his men started marching in New Jersey, they did not set any speed records there either. In the meantime, it seemed that Cornwallis could easily cross the Delaware River and capture Philadelphia—Washington begged Lee to hurry to help defend the city.

Lee reached Morristown, New Jersey, on December 8 and his troops met him there on December 10. Lee let his men rest an entire day, despite good marching weather. The next day he ordered his troops to head for Bernardsville, New Jersey. Lee's second in command, Major General John Sullivan, accompanied the head of the column, while Lee and his small entourage rode at the rear. Riding with Lee were his aide-de-camp, young Major William Bradford of Rhode Island, and two French volunteers, Lieutenant Colonel de Boisbertrand and Captain de Virnejoux.

Lee had to decide where to spend the night. He apparently did not want to spend the night at a private residence but preferred an inn. He was told of Widow White's Tavern at the small village of Basking Ridge, which was three miles from the main encampment of his troops at Bernardsville. Nonetheless, Lee decided to stay there, with his three aides and a small guard of about a dozen soldiers.

Widow White's Tavern was owned and operated by Mary White, whose first two husbands died. Operating an inn was one of the few occupations deemed acceptable for a single woman. She was assisted in running the tavern by her older sister. At the time, Basking Ridge was a small collection of houses surrounded by farms.

Lee's decision to spend the night so far from his troops was a critical mistake. Unknown to him, a party of thirty-eight British cavalrymen had departed Pennington, New Jersey, to ride north to obtain reconnaissance about Lee's army. Led by Lieutenant Colonel William Harcourt, the son of a British earl, and Banastre Tarleton, an Englishman who would later gain a reputation in the

South as the most fearsome cavalry commander of the war, the party rode across the bridge at Bound Brook over the Raritan River and headed north towards Morristown.

On the way, Loyalists informed Harcourt and Tarleton of the famous General Lee spending the night at Mary White's Tavern. As was the case throughout the war, the civilian populace was very well informed of military matters in their area. Lee that very day wrote a letter to General Horatio Gates complaining that he was surrounded by Tories—"Tories are on my front, rear and flank."[61] Accordingly, he was well aware of the risk posed by Tories and should have taken great care because of it.

On December 13, after learning of General Lee staying at an inn in nearby Basking Ridge, Harcourt seized the moment: changing his mission to nabbing Lee, he and his men set out for the village. Tarleton's advance party gained valuable information along the way by threatening captured American soldiers with death if they did not reveal all the information they knew about Lee's whereabouts. One unfortunate unidentified "Rebel officer," under the threat of being hanged, was forced to guide Tarleton's advance party to Basking Ridge and the tavern in which Lee was staying, while Harcourt and the rest of his dragoons followed one hundred yards behind. When the "Rebel officer" was close enough to point out the tavern, Tarleton's advance party, according to a German officer who was later informed of the events, "dashed in all possible haste toward the house."[62]

Back at Basking Ridge, at 10:30 a.m., an unsuspecting Charles Lee was ready to depart Widow White's Tavern to rejoin his army. Major James Wilkinson, who had arrived at the tavern the prior night, then happened to glance out the south-facing window, down the roughly 100-yard-long lane that connected the tavern's grounds with the main road. According to Wilkinson, he saw:

> a party of British dragoons turn a corner of the [lane] at a full charge. Startled at this unexpected spectacle, I exclaimed, "Here, sir, are the British cavalry." "Where?" replied the General, who had signed his letter in the instant. "Around the house," for they had opened files, and encompassed the building. General Lee appeared alarmed, yet collected, and his second observation marked his self-possession: "Where is the guard? Damn the guard, why don't they fire?" After a momentary pause, he turned to me and said, "Do, sir, see what has become of the guard."
>
> The women of the house at this moment entered the room, and proposed to him [Lee] to conceal himself in a bed, which he rejected with evident disgust. I caught up my pistols which lay on the table, thrust the letter he had been writing into my pocket, and passed into a room at the opposite end of the house, where I had seen the guard in the morning. Here I discovered their arms, but the men were absent. I stepped out of the door, and perceived the dragoons chasing them in different directions, and receiving a very uncivil salutation, I returned into the house.[63]

Why had not Lee's guard of about a dozen soldiers fired their muskets to fend off the attackers? According to Wilkinson, "The morning being cold and the sun bright, they had left their station, crossed the main road, and were sunning themselves on the south side of a house about 200 yards from the tavern, which enabled Harcourt to cut them off from their arms."[64] The guards ran to pick up their muskets, but the saber-wielding dragoons, riding furiously, were quickly upon them. According to one report, one guard got off a shot before being cut down. Another account stated that the sole sentry at the door, "his piece not being loaded," advanced toward the oncoming dragoons, who "rode up to him and said, 'don't shoot; if you fire we will blow your brains out.'"[65] The sentry wisely put down his gun. William Bradford recalled that Tarleton and five of his dragoons surrounded the house, and, slashing away with their swords, "cut off the arm of one of the guards crying for quarter."[66] Once the balance of Harcourt's men arrived, Lee's guards were either subdued or chased away.

Turning their attention to capturing their intended target—Lee—Harcourt's dragoons began to riddle the tavern with carbine fire. Inside the tavern, Lieutenant Colonel de Boisbertrand, Captain de Virnejoux, and Major Bradford kept up a steady return fire, but their pistols fired at a relatively long range caused little or no harm. Neither Lee nor Wilkinson (hiding behind the chimney) joined in the shooting. Targeting its windows, Harcourt's men reportedly "fired sixty or seventy shot into" the tavern. After about eight minutes, a frustrated Tarleton fired through its door and yelled to its inhabitants: "I know General Lee is in the house. If he would surrender himself, he and his attendants should be safe, but if my summons was not complied with immediately, the house should be burnt and every person without exception, should be put to the sword."[67]

Immediately following this ominous warning, Boisbertrand, in a panic to escape, inadvisedly rushed out of the building through its back door and headed for the woods north of the tavern. Tarleton himself galloped after the fleeing Frenchman, perhaps thinking it was Lee, and quickly captured him at sword point. Boisbertrand later stated that he had been "slightly wounded in the arm and head" after being "felled with blows from the flat of a sword," presumably by Tarleton.[68]

Seeing that the defense of his guard and his staff was ineffective, and probably fearing that a fire would flush him out and risk the lives of all the others in the house, Lee felt that his fate was sealed. "The General saw then that he must submit and after walking the chamber perhaps ten or fifteen minutes, told [me] to go down and tell them General Lee would submit," William Bradford

Opposite: "The American General Lee taken prisoner by Lieutenant Colonel Harcourt of the English army, in Morris County, New Jersey, 1776." This idealized image was sculpted by J. Hawkins, was drawn by William Hamilton, and was first published in Edward Barnard's *History of England*, in 1783 (Huddleston, *Gentleman Jonny Burgoyne*).

recalled later. "[I] went to the door and on opening it a whole volley of shot came on. At the door, [I] spoke loud and opened it again and delivered his orders."

Bradford, followed by Lee, then stepped through the tavern door's entrance and walked outside toward Harcourt's troopers. According to Bradford, "General Lee came forward and surrendered himself as prisoner-of-war, saying he trusted they would use him like a gentleman. Of this, one of them [probably Colonel Harcourt] gave assurance and ordered him instantly to mount." Before doing so, Lee asked permission for Bradford to retrieve his hat and cloak from the tavern. Keenly aware of the need to depart the tavern and return to Pennington as soon as possible, the gentlemanly Harcourt nevertheless agreed.[69]

Bradford then came up with a ruse to try to fool Harcourt's men and avoid being taken captive with Lee. After Lee "requested his hat and cloak," Bradford then "went to fetch it—but changing [my] clothes on [my] return, they did not know [me] from a servant. Laying down the general's hat and cloak, [I] escaped back into the house. They immediately rode off in triumph with the general, leaving a few to get the horses from the stable and take and bring off the rest as captives."[70] Knowing that American militia would soon be hunting for them, and with General Lee and Lieutenant Colonel de Boisbertrand in tow, Harcourt's dragoons raced down back roads to safety in British-held Pennington.

After the British raiding party left, villagers buried two American soldiers who had been cut down with heavy swords. One woman later recalled that Tarleton's dragoons had "hacked them so terribly that it was found very difficult to remove their bodies to the graveyard, and they were put in boxes and interred in the field where they lay."[71]

At the time, Lee's capture was considered a disaster for the Americans. John Trumbull, Jr., the future painter of Revolutionary War scenes, but then a young officer, gave the view of many of his fellow officers: "This is a misfortune that cannot be remedied, as we have no officer in the army of equal experience and merit." The British viewed events as led by great men and expected that Lee's capture would end the war. Lieutenant Colonel Harcourt himself wrote to his brother that as Lee was the "most active and most enterprising of the enemy's generals ... it seems to be the universal opinion the Rebels will no longer refuse treating upon the terms which have been offered them." The captain of a British frigate wrote, "I think they [the Rebels] cannot stand long, as Lee was their chief man."[72]

But as is often the case in history, the law of unintended consequences took over. Had Lee not been captured, it seems clear that he would have tried to use his troops to capture a British outpost in New Jersey. This would have been hard to accomplish, since the British army was well aware of his presence. Instead, after learning of Lee's capture, Lee's second-in-command, John Sullivan, rushed his troops to join Washington across the Delaware River. Then, on Christmas Day, in the midst of a snow storm, Washington and his men re-crossed the Delaware and captured a large garrison of German troops at Trenton. This brilliant raid altered the course of the war, giving American Patriots new hope. Had Lee not been captured, and had he tried to capture an outpost, the victory at Trenton may not have happened.

Americans discussed how Lee could possibly have been captured. Some Patriots, stunned at how easily an experienced officer such as Lee was seized, wondered whether he was a traitor. Others blamed local Tories. By August 1781, not surprisingly, a myth arose involving sexual escapades. A French officer named Baron Ludwig von Closen took a short detour to visit the famous tavern "to learn the circumstances that could have caused General Lee to have fallen into the hands of the English." There Closen was informed "that believing himself to be secure, since he [Lee] was 40 miles from the English cantonment, he preferred to spend the night there with a simple guard consisting of a corporal and four men *since he was rather smitten by the lady of the house.* One of the lady's cousins, who was jealous of him, went underhandedly to Colonel Harcourt ... that the general was in this house with a small guard.... This poor General Lee ... will be blamed for this eternally."[73] However, this story lacks credibility—the timing does not work.

Other controversies arose from Lee's capture. It was then deemed scandalous for a gentleman to appear outside without his hat and coat. John Trumbull, Jr., wrote to his father, "The inhuman rascals would not permit the General to take his hat and coat, but carried him off almost naked."[74] Even Washington complained to a relative that Harcourt's party had carried off Lee "with every mark of indignity—not even suffering him to get his hat, or surtout coat."[75] However, it appears that Harcourt allowed Lee to bring his hat and coat, but in his haste to escape possible pursuers, did not allow him time in Basking Ridge to put them on.

Lee's fate as a prisoner was of intense interest in London. The British believed that since he had served in the British army, he was a deserter, and what is more, he had taken up arms against his King. One British officer's view was typical. "I am happy to hear that Mr. Lee is in custody," crowed one, "and I will be still happier to hear in the next accounts from New York that he has been tried as a deserter, condemned and hanged."[76] Another officer, serving in the 64th Regiment, assured his friend in London, that Lee "will be destined to the cord."[77]

At this time in the war, the British approach to treating captive American officers was not settled. The test case was Ethan Allen, the leader of Vermont's Green Mountain Boys who had captured Fort Ticonderoga early in the war.

But on September 25, 1775, he had sloppily got himself captured ahead of an American army under General Richard Montgomery set to invade Canada. Allen was brought before Major General Richard Prescott. Prescott was one of those British officers who considered rebels to be criminals. After all, weren't all traitors criminals? Prescott turned purple with rage and yelled at Allen, "I will not execute you now, but you shall grace a halter at Tyburn, God damn ye."[78] (Tyburn was where criminals were hanged in London.)

Allen was treated horribly as a prisoner. He was placed in dark and dank holds in British ships and fed bad food and little water. He was brought to England and placed in a common prison, where it was expected he would be hanged. But then an extraordinary thing happened. Allen became a *cause célèbre*, and British supporters of the American Patriot cause clamored for his release. British government authorities, wanting to avoid a scene, sent Allen back to North America. Finally, after more miserable treatment in the Provost (with fellow-prisoner John Fell), Allen was treated as captive officers were expected to be treated. He was allowed to live in a house in New York City with other American captive officers and during the day was permitted to walk the streets of the city.

General Howe and King George III still wanted Lee hanged. When the Continental Congress got wind of this plan, it acted immediately, passing resolutions warning that the doctrine of retaliation would be applied. If Lee was harmed, captive British army officers held by the Americans would be as well, in an equivalent manner.

John Adams, then a delegate to the Continental Congress, and his wife, Abigail Adams, exchanged letters about many pressing subjects of the day, including the doctrine of retaliation. Abigail favored a humane approach: "Let them reproach us ever so much for our kindness and tenderness to those who have fallen into our hands. I hope it will never provoke us to retaliate against their cruelties." John wrote back, patiently explaining that while he admired her sentiments, "retaliation we must practice, in some instances, in order to make our barbarous foes respect in some degree the rights of humanity."[79]

Under the threat of retaliation, Howe deferred sending Lee to the clutches of King George III. Howe was informed that in fact Lee had resigned his commission, and so it had to be determined if Lee could therefore be charged with desertion under military law. In the meantime, Howe refused to treat Lee like a normal prisoner. He had Lee confined to two rooms. He made sure Lee was well fed and provided for, but Lee had no freedom of movement. In retaliation, Congress ordered that five German officers, one British officer, Lieutenant Colonel Archibald Campbell, held as captives by the Americans be confined to their rooms. Campbell was not only an officer in the British regular army, he was a Scottish aristocrat and a member of Parliament. Massachusetts authorities threw him in a dirty, smelly, unsanitary common jail in Concord, Massachusetts, until they realized that General Lee was not being detained in a similar manner. Campbell did not like his new quarters, the public area of a roadside tavern, much better.

Shortly after Charles Lee's capture at Basking Ridge, New Jersey, Loyalist elements in Pennsylvania reportedly made plans to emulate that success by trying to carry off Washington. Virginia's Thomas Nelson informed Thomas Jefferson by letter on January 2, 1777: "The general [Washington] was informed a few nights ago that a conspiracy was formed by some people in Bucks County near his camp to kidnap him as poor Lee was, but he has more prudence than to be caught in that manner."[80]

Richard Witham Stockton, the Famous Land Pilot

In any kidnapping special operation, local guides were crucial. They knew the fastest routes or the ones most likely to raise the least neighborhood alarms. They would also know alternative routes and back roads, so as to avoid taking the same roads on return trips, thus reducing the risk of ambush.

Guides for British army parties often did not receive much credit or publicity for their important work. This may have been in part because British regular army officers did not want to share credit with American provincials for their successful special operations. In addition, identifying local guides would place them in danger of being arrested or worse treatment by Patriot authorities.

Up to now, no published book has identified with any certainty who served as the main guide for Harcourt's party that captured General Charles Lee on December 13, 1776, at Basking Ridge, New Jersey. We now know that the main guide was very likely Richard Witham Stockton of Princeton, New Jersey, who at the time was a captain of the New Jersey Volunteers, an important Loyalist unit. In a memorial seeking compensation for his war-time financial losses filed in London in 1783, Stockton was able to persuade an amazing number of top British commanders to submit letters in support of his claims. This is a testament to Richard Witham Stockton's service to Crown troops. Brigadier General Cortland Skinner, commander of the New Jersey Volunteers, and the former Attorney General of New Jersey when William Franklin was jailed, stated that Stockton performed services "conducting and bringing off the troops that took General Lee."[81] Lieutenant Colonel Harcourt, the commander of the expedition, mentioned Stockton's valuable services "as a guide." General Earl Cornwallis, who issued the orders to Harcourt for his expedition, Lieutenant General James Grant, who commanded at New Brunswick where Lee was kept for a short time, and Lieutenant Colonel Banastre Tarleton, who played the key role in capturing Lee, all wrote letters in support of Stockton's memorial.[82]

As a result of guiding Harcourt's party, General Skinner wrote that he "was

Richard Witham Stockton, the "Land Pilot." Based on a painting by Henry Benbridge, ca. 1770. Recently copied and colorized, and with New Jersey Volunteers insignia added, by H. Harvey Hildebrand, the sixth great grandson of Stockton (H. Harvey Hildebrand Collection).

desired" to promote Stockton to be a major and that he did so at Pennington in December of 1776.[83] As Pennington was where the captive General Lee was first brought by Harcourt, and was at the time the base for General Cornwallis, this is yet more evidence that Stockton served as the guide for the party. It appears that while Harcourt, Tarleton and Cornwallis were happy to recognize Stockton's important service as a guide in the famous capture of Lee by promoting him, they were not willing to mention Stockton's role in any of their contemporary accounts of the affair. This may have been because they wanted to leave most of the glory to themselves or because they wanted to protect Stockton's identity out of fear of retribution against him, or both.

Richard Witham Stockton of Princeton, New Jersey, a first cousin to the signer of the Declaration of Independence with the identical first and last names, before the war was a successful farmer and an educated man. He was appointed captain of the New Jersey Volunteers in August of 1776, when the unit was stationed on Staten Island and still gathering troops.[84] Called "Double Dick" by his enemies, Stockton's true calling was as a skilled guide, which also earned him a more complimentary sobriquet, the "renowned Land Pilot."[85]

Stockton may have been assisted in acting as a guide in the capture of General Lee by Captain Asher Dunham of Morris County, New Jersey, also of the New Jersey Volunteers. After joining Skinner's Brigade at New Brunswick in November of 1776, Dunham claimed in his post-war application for reimbursement of losses that he "was at that time frequently employed by General Skinner and others to procure information for the Royal Army" and that "he was in the country on that service at the time Colonel Harcourt took the Rebel Major General Lee, and did actually join him on that occasion."[86] Dunham presumably did not claim he was the lead guide, as that role was Stockton's.

Stockton's increased confidence gained from his role in capturing Lee did not last long. After the disastrous loss at Trenton on Christmas day, General Howe kept most of his troops in strongly held posts in New Jersey. The bulk of his army was stationed at New Brunswick.

Major Stockton was ordered to hold a post at Bennett's Island (also called Lawrence Island), about three miles southeast of New Brunswick on the Raritan River and northwest of Sayreville. Stockton commanded only Captain Dunham, Lieutenant Francis Fraser, four subalterns, and about one hundred privates of the New Jersey Volunteers.[87] Howe ordered Stockton to this post after Patriot artillery downriver threatened to close the Raritan River to British ships resupplying New Brunswick from Amboy further to the east. Presumably, Howe was concerned that if this strategic spot on the river fell into the hands of Patriot forces, they could bring even more artillery to bear on British supply ships. While the post was hidden inside swamps and woods, and was surrounded by the Raritan River to the north, the South River to the east, and the Lawrence Brook to the west, it was still exposed to attack.

On or around February 17, one of Stockton's soldiers deserted and informed the local Patriot commander, Colonel John Nielson of the 2nd Regiment of Middlesex County militia, of the location, defenses and other details of the Bennett's Island outpost. Nielson immediately took the initiative and began organizing a surprise night attack on Stockton and his force with about 150 of his militiamen at Cranberry. After sending word to Major General Israel Putnam of his plan and requesting reinforcements, the Connecticut-raised Continental officer responded by dispatching about fifty riflemen from Bedford County, Pennsylvania, to Nielson. These reinforcements arrived on time, and at sunset Neilson ordered his men to begin their march. The night was clear and frosty, and the ground was covered in snow, but the Patriot troops made good time.

Nielson's force struck just before dawn on February 18, achieving a complete surprise. The attackers suffered only one militiaman killed, while Stockton's force lost four killed, one wounded, sixty-two captured, and arms for sixty-three soldiers.[88] Among the captives were Major Stockton, Captain Dunham, and Lieutenant Fraser, all of whom were immediately hustled to General Putnam's headquarters sixteen miles to the south at Princeton, arriving late in the day on February 18.[89]

General Washington, in the same letter read to Congress in which he warned of "the weak and feeble state of our little army," was able to add the good news of Nielson's small victory at Bennett's Island.[90] Americans also exulted in the capture of the famous "Land Pilot." On March 2, 1777, Colonel Hugh Hughes, a New York deputy quartermaster general, wrote: "A few days since a part of General Putnam's division attacked a party of the enemy about three miles from Brunswick and made 60 prisoners, among whom is Stockton who led the party who took General Lee."[91] At about the same time, a New England newspaper printed the letter of an unidentified American officer, who wrote: "I have the pleasure to acquaint you, that a few days ago a party of General Putnam's division, attacked and defeated a party of Tory soldiers, in Monmouth, killed a number, and took about 40, with their arms, and one Major Stockton, an infamous Tory who commanded them." The newspaper's editors then added in italics, "*The above Major Stockton is the identical villain who betrayed his Excellency General Lee into the hands of the enemy.*"[92]

Once Stockton was identified as the guide who led Harcourt's party, he and his fellow officers suffered for it. General Putnam gave strict orders to the American officer appointed to conduct the prisoners to Philadelphia that "no indulgence be allowed the villains which affords them a possibility of escape."[93]

II. The Fall of New York City and New Jersey   47

This unidentified officer, with or without Putnam's knowledge (it is not clear), took the unusual and shocking step of having Stockton, Dunham and Fraser manacled together in irons and marched out of Princeton as if they were slaves headed towards a slave market. Even General William Howe later complained to General Washington that "Major Stockton and other officers of the New Jersey Volunteers were put in irons at Princeton—the Major and a Captain of that Regiment were put in irons and marched out of that place under a guard and handcuffed together."[94]

An unidentified Tory wrote from Philadelphia on February 24: "Major Stockton was brought prisoner here ... , as were the men who were taken with him near Brunswick. They threaten the Major very hard, as they say he assisted in taking Lee. He was brought into this city in a wagon, with his back towards the horse, in irons, and a drum going before him, beating the Rogue's March."[95] After being paraded through Philadelphia the afternoon of February 22, Stockton, Dunham and Fraser were "closely confined" (that is, manacled) in the city's New Jail.[96]

As a commissioned officer of a Loyalist regiment in the British army, both at the time of Lee's and his own capture, Stockton could not have been prosecuted in court for any role he may have played at Basking Ridge. Thus, his treatment was uncalled for, as finally even General Washington recognized in a March 10 letter to General Horatio Gates:

> I am informed that Genl. Putnam sent down Major Stockton, taken upon the Raritan, to Philadelphia in irons, and that he continues in strict confinement. I think we ought to avoid putting in practice what we have so loudly complained of, the cruel treatment of prisoners. I therefore desire that if there is a necessity for confinement, that it may be made as easy and comfortable as possible to Major Stockton and his officers. This man, I believe, has been active and mischievous, but we took him in arms, as an officer of the enemy, and by the Rules of War we are obliged to treat him as such, not as a felon.[97]

Stockton, Dunham and six other captive officers of the New Jersey Volunteers were eventually sent to Carlisle, Pennsylvania, and placed in the jail there. In October of 1777, Stockton, Dunham and the other six officers signed a letter submitted to the Continental Congress asking to be relieved of the dreadful conditions in the Carlisle jail, as winter approached:

> We crave leave to observe to your honors that this prison is perhaps the worst on the continent, being rather a ruin than a gaol. Every part of it distributes air as through the holes of a colander, affecting the body with strange sensations and destroying our health. While at the same time we have no glass in the windows, seven of us are obliged to sleep in one room without anything but one blanket each.[98]

Later moved to a room in a jail in York, Pennsylvania, on May 17, 1778, Stockton, Dunham and Fraser joined with three other captive Tory officers, all of whom had spent at least sixteen months in jail, to pen a letter to Henry Laurens, the President of the Continental Congress, objecting to their confinements in "a loathsome, crowded jail infected with contagious fever, and polluted with noisome smells throughout every part."[99] A letter from Stockton, written on behalf of him and three captains and three subalterns, indicates that Patriot authorities may not have exchanged him and his fellow captives on the ground that they did not have their commissions as military officers with them when they were captured. As Stockton pointed out, when he was captured, he had orders addressed to him for holding the post at Bennett's Island and other correspondence between him and General Skinner and regular British officers.[100] The lack of commissions may have been an excuse to keep Stockton and other Tory officers out of the conflict for as long as possible.

Stockton was not released from his imprisonment until about September 1, 1779, much later than his fellow New Jersey Volunteer prisoners, many of whom had been paroled by August 1778. Stockton's role as the guide for Harcourt's party may again explain this harsh treatment. As a result of his battalion being merged into another in the New Jersey Volunteers, he lost his position as major. In 1780, he was convicted of murder on British-held Long Island and sentenced to death, but was not executed.[101] He later moved to Canada and died there in 1801 in New Brunswick.[102]

The Retaliatory Capture of Major General Richard Prescott

William Barton, an obscure officer in a Rhode Island state regiment, worried about Charles Lee and wanted to do something about it. He knew that Lee would never be exchanged until the Americans had as a prisoner a British army officer of the same rank of major general. As it happened, opposite Barton's posting in Tiverton, Rhode Island, was a large British garrison.

William Barton was born in ordinary circumstances in Warren, Rhode Island, in 1748, and as a young man he had struggled to build a small business as a hat maker in Providence. When war broke out, he joined the Rhode Island militia as a private, but his leadership skills showed, and he rose to become a lieutenant colonel in one of Rhode Island's two state regiments. Barton had met Lee when the latter had visited Newport in 1775, terrorized local Tories for a few days, and then departed. The Rhode Islander thought Lee was a great general.[103]

In June of 1777 all of Newport and the rest of Aquidneck Island was occupied by about 4,000 British, German and Loyalist soldiers of the British army.

II. The Fall of New York City and New Jersey 49

"The Capture of Prescott." General Richard Prescott stands in his nightshirt, ready to be put on board a whaleboat and taken across Narragansett Bay following his capture. The hats worn by the American soldiers are like the ones worn in the 1830s, when the engraving by an unknown artist was made (Williams, *Biography of Revolutionary Heroes*).

At the time, Newport was one of the five most important port cities in the thirteen states. In December 1776, a powerful fleet of more than seventy-one ships had carried the British invasion force to Narragansett Bay and after landing the troops easily captured Newport and the rest of the island, as well as nearby Conanicut Island (Jamestown). British warships then assumed stations at key points in Narragansett Bay, not allowing any American ships in or out of the bay. Rhode Island and Massachusetts troops on the mainland practically surrounding Aquidneck Island could not dislodge the British army.

On June 20, 1777, a Mr. Coffin was escorted to Barton's Tiverton headquarters. Coffin, a civilian, had recently escaped from Aquidneck Island. He had news about Major General Richard Prescott, who had recently assumed the command of the British troops on the island. This was the same Prescott who had earlier abused Ethan Allen. Coffin reported that General Prescott was spending nights at an isolated farm house owned by Henry John Overing about five miles north of Newport. Prescott previously had spent the nights at the John Banister house in the heart of Newport.

Barton then had an idea. He would form a small party of soldiers with experience using boats, not hard to do in Rhode Island. On a dark night, they would take boats across Narragansett Bay, avoiding the British warships stationed there. They would land unnoticed on the shores of Aquidneck Island, sneak up to the Overing house, and surround it. They would then storm the house, capture General Prescott, and spirit him back to the mainland. Prescott could then be exchanged for General Lee.

It did not hurt that General Prescott was a hated figure in Revolutionary Rhode Island. He was a classic petty tyrant. Once, reportedly, when he interviewed a privateer captain who had been captured by a British ship and brought to Newport, he knocked him in the head and threatened to hang him. Prescott would regularly visit a militia captain sitting in jail and threaten him with being hanged. He was known to strike Newport Quaker men with his cane for failing to doff their hats in respect when he approached.

Sometimes even the British felt Prescott went too far. Previously, in Canada, Prescott put out a reward of £1,000 for the capture of America's best general at the time, Benedict Arnold. Arnold, in turn, announced a reward for the capture of Prescott, but it was only half the amount, £500. Even London newspapers admired Arnold for his cleverness, and Prescott looked like a fool.

Why was Prescott spending time in the rural part of Aquidneck Island? Later reports were that he wanted to sleep with Henry John Overing's wife or some other local woman, but that was not true. In fact, he wanted to be closer to the action. Most of the Patriot army raids at this time had been at the northern part of Aquidneck Island, while Newport was in the south. During the summer months, raids occurred several times a week, often in the evenings. If the Americans were to invade the island in force, it would likely be in the northern part of the island. Prescott therefore ordered most of his regiments to be stationed in the northern part of Aquidneck Island. If there was any action, he would be closer to it by staying at the Overing house and he could issue orders to his troops from there.

Barton received permission from his superiors to execute his plan. He gathered together five whale boats, five other officers and forty-two soldiers. Most of them had experience rowing whale boats, including a local Native American who operated Barton's boat. Another soldier, an African American, probably Jack Sisson, would play an important role in the raid.

Barton meticulously made his plans. He recognized that the weakest link in the British defense of Aquidneck Island was Prescott's reliance on British warships in Narragansett Bay protecting the west coast of the island. Prescott had regiments stationed at the northern tip, northeast and eastern parts of Aquidneck Island, but none were stationed on its northwest coast. Prescott instead relied on the Royal Navy's 32- and 28-gun frigates, each brimming with from 200 to 220 sailors and marines on board, in the bay to protect the west coast. The problem was that there were only five of the frigates in the bay, and they were typically at least four miles from each other. Barton realized this flaw and planned not to come within two miles of any of the ships. For this reason, Barton excluded using Patriot-held Bristol just to the north of Aquidneck Island as his departure point, even though it was much closer to the Overing house than his eventual departure point, Warwick Neck, on the opposite side of Narragansett Bay.

Late on the dark night of July 10, Barton and his hand-picked detachment, starting their grueling journey rowing five whaleboats, departed from Warwick Neck. Using Prudence Island as a shield, they rowed in between the southern tip of Prudence Island and the northern tip of Conanicut Island, sneaking past British navy ships in the distance along the way. After landing, Barton left behind a man to watch each of the all-important whaleboats that would be needed for the return journey. He then carefully led his men along a hidden path to the farm house one mile away in which General Prescott spent his nights, steering clear of a guard house filled with slumbering British soldiers. At the time, in addition to Henry John Overing and his adult son, and their staff of black servants, sleeping at the house were General Prescott, Lieutenant William Barrington, the nephew of the British Secretary of War, and a dragoon in the attic. Private Walter Graham stood guard at the front door, the only sentry on duty at the Overing house. Henry John Overing's wife, Mary, and their eldest daughter, Henrietta, were not present.

As Barton was about to cross the empty West Road and enter the front yard to the Overing house, he divided his men into five groups. He directed one to approach the Overing house from its rear, the south door, and a second to close on the house from the west, towards the west door. Taking a separate route, Barton would lead a third group through the property's front yard to the house's east door. The fourth group was instructed to watch the West Road, while the fifth group was ordered to stand by in reserve.

At about 11:50 p.m. Barton and the rest of his third division, walking silently uphill single file, approached the property's front gate through a stand of trees. From twenty-five yards away, Private Graham spotted a disturbance and suddenly hailed them with an urgent "Who comes there?" Barton, taking a gamble, ignored this initial challenge and kept moving forward. Graham tried again, even more urgently: "Who comes there?" This time Barton answered, "Friends." Graham responded, "Friends, advance and give the countersign"—a request for that evening's secret password. Still leading his men forward, and entirely unaware of the password, Barton sternly barked, "We have no countersign to give; have you seen any deserters tonight?" Barton was pretending that he was a Loyalist officer on the prowl to hunt and return British army deserters.

Graham allowed Barton to approach; but even had he wanted to fire his weapon, if only as an alarm to the other soldiers in the Overing house and nearby, he could not have done so—amazingly, it was not loaded. Barton repeated his query, this time with some vehemence: "Have you seen any deserters?" Before Graham could respond, Barton was upon him and seized the trembling private's musket. Barton threatened Graham with death if he made any noise. "I won't," the captive meekly responded. Barton's ploy had worked brilliantly.

Barton recalled later, "We asked him [the sentry] if General Prescott was in the house; he was so frightened that at first he could not speak but at last with a faltering voice and waving his hand toward the house, said yes." Meanwhile, Barton's other men, except those watching the West Road and held in reserve, prepared to force their way into the Overing house using the first-floor entrance doors.

At Barton's signal, the raiders "burst all the doors open in an instant." One of Barton's party, an African American, probably Jack Sisson, took a running start and used his head as a battering ram to break the hefty front door. Barton lacked intelligence on what room Prescott was using as his bedroom. On the first floor, his men barged into the Overings' bedrooms but did not find the general. In frustration Barton, at the head of the stairway, "called for the soldiers to set the house on fire, for we were determined to have the General dead or alive!" A few of the raiders began calling out for General Prescott. At this, a voice from a second-floor bedroom was heard to say, "What is the matter?" Barton recalled, "I proceeded from whence it came and entering a room saw a man just rising out of bed, and clapping him on the shoulder, asked him if he was General Prescott." Sitting on the edge of his bed in his nightclothes, the groggy and astonished Prescott answered, "Yes sir." Barton informed him, "You are my prisoner." Prescott replied, "I acknowledge it, sir."

The action is then picked up in my *Kidnapping the Enemy* book:

> Meanwhile, Lieutenant Barrington, hearing the commotion and suspecting its cause, attempted to escape by leaping out of a first-floor window, wearing just his night shirt and britches. The Americans waiting watchfully outside the house immediately grabbed him. As the nephew of Lord Barrington, the British Secretary of War, Lieutenant Barrington was also a valuable prisoner. Back inside other raiders tried to snatch Overing and his son, but changed their minds when they put up a struggle. Time was short, and Barton could brook no delays. The raiders did not discover the dragoon quartered above the kitchen, as he wisely kept silent. For the most part, Barton's men followed his orders not to remove valuables from the home—even if its owner was a despised Loyalist.
>
> Back in his bedroom, Prescott requested permission to "put on his clothes," probably his full military uniform. But the Americans had little time for such niceties. Barton directed his captive to quickly don his waistcoat, britches, and slippers, provided him with a cloak, and had his men gather additional clothes in a bundle. He then ushered his shoeless prisoner outside, where the humbled Prescott joined the

barefoot Barrington and frightened Private Graham. Barton had spent just seven minutes in the Overing house. Maintaining his efficient pace, he ordered his men to return to their boats. Prescott was literally carried there. "We desired the General to put one arm over my shoulder and the other over one of the other officers that he might go with the greatest ease and dispatch," Barton wrote. Prescott's feet barely touched the ground as he was suspended between Barton and another tall, strong, and fast-moving officer.

The raiders had been fortunate to reach the Overing house without being spotted. And now, the one-mile distance back to the beach appeared much longer. But, rushing past the guard house and through a field of prickly barley, the hustling Americans again covered the ground without being noticed. Now, just before he was placed into Barton's whaleboat, Prescott was allowed to put on his coat and other clothing. He reportedly told his captor, "I hope you will not hurt me." Barton assured him that he would not. Ensign Abel Potter guided the last of the group's boats into five feet of water, and climbed aboard. The flotilla began the long journey back across Narragansett Bay to Warwick Neck.[104]

The raiders hurried to their boats and slipped back across the bay to Warwick, avoiding a flurry of British artillery and rocket fire. Barton fulfilled his mission of capturing a major general who could be traded for Lee.

Of course, Barton and his men had been in great danger of being caught, especially by guard boats sent out by British warships in the bay. If one musket had been fired as an alert, the whole plan might have been foiled. They risked being taken prisoner and put aboard British prison ships in Newport Harbor. Later that same summer, due to overcrowded conditions, poor and scanty food, and bad sanitation, dozens on board the prison ships died. But Barton and his men avoided being caught.

A British officer, several months after the raid, wrote that during it, he was in a rowboat with the seventeen-year-old daughter of Henry John Overing, Henrietta, and her chaperone and mother, Mary. The officer said he and Barton saw each other and that after the raid Barton admitted that he had seen his boat but chose to ignore it. Henrietta later married at Newport's Trinity Church another British officer, who abandoned her when he left Newport with his regiment. In later years she married a distant relative and her portrait by Gilbert Stuart hangs in the Brooklyn Art Museum.

An elated Washington called Barton's raid "among the finest partisan exploits that has taken place in the course of the war on either side."[105] It was the outstanding special operation of the Revolutionary War, and still ranks as one of the greatest in American military history. Lee and Prescott were finally exchanged in April of 1778. The Continental Congress was so pleased that it made Barton a colonel in the Continental Army and ordered that an "elegant sword" be awarded to him. This sword is now held by the Rhode Island Historical Society. Meanwhile, Prescott was hurried to an interior town, East Windsor, Connecticut, where he would be difficult for the British to rescue.[106]

And, of course, the British were humiliated. A British officer in Newport, Major Frederick Mackenzie, wrote in his diary, "It is certainly a most extraordinary circumstance that a general commanding a body of 4,000 men, encamped on an island surrounded by a squadron of ships of war, should be carried off from his quarters in the night by a small party of the enemy ... without a shot being fired."[107] Mackenzie drew a map of the route taken by Barton's men from the shore to the Overing house, based on the wet grass that had been matted down from the shoes of the raiders.[108]

British newspapers focused immediately on two salacious points: Prescott's shortage of clothing when he was spirited away, and rumors of his female companionship. The August 19, 1777, edition of London's *General Evening Post* reported, "Rebel troops ... took him naked out of his bed, not allowing him time to put on his clothes." The August 23 edition of the *London Evening Post* stated that Prescott "had retired in the evening with his aide-de-camp, and a sergeant's guard, to sleep a mile from his post, with a *lady*, but was discovered, and taken by a party of Provincials at two o'clock in the morning."

In little time, Prescott's capture attracted London's epigram talented writers. The ridicule became too much for King George III to stomach. The *Public Advertiser* reported in its September 1 edition, "His Majesty complains of the injustice done to Prescott by the News-Writers." This rumor of royal disfavor caused the humorists some pause for several weeks. But the cease-fire ended with the September 20 edition of the *London Evening Post*. It declared, "When General Prescott was taken prisoner all he was heard to say, when the Provincials were bearing him on their shoulders, out of the court-yard of the house was, '*give me my breeches—give me my breeches.*'"

With that, English wits returned to their favorite topic with relish. Even the controversy surrounding the media's ridicule became a target of humor. This from the September 26 edition of London's *Morning Chronicle*:

> A General of late has been vilely abus'd,
> And, without any reason, most falsely accused;
> For how could a man be neglectful of duty,
> Who was taken when storming the fortress of beauty?

The *London Chronicle*, too, capitalized on the fun:

> On General PRESCOTT being carried off naked, "unannointed, unannealed."
>
> WHAT lures there are to ruin a man;
> Woman, the first and foremost all bewitches!
> A nymph thus spoil'd a General's mighty plan,
> And gave him to the foe—without his breeches.

In fact, no credible evidence exists indicating that Prescott was found with a woman in his bed or that he stayed at the farm house in order to sleep with the farmer's wife or his daughter, or any other local woman—despite the legend that persists to this day. It was extraordinary the freedom that these English writers had at this time in mocking their military leaders during wartime.

Of the two captures, Barton's feat was the more impressive, mostly because it had to be carefully planned from beginning to end, and because his men penetrated deep inside the British perimeter and then departed from it safely with quarry in hand. Harcourt's operation was the result of a last-minute adjustment on the fly. Initially out to obtain intelligence, the dragoon commander quickly switched course after learning that Lee was staying nearby, virtually unprotected. His skillful escape through enemy-filled territory nearly matched his audacity in targeting Lee.

Barton's and Harcourt's operations had some similarities. Barton and Harcourt each benefitted from their targets, Lee and Prescott, spending the night far away from the camps of their troops. Each leader relied on information supplied by civilians and opposing soldiers (prisoners in Harcourt's case, and military and civilian escapees in Barton's). In addition, on at least two occasions Harcourt's dragoons threatened captives with immediate death if they did not divulge information related to Lee's location and circumstances, and the captives, under duress, provided the demanded intelligence. Revolutionary War historian Edwin Burrows, writing at a time of criticism of the reported torture of captives held by the U.S. Army in the Iraq War, commented that Harcourt's threats constituted "one of the few instances when the mistreatment of prisoners can be linked to intelligence gathering."[109] According to one contemporary account of Harcourt's raid, Tarleton's advance guard, fearing that the sound of a gunshot would alert nearby American soldiers, threatened to kill the sentry guarding Widow White's Tavern if he fired his musket. Barton's men likewise threatened the sentry outside the Overing house with death if he did not comply with the order not to alert others inside. Neither of these guards, it appears, carried a loaded musket. And both Harcourt and Barton threatened to burn down the house occupied by their quarry if he did not surrender himself. Most importantly, of course, both Barton's and Harcourt's missions succeeded. Few other special operations launched to kidnap generals or high-ranking government officials did.

Washington immediately offered to exchange Prescott for Lee, but General Howe refused. He still had not obtained word from London as to whether Lee should be treated as a deserter and traitor. Finally, months later, word arrived from London. The King, recognizing that Lee did resign and cognizant of Congress's policy to retaliate, allowed Lee to be exchanged. It took some time for

Howe and Washington to clear their differences regarding the treatment of prisoners generally. Finally, after fifteen months of captivity for Lee and nine for Prescott, the two generals were exchanged in April of 1778. Lee arrived back in the American camp at Valley Forge in May of 1778.

In my *Kidnapping the Enemy* book, I spend a chapter explaining how Lee returned as the general second-in-command to Washington; how he opposed fighting the British army because he did not think the American army could win; how he commanded the American army at the Battle of Monmouth Court House in June of 1778 and was accused of an unnecessary retreat and insulting Washington; how he was convicted of the same at a court-martial and suspended for one year; and how the court-martial was unfair in judging Lee's performance at Monmouth but unintentionally got it right. In 1779, after receiving a rude letter from a still angry Lee, Congress kicked Lee out of the Continental army. In disgrace, Lee died of an illness in a Philadelphia tavern in 1782 and was buried in an unmarked grave at the city's Christ Church cemetery.[110]

By contrast, Rhode Island's William Barton would live for many years. He gained a tremendous reputation for his capture of General Prescott. After the war, Rhode Islanders were the last holdout of the original thirteen colonies in not joining the union under the new U.S. Constitution. Finally, on May 29, 1790, when a state convention narrowly voted to ratify the U.S. Constitution, Barton was given the distinct honor of bringing the news to President Washington himself. He was also appointed the federal tax collector for the port of Providence, and rose to become major general of the state's militia.

But then financial and personal disaster struck Barton in 1812, resulting in his spending more than thirteen years in a Vermont debtor's prison. It was not until 1825, when another hero of the American Revolution interceded, that Barton finally returned to his family in Providence, where he was again celebrated as a war hero until his death at the age of eighty-three in 1831. My *Kidnapping the Enemy* book details the tragic post-war years of Barton.[111]

By the time of his death, Barton's daring capture of General Prescott had become a nationally honored event. Indeed, many collections of famous American stories produced through at least the mid-nineteenth century included a narrative of Barton's raid. At some point, probably shortly after Barton's death, an American fort overlooking the bluffs at Howland's Ferry, in Tiverton, first built in June of 1777, was named Fort Barton. Today it is a town park that goes by the same name. Only with the coming of the Civil War, and the countless incidents of bravery and horror associated with that national conflict, did Barton's legendary capture of Prescott begin to fade from public consciousness. I hope I have played a part in bringing back to prominence William Barton as a hero of the Revolutionary War.

George Washington Supports Kidnapping Attempt Against British Headquarters in New York City

Following William Barton's capture of Prescott in July 1777, General Washington fully supported attempts by Continental, state, and militia forces to capture high-ranking British army officers. He did not consider what was essentially kidnapping beneath the dignity of his armed forces. On the contrary, he thought a successful kidnapping operation could boost Patriot morale and gain an officer to exchange for a captive American officer. Responding to other kidnappings of British military personnel in the Rhode Island theater that had been spurred by Barton's raid, the commander-in-chief wrote to Major General Joseph Spencer, "The frequent captures you make with your little parties have a very good effect and ought to be encouraged."[112]

The following March Washington himself devised a scheme to seize the British army's commander of the New York City garrison, Sir Henry Clinton. He sent the plan to Brigadier General Samuel Holden Parsons of Connecticut, then in command of West Point. Washington's spies in New York City had informed him that Clinton occupied former British navy captain Archibald Kennedy's brick house at Number One Broadway, opposite Bowling Green, on the southern tip of Manhattan Island. Because of a devastating fire in the Wall Street district on September 21, 1776, it and two brick buildings next door stood virtually alone in the area. Washington himself had once used the Kennedy house as his headquarters, and his spies even told him in which room Clinton slept.[113]

Washington sought to assure Parsons that the British commander-in-chief was a proper military target. "I think it one of the most practicable

General Sir Henry Clinton, the target of more than one kidnapping plan (Author's collection).

58 Abductions in the American Revolution

(and it will be amongst the most desirable and honorable) things imaginable taking him prisoner," he wrote.[114] The remainder of his letter to Parsons indicated the time and effort he had spent considering the details of the proposed operation:

> This house lying close by the water, and a retired way through a back yard or garden leading into it, what, if you have whaleboats (8 or 10), but want of secrecy, can prevent the execution in the hands of an enterprising party? The embarkation might even be (and I should think the best), at King's Ferry on the first of the ebb [tide],

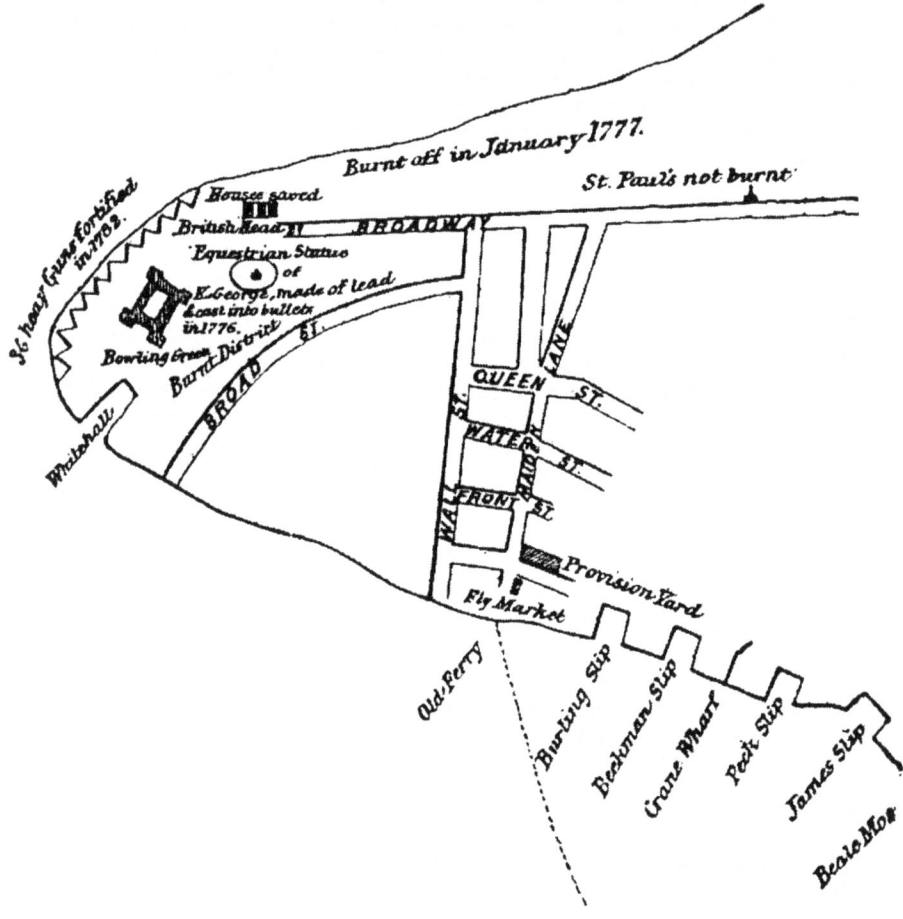

Part of a map showing Lower Manhattan Island during the occupation of New York City by British forces during the Revolutionary War. It shows large swaths of the city west of Broadway that burned down in the fire of September 1776, but also shows the surviving buildings at Numbers 1, 2 and 3 Broadway (Number 1 was Clinton's headquarters). Jeremiah Johnson, ca. 1786 (Trask, *Bowling Green*).

and early in the evening. Six or eight hours with change of hands, would row the boats under the west shore and very secretly to the city, and the flood tide will hoist them back again; or a party of horse might be sent to meet them at Fort Lee.

I had like not to have mentioned that no ship-of-war is in the North [Hudson] River (was not as least ten days ago), nor within 400 yards of the point [the southern tip of Manhattan Island], all of them being in the East River. I shall add no more. This is dropped as a hint to be improved upon or rejected as circumstances point out and justify.[115]

Conveniently for the would-be raiders, the garden in the rear of the Kennedy house extended 300 yards to the Hudson River.[116] This fact was also noted by Major James Wilkinson (he had been present at Widow White's Tavern when Charles Lee was captured), who recalled that "there were no buildings at that time between" the Kennedy house "and the river," and that Clinton was "relying on naval protection for safety in his rear."[117] Relying on Royal Navy ships for protection was the same mistake Prescott had made on Aquidneck Island in July 1777.

Three days later Washington followed up with another letter to Parsons containing an idea for a deception, "namely to let the officers and soldiers in the enterprise be dressed in red, and much in the taste of the British soldiery." Colonel Samuel B. Webb's Additional Continental Regiment, he noted, could supply the uniforms. The many New London, Hartford, and New Haven natives of Webb's regiment were renowned for wearing scarlet red uniforms taken from the massive British supply ship *Mellish*, which John Paul Jones had captured in December 1776.[118] Washington must have realized that American soldiers caught wearing British uniforms inside British lines would likely be treated—and hanged—as spies.

In a postscript, Washington reminded Parsons that Clinton's "official papers would be a vast acquisition and might without much difficulty accompany the person."[119] As the highest ranking general, behind only General Howe, in the British army in North America, Washington hoped that the raiders could seize Clinton's correspondence and plans.

Major Wilkinson later described an exchange in which Lieutenant Colonel Alexander Hamilton, then a young aide to General Washington, expressed his opposition to the plan:

> Colonel Hamilton took occasion to observe to the General [Washington] that "there could be little doubt of the success of the enterprise, but," said he, "have you examined the consequences of it?" The General inquired "in what respect?" "Why," replied Hamilton, "as it has occurred to me that we shall rather lose than gain by removing Sir Henry Clinton from the command of the British army, because we perfectly understand his character, and by taking him off we only make way for some other, perhaps an abler officer, whose character and dispositions we may have to learn." The General acknowledged these reflections had not occurred to him, but

with noble frankness admitted their force, thanked Colonel Hamilton for his suggestion, and the expedition was abandoned.[120]

Hamilton might also have mentioned another consequence of capturing Clinton, based on the experience of Charles Lee. If Clinton was seized, the British would likely have reciprocated by targeting an American of equal rank, in this case, probably Washington himself. The operation was laid aside—at least for the time being. It is not known if the operation was suspended for the reasons stated in Wilkinson's recollections.

Washington's plan to abduct Clinton at British headquarters in New York City represented the first time that the Continental army had laid formal plans to capture a high-ranking enemy general. (Barton and his men who captured General Prescott hailed from one of Rhode Island's state regiments). It would not be the last time.

III

The Fall of Philadelphia (September 1777 to April 1778)

Delaware's Chief Executive Is Abducted from His House

Near the start of British commander-in-chief William Howe's campaign to seize Philadelphia, at Wilmington, Delaware, on September 5, 1777, Washington learned from several persons that there was "a Hessian general quartered at one Fisher's, covered only by a small guard." Washington dashed off a note to Brigadier General William Maxwell, who two days earlier had led American militiamen in a skirmish against British troops near Fisher's house, stating that the German general's close proximity offered "a glorious opportunity for a partisan exploit."[1] By September 10, General Howe's army was back on the march toward Philadelphia, and the opportunity to capture the German general (probably Knyphausen) was lost. On September 11, 1777, both sides were busy fighting the Battle of Brandywine outside Philadelphia.

On the night of September 12, 1777, the evening after General Howe's victory at Brandywine, Delaware residents thought themselves safe. Surely, the British would now focus on taking Philadelphia, the great prize of the new United States. But Howe ordered the British 71st Regiment, known as Frasier's Highlanders, to seize Wilmington, Delaware, and to establish a hospital for the wounded there. The detachment sent for the purpose, soon after its arrival, was informed by local Loyalists that Delaware's governor (with the title of President), John McKinly, was staying at his residence in the town. At night the soldiers found McKinly at home in bed and made him a prisoner, and they seized the governor's state papers as well.[2]

The fifty-six-year-old Scotch-Irishman was kept in Wilmington for eight days, until on September 20 Captain Andrew Snape Hammond of the H.M.S. *Roebuck*, "for the more certain security" of retaining the valuable prisoner, ordered Captain Thomas Symonds of the H.M.S. *Solebay*, which lay in the Delaware River off of Newcastle, to take McKinly on board his ship. Hammond ordered that McKinly "be accommodated an officer's berth, allowed the liberty of being upon deck (at proper times) during the day time ... and in all respects treated with civility."[3] In a letter to his wife, McKinly conceded he was treated with "much civility" on board the *Solebay*.[4] He was detained there until Howe's army finally took Forts Mercer and Mifflin below Philadelphia in late November and British ships could pass freely up to Philadelphia. Allowed to reside in the house of an acquaintance, McKinly stayed there until General Henry Clinton evacuated the city in June of 1778. McKinly was then brought by sea with other prisoners to Flatbush, Long Island, where he stayed until he was paroled in August for one month in order to seek his formal exchange.[5]

While serving the Patriot cause as the chief executive of Delaware, McKinly was a moderate, and not a zealous, Whig. His moderation was key to his election in conservative Delaware, but it hurt him later in the halls of the Continental Congress. The logical decision was to exchange McKinly for William Franklin, the former governor of New Jersey held by the Americans. However, some Congressional delegates reportedly expressed the concern that the passionate Tory William Franklin, if freed, would "do more mischief than the president [McKinly] can do good."[6]

As a result of his being captured and held by the British, McKinly's loyalty also began to be questioned. On February 12, 1778, the man who replaced McKinly temporarily as president of Delaware, Thomas McKean, wrote to George Read, who was McKinly's permanent successor as president, discussing McKinly's captivity in Philadelphia: "I was told the other day that he lodged at widow Jenkins's, along with his *old friends* Robinson and Manlove, and seemed *very happy*."[7] Thomas Robinson and Boaz Manlove were two Delaware Tories who had fled to the protection of British-held Philadelphia.[8] In responding to McKean's veiled charge against McKinly, Brigadier General Caesar Rodney defended the former executive: "It may be that those traitors to their country have visited him, though it be merely to insult him in his unfortunate situation. But, Sir, I am well informed that Robinson has lodged at Joshua Fishers ever since he first went to the City and that Manlove's place of abode is at one Snowden's over the drawbridge."[9] In fact, when McKinly first moved to the "widow Jenkins's" house, he had been invited by three captive American officers to join them.[10] Rodney hoped that an exchange could be worked out, even though McKinly "might never have discharged the duty of that station [as President of Delaware] with that energy that you and I could have wished."[11]

Still, Congress delayed in making the obvious exchange of McKinly for William Franklin. One reason for the delay was that no Whig leader from

Delaware pushed for the exchange. Finally, General Henry Clinton, then commander-in-chief of the British army, released McKinly for one month to travel to Philadelphia to negotiate his exchange. General Caesar Rodney came to McKinly's defense, informing the President of the Continental Congress, Henry Laurens, in an August 24, 1778, letter, that from the date of his appointment as president of Delaware "until he was taken prisoner, all his letters and orders to me as commanding officer of the militia breathed the same spirit of patriotism."[12] On the verge of his one month pass expiring and being forced to return to captivity in New York, Congress finally agreed to formally exchange McKinly for William Franklin in mid–September of 1778.[13]

Even as he was being freed, McKinly was insulted. General William Thompson had been captured by the British in 1776, but after a few months of captivity had been released on parole and allowed to return to Pennsylvania. But under the terms of his parole he was not allowed to take up arms against the British until he was formally exchanged for a high-ranking prisoner held by the Americans. When Congress passed by Thompson in order to exchange McKinly for Franklin, the general was heard to complain loudly, "Some who were taken sleeping in their beds [referring to General Lee, in addition to McKinly] were exchanged, whilst he who was taken fighting in the field was not exchanged."[14]

McKinly never again held public office. Franklin, as anticipated, would cause Patriots trouble, including coming up with a plan for kidnapping New Jersey's Governor William Livingston and supporting other kidnapping efforts.

In the aftermath of the Battle of Brandywine, with Philadelphia exposed to be captured by Howe's army, members of the Continental Congress were warned by Washington's aide, Colonel Alexander Hamilton, to evacuate the city immediately. Delegate James Lovell of Massachusetts wrote to another state delegate, "with the capture of Governor McKinly fresh in memory, your colleagues with their brethren of Congress took to the saddle without loss of time, governed by different fancies as to roads."[15] None of them were seized by the British army. McKinly's immediate successor as chief executive of Delaware, Thomas McKean, complained to John Adams that following the Battle of Brandywine "I was hunted like a fox" and that he had to avoid being kidnapped by moving his family five times in two months.[16]

Congress Responds to Tory Kidnappings

Most operations during the Revolutionary War to kidnap officers and government officials were conducted either by irregular Loyalist forces or Patriot militia forces. And most of these targeted low-ranking military and minor government officials.

Loyalists became emboldened by the British September 26 capture of Philadelphia. On February 14, 1778, Colonel Joseph Kirkebride of Bordentown, New Jersey, informed Thomas Wharton, President of the Pennsylvania Supreme Executive Council, sitting at Lancaster, "You have undoubtedly before this heard of the unhappy capture of poor Colonel Coates, which was entirely done by treachery and for want of a proper guard upon the roads in that quarter." William Coates had been put in the new common jail in Philadelphia, where "a violent fever prevails very much among the prisoners and carries numbers of them off." Kirkebride complained that "I am almost every day warned by one or other of my friends to be upon my guard, as I have for some time past been threatened by the enemy.... I am afraid a plan is forming, through treachery, to kidnap as many as possible of the Friends of Liberty, for which a handsome reward is offered" by British authorities in Philadelphia.[17] The February 17 issue of the British-controlled *Pennsylvania Evening Post*, distributed in Philadelphia, gleefully published a list of captured "militia officers, justices of the peace, and collectors of fines under the new state, and some other disaffected persons."

Writing to President Wharton on February 23, General Washington, from his headquarters at Valley Forge, expressed his astonishment that "the insolence of the disaffected in Philadelphia and Bucks Counties had arisen to a very alarming height." The Tories, he added, had "seized and carried off a number of respectable inhabitants in those counties, and such officers of the army as fell their way," including Major Francis Murray of the 13th Pennsylvania Regiment, who was captured on February 21 at Newtown, along with five of his subordinate officers, by a raiding party of Pennsylvania Loyalists operating out of Philadelphia.[18]

One Loyalist kidnapper, who had tried to seize a Whig justice of the peace, was captured, but the Continental army hesitated to try the man by court-martial, concerned that it did not have the statutory authority to try a civilian.[19] Joseph Reed, representing a group of officers in the Continental army at Valley Forge, in a letter to Henry Laurens, the President of the Continental Congress, focused on the lack of statutory authority "to try persons other than of the Army," even though "those villains ... come out to kidnap and deliver to the enemy the active friends of their country." Reed further lamented that "there are a number of these offenders now in custody who must either escape with impunity (the court-martial having declined passing upon them)" or the accused kidnappers must be turned over to the state to be prosecuted under general state laws.[20]

In late February 1778 Congress, meeting in York, Pennsylvania, finally took official notice of Tory-run kidnapping operations. In a formal resolution, it denounced Tories who banded together "for the purpose of seizing and secretly conveying to places in possession of the British forces, such of the loyal citizens, officers, and soldiers of these states, as may fall into their power." The resolution called this "nefarious" practice "repugnant to the rules of war"—despite the fact that Americans were conducting similarly secret work. Congress declared that any person who "shall kill or seize, or take any loyal citizen or citizens thereof, and convey him, her or them, to any place within the power of the enemy," or who gave intelligence or acted as a guide in such an effort, "shall suffer death by the judgment of a court-martial, as a traitor, assassin and spy," if the offence was committed within seventy miles of the headquarters of any American army.[21]

While the Congressional resolution was a significant one, it had its limits. In a May 19, 1778, letter Washington declared that one "Jetson," despite his "atrocious" Tory conduct, could not be tried by Continental army court-martial unless the charge of "kidnapping as one of Jetson's offenses" was supported by evidence and fell within the new law passed by Congress.[22]

Although the resolution was widely publicized, the threat contained in it did not deter nineteen-year-old William Hammet, described by a Loyalist gazette as "an intrepid young man who had suffered much by the Rebel plunders."[23] Learning that two Whig officers were staying at Dr. Benjamin Vanleer's house in Haddonfield, New Jersey, Hammet rounded up four other Loyalists from British-occupied Philadelphia to take them on the night of March 15, 1778. After crossing the Delaware River, they approached Vanleer's house, "broke open the door, passed up to the room where the two officers lay, and with a fixed bayonet at their breasts, demanded their arms." Hammet transported his two captives to military authorities in Philadelphia.[24]

New Jersey authorities apprehended Hammet later in the year. Under Congress's tough, kidnapping-related law, Hammet could have been court-martialed. Instead, he and seventeen others were tried and convicted of high treason, under state law, in Gloucester County Court, New Jersey, and on December 5, 1778, sentenced to death. While the New Jersey Privy Council pardoned the other seventeen men, it chose not to extend mercy to the unrepentant Hammet, in part because of his role in kidnapping the two Whig officers.[25] On the day of his execution, January 29, 1779, Hammet "passed a great crowd of spectators" to reach the gallows where "he was hung and died quickly."[26]

It does not appear that any civilian Tory was ever hanged under the law passed by the Continental Congress designed to discourage kidnappings of Patriot leaders within seventy miles of an American army. Patriot leaders were probably hesitant to apply the law, knowing that Tories and the British could retaliate in kind. Moreover, state law could be vigorously applied to the same ends, as was demonstrated in Hammet's case.

A notorious Tory marauder operating out of British-held Newport, Rhode Island, William Crossing, was overtaken by a sailboat filled with Patriot militiamen and caught in his whaleboat in the Sakonnet River, within hours of his raiding nearby Dartmouth, Massachusetts, and taking with him in his whaleboat two prisoners, both local Whig officials. At a court-martial held in Providence, the headquarters of the American army near where Crossing was taken, Crossing was found to lack a commission as an officer in a military regiment and was convicted of marauding, robbing and plundering. Crossing was sentenced, "according to the custom of war" to "suffer death by the cord."[27] Even though Crossing was caught having kidnapped two victims within twenty-five miles of the American headquarters at Providence, no mention was made of the law enacted by Congress to address such conduct.

The American commander in the Rhode Island theater of war, Major General John Sullivan, forwarded the court-martial transcript to Congress and sought approval of the death sentence.[28] Sullivan clearly had authority to approve the hanging of Crossing under the Continental Congress's legislation, without in turn seeking the approval of President Henry Laurens of the Continental Congress. But Sullivan may not have felt comfortable acting on his own, perhaps out of fear of retaliation by the British in Newport or the factual question of whether Crossing was a commissioned officer (General Richard Prescott, back as commander of the Newport garrison, argued that Crossing was a commissioned officer, but he never produced a copy of the commission). But before Congress acted, Crossing managed to escape from his jail cell and make it safely back to Newport.[29] With a death sentence still looming, Crossing went underground and was essentially not heard from again.

Kidnapping and marauding continued on both sides near any British garrison, but particularly in the area of northern New Jersey and Staten Island. Cornelius Titus, a fugitive slave from Monmouth County, formed a small, but effective, band of African American Loyalists, using British-occupied Staten Island and Sandy Hook, New Jersey, as bases to raid Whig households in Monmouth County. General Clinton, in a June 30, 1779, manifesto, had adopted a policy of freeing slaves for serving in the British army, and Titus and his men meant to benefit from it.

In one of his first raids in 1779, Titus raided a farm at Shrewsbury, New Jersey, near where he had served as a slave, taking cattle, horses and two prisoners. On March 30, 1780, "Colonel Tye," as Titus came to be known, and his men raided the home of John Russell, again in the town of Shrewsbury. Russell himself had participated in Whig raids on Staten Island. Titus's party burned

Russell's house, killed his father, and wounded his son. In a two-week period in June, Titus and his men killed a Whig known for executing Loyalists in Monmouth County at his house, took twelve prisoners at the house of Barnes Smock (one of the Whig leaders in Monmouth County), and led another raid in the county that netted eight prisoners, including a captain and major of the militia. Titus's raiders suffered no casualties.

Titus created such fear among white Whigs in Monmouth County that in July 1780, led by former New Jersey militia general David Forman, they organized the Association for Retaliation. On September 1, 1780, Titus attempted what would have been his greatest feat—the capture of Captain Josiah Huddy, who was renowned for raiding Staten Island and Sandy Hook, and was accused of executing several Loyalists seized in his raids. Huddy was eventually burned out of his Colt's Neck house, but he later escaped by jumping off the whaleboat taking him to New York City. During the gun battle with Retaliators at Huddy's home, Titus was struck in the wrist by a musket ball. Although Titus's wounds were initially thought to be minor, he contracted lockjaw, and after several days he died.[30]

Huddy was again captured on March 23, 1782, by a party of 120 Associated Loyalists, a group of militant Loyalists organized by former New Jersey governor William Franklin. Meanwhile, Philip White, a Loyalist who had killed the son of another New Jersey militia captain, was captured by Huddy's men and executed. In revenge, Captain Richard Lippincott and other Loyalists took Huddy from his prison ship—without receiving proper permission from British General Clinton—and hanged him. "Up goes Huddy for Phillip White," said the placard left on the victim.

After Lippincott was found not guilty in a British army court-martial, Washington ordered the execution of a British prisoner of the same rank as Huddy. At a prisoner of war camp in Pennsylvania, lots were drawn, and young Captain Charles Asgill was selected. He was an unfortunate choice as he was the son of a merchant-banker who had been Lord Mayor of London and had been knighted as a baronet. Washington delayed Asgill's execution, hoping that the new British commander-in-chief, Sir Guy Carleton, would convict Lippincott. Eventually, the case became a *cause célèbre*, with Asgill's mother travelling to Paris and writing to the Comte de Vergennes, the French minister of foreign affairs. Vergennes was so moved by the letter that he showed it to King Louis XVI, who ordered his minister to request Washington to release Asgill. Vergennes reminded Washington that Asgill, captured at Yorktown by allied French-American forces, was also a prisoner of the French. After forwarding Vergennes's appeal to Congress, following a spirited debate, the delegates voted to spare Asgill's life as a gift to Louis XVI.[31]

"Paul Jones, the Pirate." Some British considered John Paul Jones to be akin to a pirate. Engraving of caricature published by A. Park, London, 1825 (National Archives).

John Paul Jones Strikes Fear in Great Britain

The Continental navy's only prominent kidnapping attempt occurred within the borders of Great Britain itself. Not surprisingly, it was conducted by the navy captain who gained the greatest reputation for boldness and courage, John Paul Jones. One man who knew Jones described him as "a man about five feet six inches high, well-shaped below his head and shoulders, rather round shouldered, with a visage fierce and warlike." This contemporary also called him an "excellent seaman," as knowledgeable of navy tactics as the best captains, and brave.[32]

Sailing from Brest, France, on April 10, 1778, Jones, then captain of the 18-gun *Ranger*, sought to bring the war home to the British people and capture high-ranking Britons to exchange for American sailors rotting in jails in Great Britain.[33] Jones and his crew were about to undertake one of the Continental navy's most celebrated cruises of the war.

Boldly sailing into the Irish Sea, Jones and his crew captured and sank several small British commercial vessels, after seizing their sailors. Then Jones set his site on Whitehaven, of which he was well acquainted, having grown up near the town. He landed with thirty-one men in two small boats at Whitehaven at 3 a.m. in the morning of April 23, while townsmen slumbered and the town's two forts were unmanned. The *Ranger* crew spiked about thirty 32-pounder and 42-pounder guns at the forts, and tried to start a fire in the harbor hoping it would catch on and burn some two hundred merchant vessels anchored there. This attempt, as well as a deserter from Jones's crew, awoke townsmen, who rushed to contain the fire and lost only two vessels, while the *Ranger's* raiders retreated back to their ship.[34]

Later the same day, Jones then crossed Solway Firth and landed at St. Mary's Isle in Scotland to try to kidnap Dunbar Hamilton, the fourth Earl of Selkirk, whose estate was near Kirkcudbright. Jones's father had worked as a groundskeeper on the estate. Now he had returned to seize the area's most prominent aristocrat, even if he was a minor nobleman by overall British standards. The sea captain probably selected his target because of his familiarity with the local area.

Coming ashore with about a dozen armed men in the morning, Jones used a clever ruse to chase off the male servants on Lord Selkirk's property by announcing that he was leading a Royal Navy press gang seeking men for dreaded service on board British war ships. But he also soon learned from some men onshore that the earl was away, in London. A disappointed Jones wanted to return to the *Ranger*, but some of his crew insisted that they had a right to plunder Selkirk's rambling Georgian manor house. Jones, who had had a number of troubles with his rambunctious crew, argued against it but ultimately felt he had to compromise and allow his men to enrich themselves somewhat to compensate for the risks they were taking on this dangerous voyage. It appears that Jones permitted his crew to liberate Selkirk's manor house of its valuable set of silver plate, but not more.[35] Jones, who did not want his local reputation tarnished by participating in a mere seizure of plunder, returned to the *Ranger*.

Meanwhile, the raiders, led by Lieutenant Samuel Wallingford of the Continental Marines, marched to Selkirk's house and surrounded it. According to an account in a London newspaper, the Connecticut-born Wallingford and two others, each armed "with two horse-pistols at his side, and with bayonets fixed … demanded to see the lady of the house; and upon her appearing, told her, with a mixture of rudeness and civility, who they were, and that all the plate must be delivered to them." A pregnant Lady Selkirk (Helen Hamilton) cooperated by handing over the silver pieces. Wallingford explained to her that "their intention was to size Lord Selkirk, who is now in London."[36] If some of the Americans were "horrid-looking wretches," she later wrote to her husband, "I must say they behaved civilly."[37] The London newspaper marveled that "without doing any other damage, or asking for watches, jewels, or anything else (which is odd) the *gentlemen* made off." Wallingford and his men returned safely to the *Ranger* and were fortunate to avoid armed men from Kirkcudbright who rushed to confront them.[38] However, before leaving, a few of Jones's men let it be known that they would return, causing the local militia to be on guard for several days and Lady Selkirk to flee to the estate of a nearby aristocrat that was located farther from the coast.

On the morning of April 24, shortly after leaving St. Mary's Isle, while sailing off Carrickfergus near Belfast in the North Channel, Jones and the *Ranger* were challenged by the 20-gun Royal Navy sloop-of-war *Drake*, whose commander had been informed of Jones's Whitehaven raid. The two ship commanders spent time maneuvering for the inevitable engagement, until Jones at about 7 p.m. pressed in and fired the first broadside. A fierce battle ensued that lasted for one hour and five minutes, until the commander and lieutenant of the *Drake*, as well as some forty others of the British ship's officers and men, fell and the British ship surrendered. Had the Earl of Selkirk been on board the *Ranger*, Jones later wrote to Lady Selkirk, "he would have seen the awful pomp and dreadful carnage of a sea engagement."[39] Jones did not have the heart to inform Lady Selkirk that the leader of the party that raided her house and took the family silver, Lieutenant Samuel Wallingsford, was killed in the contest after being shot in the head by a musket.[40]

On his voyage to the coast of Britain, in addition to claiming the damaged *Drake* as a prize, Jones captured a merchant brig and sank three other small vessels. When he arrived at Brest, France, on May 7, 1778, he had with him some two hundred captive British sailors, whom he hoped to exchange for American prisoners.[41]

While his raid on Whitehaven was a minor affair, it was nevertheless the first on a British seaport since the Dutch wars of the seventeenth century.[42] The British public also took note. Those living on the coast were apprehensive of where Jones might strike next. "We are all in a bustle here," a Whitehaven correspondent reported in the *London Morning Press*, as a result of the "late insolent attack of the provincial privateer's men." The report identified Jones as "John Paul," who had apprenticed on a Whitehaven ship and "was well known by many people in this town." The *Morning Chronicle* reported that the northern coasts of England and Scotland were so fear-stricken "that a general intimidation discovers itself on every appearance of a sail."[43] Shortly after Jones's raid, Lord George Germain, the British cabinet official leading the war effort, declared in a letter to the Admiralty that "the Rebel privateer which plundered Lord Selkirk's house has thrown the whole western coast into consternation."[44]

Jones had made his mark. British navy ships dispatched to find Jones returned empty handed. Insurance rates on shipments across the Irish Sea increased fourfold. In later years, British mothers would warn their children to behave, or the "Pirate Jones" would come and take them in the night.

After the affair, Jones wrote to Lady Selkirk, promising to return the family silver and stating that he had merely "wished to make [Lord Selkirk] the happy instrument of alleviating the horrors of hopeless captivity, when the brave are overpowered and made prisoners of war." As another defense of his men's actions he added, "Some officers who were with me could not forbear expressing their discontent, observing that in America no delicacy was shown by the English, who took away all sorts of movable property, setting fire not only to towns and to the houses of the rich without distinction; but not even sparing the wretched hamlets and milk cows of the poor and helpless as the approach of an inclement winter."[45] Jones compensated his officers and crew for their share of the silver, while the Continental Congress agreed to waive its one-half share.[46] Lord Selkirk pompously delayed matters by taking the position that while "he might not refuse it if offered him by a public body" such as the Continental Congress, "he could not accept it from any private person whatever," meaning from Jones.[47] Finally, after seven years and much time and expense, Jones successfully had the plate returned to the Selkirks.[48]

IV

The War in the North (January 1778 to February 1781)

Multiple Attempts to Kidnap Governor William Livingston of New Jersey

William Livingston, the Whig governor of New Jersey, was probably targeted for kidnapping more often than any other leader in the war. This dubious honor was due in part to his firm anti–Tory policies and in part to his close proximity to British headquarters in New York City. Liberty Hall, his home, was near Elizabethtown, little more than a cannon shot's distance from British and Loyalist forces stationed across the bay on Staten Island.

Livingston hated Tories. He once wrote to Washington, "A Tory is an incorrigible animal and nothing but the extinction of life will extinguish his malevolence against liberty."[1] It is little wonder that both the British and Loyalists would endeavor on numerous occasions to kidnap and remove Livingston from his post as governor.

Livingston first expressed concern for his personal safety in early 1778. "I have this

New Jersey Governor William Livingston, the frequent target of kidnapping attempts. Silhouette, capturing Livingston's prominent nose (Moody, *Narrative*).

moment received intelligence that a party is engaged to way-lay me between this place [Morristown] and my house," he wrote to Washington on January 13.[2] Two weeks later, he briefed the commander-in-chief that he had uncovered "our enemies ... in offering a bribe to assassinate me."[3] In response the New Jersey governor took to staying at the homes of friends or in rented quarters in the northwest interior of the state at Parsippany. On March 28 the New Jersey legislature passed a resolution permitting him to call on a "guard for the security of his person" consisting of six light horsemen and six militiamen whenever he thought fit.[4] These efforts failed to discourage his enemies. On April 10 Livingston wrote to Levinus Clarkson, a New Brunswick merchant, thanking him for alerting him to "the friendly designs of some British scoundrels in New York. I was before apprised of their infernal assassinating purpose and am provided for a small skirmish with them."[5]

In February 1779, General Clinton personally authorized a secret expedition by 1,000 soldiers (an especially substantial raiding force) to seize Governor Livingston at Liberty Hall. In the overnight darkness of February 25–26, Lieutenant Colonel Thomas Stirling of the 42nd Regiment (also known as the Black Watch) led his boated force from Staten Island to a spot about two miles north of Elizabethtown. Marching "with the most profound silence," the raiders surrounded Liberty Hall at 5:00 a.m., but, as Stirling informed Clinton, "the Rebel governor Livingston had notice and left his house before we got there."[6] The *New Jersey Journal* later reported that Livingston had spent the night at the home of a friend.[7]

Determined to salvage something from the operation, Stirling roused the governor's daughters, Catherine and Susannah, from their beds and demanded that they turn over their father's public papers. Susannah reportedly concealed her father's most important documents, and handed over papers of minimal significance.[8] Stirling and his troops then raced from Liberty Hall to Elizabethtown, hoping to surprise in their barracks the men of General William Maxwell's Brigade. But again the British were disappointed. Maxwell's men, warned of Stirling's intent, had retreated safely toward Perth Amboy.[9]

Several weeks after this incident, Livingston wrote a letter of complaint to Clinton. It was not the kidnapping attempt that troubled him, but the fact that he had in his possession "the most authentic proofs of a general officer under your command having offered a large sum of money to an inhabitant of this state to assassinate me, in case he could not take me alive." Livingston wrote that, because he doubted that the British commander-in-chief could be a party "to a design so sanguinary and disgraceful," he would give Clinton the opportunity to disavow "such dark proceedings." The New Jersey governor added menacingly that, if the British leader had approved such a plot, he should beware since "your person is more in my power than I have reason to think you imagine."[10]

In British-held New York City, prominent Loyalists "ridiculed" Livingston's charges.[11] Clinton answered Livingston's letter with a published statement in which he denied he had "a soul capable of harboring so infamous an idea as assassination," especially "to obtain so trifling an end." With undisguised sarcasm, Clinton added: "Sensible of the power you boast of being able to dispose of my life by means of intimates of yours, ready to murder at your command, I can only congratulate you on your able connections."[12] Rivington's *Royal Gazette* published the two men's letters with Clinton winning plaudits for his cleverness. Loyalist William Smith, a friend of Governor Livingston prior to the war, wrote in his journal, "It is no compliment to the General [Clinton] that people wonder who penned it."[13] Livingston responded with a second missive in which he denied threatening to murder the British general.[14]

In fact, Lieutenant Colonel Stirling's orders were merely to kidnap Livingston. The operation was apparently the brainchild of William Franklin—the son of Benjamin Franklin and New Jersey's last royal governor—who had been held by Patriot authorities as a prisoner from June 1776 to October 1778 until he was exchanged for Delaware's John McKinly. Now the head of a New York-based Loyalist ring, the younger Franklin had suggested on February 3 that Clinton send a force into New Jersey "to bring off a number of committee men and other Rebels to keep as hostages for their own security and in case any of their body should happen to be taken prisoners."[15] Thus, the former governor's motive was to help the English secure a prominent public official who might be exchanged for Franklin himself, in the event that Patriots kidnapped him.

One kidnapping effort against Livingston, possibly orchestrated by New York City Mayor David Mathews, suggested that the dangers on such missions were not all faced by the targets. In mid–June 1779, Livingston learned of a plot to kidnap him while he travelled from Trenton northward to his second home in Parsippany. Deciding to remain in central New Jersey, the governor allowed his son, William Livingston, Jr., to spread word that his father would be at his rented house in Parsippany on June 22.[16] At about 2:00 a.m. on June 23, kidnappers approached the house, where they were surprised by Livingston, Jr., and a small force. One of the Tories was captured.[17]

In January 1780, Livingston gave up his Parsippany home and moved to the house of a friend two miles from Washington's Morristown headquarters. He politely declined Washington's offer to send guards for his protection should he want to return to Parsippany, responding that he could "not think of putting the men to that trouble for my sake."[18]

In May 1780, Lieutenant General Wilhelm von Knyphausen authorized another attempt against Livingston. This one would be led by Knyphausen's aide-de-camp, Captain George Beckwith of the 37th Regiment, and Ensign James Moody of the New Jersey Volunteers, a Loyalist regiment. Both were remarkable men. Beckwith's role in the British secret service is often overlooked, but it should not be. Just in his twenties, Beckwith established himself as a resourceful intelligence officer during the latter years of the British occupation of New York City. He developed extensive contacts with Loyalists stretching from Rhode Island to the north and Pennsylvania to the south. He once even obtained from Philadelphia "a good many secrets of Congress that he could have got only from intimate acquaintance with members." Using a go-between, he initiated the correspondence with Benedict Arnold, using the alias G. B. Ring. After John André's capture, he became the liaison with Benedict Arnold, and after André's hanging as a spy on October 2, 1780, he assumed the dead officer's responsibilities leading the British intelligence effort from British headquarters. After the war, he was appointed governor of Bermuda in 1797, knighted in 1809, and promoted to general in 1814. During the Napoleonic wars, he commanded a British invasion force that captured the French island of Guadeloupe in 1810.[19]

James Moody, born in Little Egg Harbor in New Jersey in about 1744, married and raised a family on his father's 500-acre farm in Sussex County (present-day Warren County). At the outbreak of the Revolution, although he was a "lover of peace & good order, and loyal on principle," he had taken no active part in the struggle. On Sunday, March 28, 1777, a party of Patriot militia arrived at his house to arrest him for refusing to renounce his allegiance to the Crown and swear loyalty to the United States. Shots were fired, but he managed to escape.

In September 1777, Moody was at the head of a Loyalist force of about 130 men who had gathered from Bucks County, Pennsylvania, Hunterdon County, New Jersey, and other areas in between, guiding them to British-held Staten Island. But before they reached their destination, they were set upon by a stronger force of local Patriot militia. Most of the Loyalists were captured and imprisoned in Trenton, but Moody and eight others escaped. As discussed in connection with the parole of John Fell, two of the captured men, Lieutenant John Iliff of the New Jersey Volunteers and John Mee, a British soldier out recruiting for the same Tory regiment, were hanged for the crime of treason at Morristown on December 2, 1777.[20] (It may have been after this ugly episode that the British began to target Livingston for kidnapping, given that the governor first mentioned he was a potential kidnapping victim in early 1778.)

After arriving in New York City, Moody became an unpaid volunteer in the New Jersey Volunteers under Brigadier General Cortlandt Skinner, the last Crown-appointed attorney general of New Jersey. Because of his knowledge of northern New Jersey, Moody was often sent back there to observe Patriot troop movements, enlist Loyalists in military service, and generally annoy northern New Jersey Whigs.

On May 10, 1778, Moody departed New York City for Sussex County on a mission to recruit more men for the New Jersey Volunteers. Due to the presence of Whig authorities, Moody was "obliged to stay in the woods" for almost two months and was able to spend "one day only in his own house" in Knowlton township. Moody had a second mission—"to take Martin, one of the Rebel commissioners employed in selling" Tory estates. (The target was Isaac Martin of Hardyston in Sussex County, who not only served as a colonel of the militia, but also as a commissioner supervising the sale of forfeited Tory property.) According to an account Moody later told to a British secret service agent, Moody and three other recruits kidnapped Martin on July 14 "at his own house" but that two days later, a party of sixty Whig militiamen sent to rescue Martin caught up with them. Moody released Martin in order to escape safely back to New York City, which he reached about August 9.[21] One of Martin's rescuers, in his pension application submitted after the war, stated that when news arrived that "Moody took Col. Martin from his house in Sussex County and attempted to take him to New York ... squads of militia & volunteer citizens" immediately pursued the abductors, until they overtook them "at a place called Sprowles Meadow."[22]

Moody survived several other narrow escapes. He once stood erect inside a haystack for two days, without food, and without alerting enemy soldiers camped nearby. On another occasion after he completed a dangerous mission for General Clinton, the commander-in-chief scolded Moody, warning that he should not undertake any more "such hazardous enterprises." But as Moody later recalled in his memoirs, "these and his other intentions seldom lasted longer than a day."[23]

Knyphausen's May 10, 1780, orders, written and delivered by Beckwith, instructed Moody "to proceed without loss of time, with a small detachment, into the Jerseys, by the most convenient route, in order to carry off the person of Governor Livingston."[24] Moody probably kept this letter with him, so that if he were captured, he could show that he was on a military mission and not a spy mission. For the same reason, the Tory raider kept his regimental commission with him and had his uniform on underneath his civilian clothes. On the other hand, by not outwardly wearing his green regimental uniform on his mission, he still risked being charged as a spy.[25]

Livingston frequently claimed that the British hoped to assassinate him. However, Beckwith's orders, at least, made it clear that the governor was not to suffer "any violence to his person."[26] Knyphausen had himself been a kidnapping target and approved of such efforts. For his operation with Beckwith,

Moody received funds from one of the top commanders in New York City, Major General James Robertson—more proof that attempts to kidnap Patriot leaders were authorized in the highest councils of the British army.[27]

Moody apparently conceived of the idea for this particular operation.[28] He also later claimed that "one of the Governor's Council was privy to and had promised his assistance in accomplishing the above design" to abduct Livingston.[29] As he later described in his memoirs he "took with him four trusty men and went into Rebel country with the intention of surprising Governor Livingston, a man whose conduct had been, in the most abandoned degree, cruel and oppressive to the loyal inhabitants of New Jersey."[30] Moody and his men were frustrated to discover that Livingston was not home in Parsippany, but instead was in Trenton on government business. After Moody took his small party to Sussex County to be surreptitiously supported by local sympathizers and await Livingston's return, one of his men, Corporal Joseph Lowery of Sussex County, while unwisely walking on a public street with a woman on Sunday, June 4, was accosted by an alert Major Robert Hoops. When Lowery tried to dash away, Hoops chased and wounded Lowery in a hand-to-hand struggle. The Whig officer then, according to the *New Jersey Gazette*, "presented one of the pistols he had taken from [the captive] to his head, and resolutely declared he would put him to death if he did not inform him of his designs in coming to this part of the country."[31] Under this threat, Moody's accomplice revealed the plot—this was another example of a death threat successfully resulting in the extraction of demanded information. Lowry added that Moody had received his instructions from General Knyphausen himself. The intelligence, according to the *New Jersey Journal*, "was instantly sent to Livingston, who ... took every precaution to prevent surprise."[32]

Lowery's capture and confession, as Moody explained, "blasted the whole project."[33] He and his men moved on to the Sussex County jail at Newton, where they freed several British soldiers who had been captured in Burgoyne's army, as well as Loyalists, some of whom immediately joined his band. Moody's liberation of one of the British soldiers, Robert Maxwell, was memorialized in a print, which is on the cover of this book. Moody and his men later captured and paroled about thirteen American militiamen and officers.[34]

On their way back to New York, Moody and his men had the misfortune of trying to enter Paulus Hook (now Jersey City) just as several regiments of Continental troops were preparing to attack it. Moody and his entire band were captured.[35] Gloating over this turn of events, the *New Jersey Journal* added that "another party was sent from Staten Island last week for the express purpose of assassinating his Excellency our governor."[36]

The resourceful Moody, after some rough treatment, was eventually able

HUE and CRY,
TWO HUNDRED GUINEAS REWARD.

Whereas a certain WILLIAM LIVINGSTON, Late an Attorney at Law, and now *A Lawless Usurper, and incorrigible Rebel*, stands convicted in the minds of all honest men, as well as in his own conscience, of many attrocious crimes and offences against God and the King, and among many other treasonable practices, has lately, with malicious and murderous intention published a seditious advertisement in a rebel news-paper, offering a reward of what he calls Two Hundred State Dollars to an Assassin who shall take and deliver me, and three other Loyalists into the power of him the said William Livingston.

I do therefore hereby promise to pay the sum of Two Hundred Guineas, *true money*, to the person or persons who shall bring the said William Livingston *alive* into this city, and deliver him into the custody of Capt. Cunningham, so that he may be duly lodged in the Provost, till the approaching extinction of the rebellion, then to be brought to trial for his numerous crimes and offences aforesaid. In the mean time, if his WHOLE person cannot be brought in, half the sum above specified will be paid for his

EARS and NOSE,

which are too well known, and too remarkable to be mistaken. — Observe, however, that *his life* must not be attempted, because that would be to follow *his* example of exciting the villainous practice of *Assassination*, and because *his death*, at present, would defraud *Jack Ketch* of a future perquisite.

Given under my Hand and Seal at Arms, in New-York, this Twenty Third Day of August, 1781.

(A stile which I have surely as much right to assume as William Livingston, or any other rebel usurper.)

J. MOODY.

The several Printers on the continent are requested to insert the above in their newspapers.

to break loose from his handcuffs, escape from jail, and return safely to New York. To counter Livingston's subsequent offer of a reward for the capture of his brother, John Moody, for a recent theft of Washington's mail, Moody issued his own joking proclamation, offering 200 guineas for "a certain William Livingston, late an attorney at law and now a *lawless usurper and incorrigible rebel*." If "Livingston's entire body" could not be returned, Moody offered half the reward money for the governor's "ears and nose, which are too well known, and too remarkable to be mistaken."[37]

In July 1780, now an ensign, Moody was again captured, this time near Englishtown, New Jersey. Imprisoned at West Point, he was treated cruelly by General Benedict Arnold, who still commanded there, and it was not until George Washington himself intervened that his conditions improved. In September, Moody was transferred to Washington's main camp, where he was to be tried by court-martial for participating in a skirmish in which two Patriot officers were killed. Learning that he would likely be convicted and hanged, he decided to escape. But that was not easy, given that he was manacled, guarded by a sentry in his jail cell, with five other sentries nearby, and in the middle of a Continental army camp. The incredibly resourceful Moody, however, pulled off his escape one stormy night, managed to evade patrols, and arrived safely at New York City.

Moody soon gained the new specialty of intercepting the Continental army's mail in the

James Moody's satirical advertisement, offering a reward for Governor Livingston's "ears and nose, which are too well known, and too remarkable, to be mistaken." From Rivington's *Royal Gazette*, Aug. 25, 1781 (Library of Congress).

New York and New Jersey areas. On March 29, 1781, he intercepted a post rider carrying in his mail bag several letters from General Washington, including one that contained a detailed description of a council of war between Washington and the commander of French troops stationed at Newport, Rhode Island. Loyalist newspapers giddily published the letters, to the embarrassment of Washington.[38] On another mission to capture enemy mail, he again flirted with death when some seventy soldiers fired at him from close range but missed.[39]

After promotion to lieutenant in August 1781, Moody's luck finally ran out after an audacious attempt to steal the Continental Congress's papers from the State House in Philadelphia went awry. After the plan was exposed, James Moody barely escaped to safety, but his brother, John Moody, was caught, convicted as a spy, and hanged on the Philadelphia Commons on November 13, 1781. The day before his death, John wrote to his brother, advising him to "not hereafter so often venture yourself out of British lines."[40] There was understandable anxiety among Whig leaders that Moody would take revenge for his brother's execution. In a January 1, 1782, letter, Governor Livingston alerted Washington that Moody had again entered New Jersey, this time to kidnap a member of Congress in Philadelphia.[41] But the governor was misinformed; Moody's days working behind enemy lines were over.[42] Amazingly, Moody survived the war, settling with his wife and some of his friends in what would become Weymouth, Nova Scotia, where Moody became a shipbuilder and the area's most influential citizen.[43]

General Clinton, meanwhile, claimed he had proof that in August 1780, Governor Livingston had bribed "my servants to poison me" as a result of the "ridicule" with which the British commander-in-chief had dismissed Livingston's kidnapping charges the previous April.[44] Clinton's biographer, William Willcox, doubted that any such attempt was made to poison the general and believed that Clinton's wine was simply tainted.[45]

In April 1, 1781, Washington alerted Livingston of his being informed "by a gentleman living near the enemy's lines" that "four parties had been sent to take or assassinate" Livingston, New York's Governor George Clinton, Washington, and a fourth person, who turned out to be Joseph Reed, then the president of Pennsylvania's state legislature.[46] In October, thirty Tories went ashore at Woodbridge and split up into smaller parties, each intent on capturing Governor Livingston. Livingston evaded all attempts "to take or assassinate me."[47] Because none of the suspected raiders was captured, it cannot be confirmed whether either of these reports was accurate, or whether they had been instigated by Beckwith and Knyphausen.

Livingston went to great lengths and sacrifice to avoid putting himself in a position where he was vulnerable to capture. In taking such precautions, he performed a substantial service to the Whig cause. By contrast, General Richard Prescott, who was captured by William Barton the night of July 10–11, 1777 on Aquidneck Island north of Newport, Rhode Island, argued that he kept only nine privates and a corporal as a guard at or near his temporary quarters because increasing his guard would have left fewer troops to defend other parts of Aquidneck Island. Yet his capture was a greater blow to the British war effort than would have been experienced had his guard at his temporary quarters been increased. Similarly, General Charles Lee chose to spend the night of December 12, 1776, at a tavern three miles from his division and closer to the enemy, yet he brought with him only a dozen guards. At the time it occurred, Lee's capture was viewed by many as a crippling blow to the Patriot cause.

Retaliatory Kidnappings: The Cases of Connecticut's General Silliman and Long Island's Judge Jones

After the British seized New York City in the fall of 1776, a "whaleboat war" erupted along Long Island Sound. Connecticut Whigs raided British-controlled Long Island, and, in turn, Long Island Loyalists raided the Connecticut coast. To carry out their low-intensity sea-land assaults, the two sides counted on versatile whaleboats. The primary objective of many of these operations was abduction. Prominent local military or government personnel could be held for ransom or turned over to military authorities to be exchanged for captives of equal or similar rank held by the other side. The best known example of reciprocal kidnappings of local leaders involved American Brigadier General Gold Selleck Silliman of Connecticut and Loyalist Judge Thomas Jones, then residing on Long Island.[48]

In the spring of 1779, Captain Isaac Bonnell of the King's Militia Volunteers, a New York Loyalist outfit, received orders from British headquarters in New York City—reportedly from General Clinton himself—to try to capture Silliman, then commander of Connecticut's coastal militia.[49] Bonnell obtained as a guide Captain Isaac Glover, who had once helped build a cider mill on Silliman's property near Fairfield, Connecticut.[50] Bonnell attracted seven more men for the enterprise—all but two Loyalists who had been forced to flee their Connecticut homes for the safety of Long Island. During the night of May 1, 1779, Bonnell's party departed Lloyd's Neck in a whaleboat, crossed Long Island Sound and landed about two miles north of Fairfield at Black Rock Harbor. Leaving one man with the boat, Bonnell led his party the two miles to Silliman's residence.

Mary Silliman, the general's wife, recalled the terrifying events that followed:

Between midnight and one o'clock in the morning, when we were all asleep, the house was attacked. I was first awakened by my husband's calling out, "Who's there?" At that instant there was a banging at both doors, they intending to break them down or burst them open, and this was done with great stones as large almost as they could lift. My husband then sprang up, caught his gun (two guns always stood loaded at the head of his bed) and ran to the front of the house, and as the moon shone he saw the men through the window.... He then thrust his gun through a pane of glass and attempted to fire, but the powder only flashed in the pan and misfired. At that instant the enemy burst in a window, sash and all, jumped in, seized him, and said he was a prisoner.... [T]heir appearance was dreadful.... I heard them breaking the windows, which they wantonly did with the breeches of their guns. Then they asked him for money, he told them he had none but Continental bills, which would do them no good. They then asked for his papers. He replied that his public papers were sent abroad, and his private papers would be of no use to them. Then some of them wanted spoils and began to take one thing and another. He told them mildly he hoped he was in the hands of gentlemen ... and that it was beneath them to plunder. With these arguments, he quieted them so that they plundered very little.[51]

According to Mary Silliman, who was pregnant at the time, "these ruffians" told her husband that "it was fortunate for him that his gun misfired, for had he killed a man they would have burned the house and murdered all who were in it."[52] The raiders then tied up Silliman and his son, Major William Silliman, and forced them to run the two miles back to the coast. Meanwhile, Mary sent a black servant to inform neighbors, who fired alarm guns, but the raiders were able to reach their whaleboat and depart safely.

Rowing back to Lloyd's Neck, Bonnell's group was met by Lieutenant Colonel John Graves Simcoe, the British dragoon officer who, the following year, would endeavor to capture General Washington himself. "Have you lost any men?" Simcoe asked. "No" was the answer. "That's well," Simcoe responded. "Your Sillimans and your Washingtons are not worth a man."[53] Silliman was treated well enough in his captivity and was permitted to move freely about Flatbush, in Brooklyn. Soon afterwards Simcoe himself was targeted for abduction, as he recalled in his memoirs, by "a party of twenty men" from Connecticut who lay "concealed" on Long Island for three weeks. They were unsuccessful.[54]

When it became clear that the Continental army lacked a captive general who could be exchanged for Silliman, his friends in the Connecticut militia decided that they would have to take matters into their own hands by abducting a prominent civilian Loyalist for a prisoner exchange. Their attention focused on "that great Tory," Judge Thomas Jones, formerly a neighbor of the Sillimans.[55]

On the evening of November 4, 1779, Captain David Hawley of Stratford, Connecticut, and Samuel Lockwood of Norwalk, with a crew of twenty-five volunteers, crossed Long Island Sound in whaleboats, which they dragged ashore and hid in the woods. The men then "lay concealed all the day and travelled in the night."⁵⁶ After traversing an astounding fifty-two miles, mostly in darkness, they arrived at Judge Jones's home at about 9:00 p.m. on November 6. As luck would have it, Jones was inside, hosting a dinner party. When rapping on the door did not produce an immediate response, Hawley broke a panel and forced the door open, just as Jones and his nephew were approaching the doorway. Hawley and his men seized both of them and whisked them away into nearby woods. British troops subsequently captured six of Hawley's men (who may have lagged behind to try to plunder local houses) but most of the kidnappers and both of their captives made it back to Connecticut.

Ironically, Mary Silliman ended up hosting at her home the understandably disgruntled Jones for several days. Shortly thereafter Jones's nephew and William Silliman were exchanged. On April 27, 1780, almost a year after Gold Selleck Silliman was seized at his home, he and Judge Jones were exchanged.⁵⁷ The exchange occurred as follows: each side brought its prisoner in a vessel to a spot off Hart Island in Long Island Sound, and the prisoners swapped boats and were then sailed to freedom. The British vessel, the *Grand Duke*, had the benefit of the wind and tide and was able to carry Judge Jones to New York City that evening, while Gold Selleck Silliman had to wait and did not arrive home until the following evening.⁵⁸ After Silliman's vessel docked at Black Rock Harbor and the freed general made his way home amidst throngs of well-wishers, he was, as he later wrote, "received at the gate, by the dearest and most affectionate of women."⁵⁹

Raid Across the Frozen Hudson River: The Attempt to Kidnap Washington at Morristown

In February 1780 General Knyphausen and Captain Beckwith planned and attempted a mission that could have changed the course of the war: the capture of General George Washington, then quartered near Morristown, New Jersey. Credit for the remarkable plan lay with Lieutenant Colonel John Graves Simcoe, an exceptionally courageous British cavalry officer who was just twenty-eight years old and only a few weeks earlier had returned from a three-month stint as a captive of the Americans.

The commander of the Queen's Rangers, an elite legionary corps composed of Loyalist cavalry and infantry then stationed on Staten Island, Simcoe "thought that it would not be difficult" to lead a party of his mounted hussars over the winter ice to the New Jersey shore and make off with the American commander-in-chief who, according to Simcoe, "was quartered at a considerable distance from his army, or any corps of it."⁶⁰ Obtaining the assistance of a Loyalist sympathizer who had once lived near where Washington was staying, Simcoe soon had "a very minute and perfect map of the country." His plan was to personally select eighty of his cavalrymen, to be led by thirteen officers. The force "was to march by secret ways, made the more so by the inclement season, and to arrive near General Washington's quarters by day-break, to tie up his horses in a swamp, and to storm the quarters, and attack his guard on foot. For this purpose, his party was to carry muskets as well as swords.... The party was to halt at two cottages in a wood, if they should arrive before the appointed time."[61]

Simcoe likely would not have even considered the idea of a raid to capture Washington, but for the fact that the Hudson River had iced over. Usually, the Hudson River did not turn to ice during the winters, but the bitterly frigid winter of 1779–1780 in the area of New York City was one of the coldest of the century.[62]

It seems odd that Simcoe would choose to attack on foot, when on horseback he had the advantage of speed. By comparison, Lieutenant Colonel William Harcourt's party used horses to surround Widow White's Tavern at Basking Ridge and to depart it quickly once General Charles Lee had been secured. Perhaps Simcoe thought that approaching Washington's headquarters by foot would be quieter and less likely to create an alarm. In any event, Simcoe decided he would not kill Washington, but he worried how he could prevent the death of the American commander-in-chief should he "personally resist."[63]

Since December 1, 1779, Washington's headquarters had been located outside Morristown in the area's finest house, built by Colonel Jacob Ford, Jr.[64] Shortly after returning from a mission commanding Morris County militia, Ford had died of pneumonia in January 1777. His house was now occupied by

John Graves Simcoe, who conceived of a plan to kidnap General Washington. This image shows him as Governor of Upper Canada in about 1791. Engraving, 1873 (Library of Congress).

84   Abductions in the American Revolution

The Jacob Ford, Jr., mansion, Morristown, New Jersey. It served as George Washington's headquarters during the winter of 1779–1780 (National Park Service, Morristown National Historic Park).

the wife he left behind, Theodosia, and their four young children. Lying roughly a half-mile east of the main part of Morristown, and three miles northeast of the main American encampments at Jockey Hollow, the Ford house was vulnerable.[65] Washington was doing what General Lee had done at nearby Basking Ridge more than four years earlier—spending nights three miles from the main body of his troops.

Still, Simcoe's cavalry would have had to ride some thirty miles, through the foothills of the Watchung Mountains and then across rough-hewn back roads regularly watched by local militia and Continental troops. Moreover, the raiders' escape route would be exceedingly long—to New York City—a fact that alerted enemy troops would surely know. The weather was also unpredictable and potentially dangerous. That winter more than twenty snowstorms would pound the Morristown area, sometimes blocking roads with six-foot high snowdrifts.[66] Simcoe's proposal was indeed a daring one.

In addition, some eighty-seven soldiers, whose specific job was to protect Washington, lurked in the vicinity of the Ford house. Unlike British commanders, Washington had established his own security detail, commonly known as Washington's Life Guard, in March of 1776 at Cambridge, Massachusetts. The unit's purpose was to provide personal security for Washington, as well as handle the baggage of his headquarters and the money and official papers of the Continental army.[67] However, the size of the Life Guard had shrunk from about 150 men in March 1778 to about 115.[68] Led by Major Caleb Gibbs, the number of soldiers in the Life Guard available to defend against a raid was further reduced by the fact that about twenty-eight of them were away from camp on permitted leave, around six of them worked as servants for Washington (including one as a steward and another as a cook), three more worked as stable hands, and more served as messengers or to procure supplies.[69]

Historian Benson J. Lossing, who travelled the country in the 1840s interviewing elderly, surviving veterans, interviewed Gabriel Ford, who then owned the Ford Mansion and resided there. New Jersey historians John W. Barber and Henry Howe did the same. No doubt Lossing, Barber and Howe relied heavily on Gabriel Ford in discussing the defenses at the Ford Mansion.

Barber and Howe, in their book on the history of New Jersey published in 1846, wrote: "Two sentinels paraded in front" of the Ford Mansion, "and two [patrolled] in the rear constantly, day and night. The Life Guard, composed of about 250 men, under Gen. Wm. Colfax, were barracked in about 50 rude huts which stood in the meadow formed by an angle of two roads a few rods southeast of the dwelling." Gabriel Ford's recollection is likely generally accurate, except that due to the lapse of time he exaggerated the number of Life Guards and huts. If the Life Guards had a total of about eighty-seven men in early February 1780, perhaps only about eleven huts were needed.[70] (Additional huts could have been built to accommodate more soldiers assigned to guard duty at the Ford Mansion in March of 1780.) Gabriel Ford's description of the location of the huts is consistent with a contemporary map, showing the huts on the south side of the road and about one hundred yards to the east of the Ford house.[71] One soldier's diary indicates that the Life Guard, after arriving at Morristown on December 4, finished their huts and moved into them on December 9.[72]

According to Barber and Howe, "Several times in the course of the winter false alarms were given of the approach of the enemy. First, a distant report of a gun would be heard from the most remote sentinel, and then one nearer, and so on, until the sentinels by the house [the Ford Mansion] would fire in turn. From them, it would be communicated on towards Morristown, until the last gun would be heard far to the westward at camp," at Jockey Hollow about three miles away. Upon hearing the discharge of the muskets, Barber and Howe continued, "Immediately, the Life Guard would rush from their huts into the [Ford] house, barricade the doors, open the windows, and about five men would place themselves at each window, with their muskets brought to a charge, loaded and cocked ready for defense. There they would remain until the troops from camp were seen marching, with music, at quick-step down towards the mansion."[73]

Benson Lossing wrote a similar account in his history of the Revolutionary War published in 1851, and added: "These occasions were annoying to the ladies of the household, for both Mrs. Washington and Mrs. Ford were obliged to lie in bed, sometimes for hours, with their rooms full of soldiers, and the keen winter air from the open windows piercing through their drawn curtains."[74] (Martha Washington arrived to stay at the Ford Mansion on December 31.[75]) Lossing further wrote that Washington's "tender care for the comfort of Mrs. Ford was often evinced. On the occasions when the alarms ... were given, he always went to her room, drew the curtains close, and soothed her by assurances of safety."[76]

Richard Kidder Meade, one of Washington's aides who stayed at the Ford house, stated that Washington and his staff "occupied two rooms below, all the upper floor, the kitchen, cellar and stable."[77] Still, the Ford house, even though spacious, was cramped with bodies. On January 22, Washington complained to General Nathanael Greene that "eighteen belonging to my family [meaning his staff] and all of Mrs. Ford's family are crowded together in her kitchen," presumably to keep warm from the freezing temperatures. The commander-in-chief further complained that there was nowhere in the house "at this moment in which a servant can lodge with the smallest degree of comfort."[78]

On January 31, 1780, Simcoe obtained approval to execute his plan from Brigadier General Thomas Stirling, the same officer who had tried to nab Governor Livingston a year earlier. Not only was Stirling now a general, he was the commander of British forces on Staten Island. "Your ideas are great, and would be of importance if fulfilled; as I am confident of your zeal and capacity, I should be sorry to check them," Stirling told the raid's designer.[79] Simcoe may have wanted Stirling's troops to provide cover for his returning men as they approached the coast—perhaps the British outpost of Paulus Hook—before they re-crossed the ice to the safety of Staten Island.

On the very day that Stirling approved Simcoe's plan to capture Washington, Silas Condict, a member of New Jersey's executive council, wrote Washington expressing his concern "respecting Your Excellency's situation, which I do not think so secure as I would wish, while the frost [ice] makes firm passing into Jersey from every part of the enemy's lines." The prescient councilman thought the solid ice could make a "bold" attempt to surprise Washington possible and that a party of cavalry could reach Morristown "undiscovered." Condict warned, "The importance of the object may induce them to hazard an attempt and it will fully justify every means to be ready to receive them."[80] Washington, however, seemed nonplussed by the warning. He responded to Condict that he had already taken "precautions" that he thought would be "effectual" in preventing a surprise cavalry raid on the Ford Mansion.[81] It is not known what steps Washington took to improve security at his headquarters, other than have soldiers in his Life Guard set up their barracks nearby.

Meanwhile, while waiting "with great impatience" for scouts to confirm Washington's continued presence at the Ford Mansion, Simcoe "to his great surprise" learned that Captain George Beckwith had come up with his own plan to seize Washington.[82] General Knyphausen, then serving as interim commander-in-chief of New York–area forces while General Clinton was sailing with 8,700 troops to invest Charleston, South Carolina, agreed that a raid on Morristown was feasible. In a report to Clinton, the German general wrote, "General Washington, having taken up his quarters at a distance from his army, under the protection of a small corps of infantry, it appeared practicable to surprise that body with cavalry and to penetrate to the neighborhood of Morristown."[83] Knyphausen was bold since Clinton had left him with few troops to defend New York City.

Knyphausen preferred Beckwith's plan to Simcoe's proposal, since Beckwith's plan would require the deployment of many more troops than did Simcoe's plan, resulting in less risk. Beckwith proposed staging various diversions in New Jersey. By "different movements from Staten Island," British forces would attack American outposts at Crane's Mills, Elizabethtown, Rahway, and Woodbridge. Then, according to Knyphausen, "120 dragoons were to cross the North [Hudson] River from the City of New York to penetrate by a particular route to the neighborhood of Morristown and in their retreat to fall back upon a body of infantry posted at Newark to receive them."[84] This force of mounted men would consist of about sixty cavalrymen each from the British 17th Light Dragoons and from Simcoe's Queen's Rangers. Beckwith ordered a disappointed Simcoe, who would not have the glory of capturing the American commander-in-chief, to send him the mounted troops of the Queen's Rangers for the operation.

Knyphausen originally also planned to use one force to march across the ice from King's Bridge and attack the American outpost at Paramus, manned by a detachment of 200 to 300 men, while another force was to hit the American outpost at Newark Mountain Meeting, believed to hold about 300 soldiers. But after the German general was informed that Washington had withdrawn his troops from these two outposts, he canceled those attacks.[85]

In late January and early February, Knyphausen made his preparations for Beckwith's planned raids. He newly assigned a regiment of infantry to Paulus Hook to await the return of his mounted men from Morristown.[86]

Either Simcoe or Beckwith may have received confirmation that Washington continued to use the Ford Mansion as his headquarters from John Jones, a deserter from the Continental army at Morristown. Originally from Merionetshire in Wales, Jones reported to William Tryon in New York City on February 15 that "the Horse [cavalry] sent to distant quarters. Washington has a few about him and a small foot guard."[87] Presumably, to be in New York City on February 15, Jones must have deserted in late January or early February, and he may have been interviewed first at that time by Simcoe or Beckwith.

While not clear, Knyphausen may have increased the size of his main cavalry strike force from 120 to more than 300. Three sources suggest that he kept the number of mounted men at about 120. First, in his journal, Knyphausen never mentioned any increase. Second, records of the British 17th Light Dragoons suggest that only about sixty cavalrymen departed the regiment's main camp at Jamaica in Queens County (then considered part of Long Island) in early February.[88] Third, William Smith, the prominent New York City Loyalist, wrote in his diary that 400 to 500 men crossed the Hudson River for the operation.[89] Smith's estimate likely included the infantry regiment that accompanied the cavalry, which may have numbered about 350 foot soldiers, leaving about 100 to 150 mounted men as the remainder of the force.

On the other hand, three sources support a finding that Knyphausen increased the size of the mounted strike force to 300 or more. First, an American spy who rode with the raiders estimated the number of enemy cavalry at 300.[90] Second, a resident of Elizabethtown informed a Continental officer that the raiders included about 400 to 500 cavalry and 3,000 infantry.[91] Both estimates are likely exaggerations; the British did not even have a total of 400 mounted soldiers in the New York City area. Nonetheless, the 400 or 500 estimate for cavalry suggests that the actual number may have substantially exceeded 120. Third, Captain Frederick Diemar's "Black Hussars," about seventy German cavalrymen, were reported to have ridden from Long Island to Richmond on Staten Island on February 4.[92] They made this move presumably to ride with the Queen's Rangers, which they often did. (Indeed, in October of 1779, Diemar's Hussars were transferred to Richmond on Staten Island, along with Simcoe's Queen's Rangers.[93]) If Knyphausen's mounted force consisted of about 300 men, they likely would have included about 175 cavalrymen from the British 17th Light Dragoons, sixty hussars from Simcoe's Queen's Rangers, and about seventy of Captain Frederick Diemar's "Black Hussars."[94]

The core of the mounted attack force poised to ride to Morristown and capture General Washington was the British 17th Light Dragoons, commanded by Lieutenant Colonel Samuel Birch. This regiment left Ireland in 1775 and landed in Boston just before the Battle of Bunker Hill. Some of them had infamously ridden their mounts inside Boston's Old South Meeting House. Since then the regiment had participated in most of the significant engagements in the North, including those of Long Island, White Plains, and Monmouth, as well as dozens of small skirmishes in New Jersey and around Philadelphia and New York City. After the British evacuation of Philadelphia in 1778, its sister regiment, the 16th Light Dragoons, the only other British regular cavalry regiment used in the Revolutionary War and whose dragoons had captured General Charles Lee, transferred many of its men and horses to the 17th and its officers returned to England. After arriving in the New York City region, its headquarters was usually at Hempstead, on Long Island, but its men constantly patrolled the lines around New York City.

The uniform of the 17th dragoons included a red jacket with white facings, buckskin breeches and black top boots, and a leather helmet with a skull-and-crossbones or death's head figure on it, with the words beneath it, "or glory." The helmet was topped with a red flowing crest of dyed horsehair. The dragoons were armed with a straight saber that had a single blade and a light carbine. They were trained to fire from the saddle.[95]

The Black Hussars was composed mostly of escaped German prisoners of war who had accompanied Burgoyne's army to Saratoga. After they had gathered in New York City and had gained a reputation for being unruly, they were formed into a hussar outfit in 1779. The men wore a hussar cap and black coat with blue trousers and boots of the hussar style (that is, a short boot with the trousers worn tucked in).[96] In turn, Simcoe's Queens Rangers were similarly attired, wearing a hussar-type cap, with the crescent or half-moon insignia of the Rangers mounted on front, a green wool jacket, green trousers tucked into short boots, and a sword belt over the right shoulder.[97]

It is not known for certain who commanded this expedition, but it was probably Lieutenant Colonel Samuel Birch of the 17th Light Dragoons, since he was the senior commander of the only regular British army cavalry regiment in the attack force. Birch had not yet made much of an impression as a military leader. As commander of his dragoons on Long Island, and later as a brigadier general and commandant of New York City, according to Loyalist Judge Thomas Jones (the same man who had been a kidnapping victim and exchanged for General Silliman), Birch gained a reputation for corruption, stealing the houses and possessions of Loyalists, allowing his soldiers to plunder the churches of Loyalists, and even ordering the tearing down of a Quaker meetinghouse on British-held Long Island and personally selling the wood.[98] As mentioned previously, he also had ordered signer Francis Lewis's estate at Whitestone to be burned in 1776.

Knyphausen also augmented Stirling's Elizabethtown-bound force with additional troops and a second senior officer, Brigadier General Cortland Skinner, the former attorney general of New Jersey. The exact size of Stirling and Skinner's combined force is unclear; local civilians later estimated it at 2,000 men, but that was probably an exaggeration.[99] Stirling commanded two regiments of British regulars and Skinner probably commanded his first and fourth battalions of New Jersey Volunteers, for a total of about 1,200 men.[100]

The British seized sleds from civilians. At least eighty-six were used on February 6 to carry munitions, provisions, and other military supplies to British posts at Paulus Hook and Staten Island.[101] The ice on Newark Bay was so firm that 24-pounder cannon hauled across it to Paulus Hook on February 8 and 13 "made no impression" on the frozen surface, "an event unknown in the memory of man," wrote Major General James Pattison.[102]

On February 7, the mounted men of Simcoe's Queen's Rangers and Diemar's Hussars rode on the ice over from Staten Island to New York City, and by the next day the 17th Regiment of Light Dragoon had joined them, after departing from their base at Jamaica in Queens County.[103] The British also called upon prominent New York City Loyalists to make maps detailing the network of roads between Elizabethtown and Washington's headquarters, and the more distant Continental camps at Morristown.[104]

While Knyphausen finalized plans for his move against Washington at Morristown, much of the British activity related to efforts to increase New York City's and Staten Island's defenses. The American army could just as easily cross the ice to attack them. And with Clinton approaching Charleston, South Carolina, with the bulk of the British army, New York was vulnerable. The British navy, having departed Upper New York Bay for the winter to avoid being iced-in, could not protect army outposts. In desperation, Major General James Pattison, commander of the British army's New York City garrison, buttressed his force by drafting more than 2,500 Loyalist militiamen in a single week.[105]

News of British preparations was speedily conveyed to Washington and his commander of American outposts in northern New Jersey, Major General Arthur St. Clair.[106] Washington believed that with Continentals and local militia manning guard posts at various key points, "our main body cannot be surprised" and that the main object of a raid would be his army's "magazines of hay."[107] He had no idea that he was the primary target of the raid, and that the British planned to have him on his way to Paulus Hook well before Continental troops could interfere.

Historian Benjamin Huggins has described the defenders along New Jersey's shoreline that Washington had at his disposal in early February:

> To guard against raids from Staten Island, General Washington kept two brigades of his main army stationed west of Elizabethtown. In February, Major General St. Clair commanded these brigades. On his arrival to take the command on 27 January, St. Clair ordered his commanders to post guards at Rahway, Cranes Mills, Connecticut Farms, Elizabethtown, and Newark. In addition to St. Clair's brigades, the New Jersey militia could be called into the field on an alarm. Washington also kept a detachment of about 200 infantry at Paramus. (Knyphausen's information that Washington had recalled the detachments at Newark and Paramus was false).
> Washington and St. Clair had also put another force into operation that proved critical in deflecting one of the raiding parties. Due to a lack of Continental cavalry to patrol the areas between his guard posts, St. Clair asked the New Jersey authorities to raise a company of light cavalry at Continental expense to patrol the coast

roads between Newark and Amboy. The company eventually numbered forty-five light cavalry raised from militia volunteers. St. Clair stationed these light cavalry at Rahway, Newark, and Woodbridge, with fifteen at each town. They would prove their worth in the coming fights.[108]

The mission to grab General Washington was scheduled for February 8, but a fierce snowstorm intervened.[109] It started to snow on the evening of February 7 and continued all the next day.[110] General Knyphausen, however, was unwilling to put it off for long. With no new snowfall on February 10, the German general boldly ordered the Morristown raid and diversionary attacks to begin the next evening. During the night of February 11–12, either 120 or some 300 cavalrymen (with their unknowing mounts), all probably commanded by Lieutenant Colonel Samuel Birch of the 17th Light Dragoons, accompanied by an infantry regiment crossed the ice-sheeted Hudson River and Newark Bay to Paulus Hook, on the New Jersey mainland.[111]

Meanwhile, Lieutenant Colonel Simcoe ventured out to create his diversion. At the head of 200 infantrymen, Simcoe passed over the ice at 1 a.m. in the morning on February 11. Stirling's orders called for Simcoe to send a party to surprise the enemy post at Woodbridge or Rahway "and to give a general alarm." Simcoe posted Major Richard Armstrong with some of the regiment's infantry, his remaining cavalry, and some cannon at the heights overlooking Old Blazing Star Ferry (now Rossville, Staten Island) to cover his return. He then took the rest of the Rangers and headed toward Woodbridge, but they were forced to march "on the beaten road" due to the deep snows. When Simcoe and his men arrived at Woodbridge, they found the enemy guard post abandoned. Still, Simcoe was determined to "beat up some of the enemy's quarters, or fall in with their patrols" in order create a diversion to "give every assistance in his power to his friend," Captain Beckwith.[112]

After marching on, at a crossroads on the road from Perth Amboy to Elizabethtown, Simcoe's troops were challenged by Patriot sentries. All of Simcoe's men halted and stood still "in profound silence," which was accentuated by the deep snow drifts and dark night. The sentinels, talking about themselves, thought themselves mistaken in spotting the enemy. But soon, one of the New Jersey militia on horseback, rode up on the flanks of Simcoe's unit and yelled an alarm and the sentries opened fire. As historian Benjamin Huggins wrote, "The horse patrols had done their job."[113] Simcoe, with "bugle-horns, drums, and bagpipe of the Queen's Rangers sounded," ordered his men to retreat. One of Simcoe's Rangers was struck and killed by a "chance shot of the sentinels."[114]

Patriots took time to gather their forces and organize themselves. Once they did, they set out after Simcoe and his men, using the same snow-trodden path. Finally, at 8 a.m., after crossing Woodbridge Creek, the Americans caught up with the raiders. However, their inability to attack the flanks of the enemy force due to the deep snow benefitted Simcoe. As he approached the road to Old Blazing Star Ferry, Simcoe dispatched a sergeant to ride over the ice to alert Major Armstrong to prepare his cannon, and he ordered Captain David Shank to take a small detachment, cross back over the ice, and man a ridge in order to cover his retreat. That done, Simcoe suddenly ordered the remainder of his men to "turn about" and charge at "a steady run" at the pursuing Americans who, surprised, "immediately fled." When Simcoe's men then began passing over the ice to Staten Island, some Americans pursued. At this point, Captain Shank's men rose and fired upon the retreating Americans, driving them back, and Armstrong opened up his cannon on some ferry buildings sheltering some of the other American soldiers. This dispirited the attackers and allowed Simcoe and his men to return over the ice to Richmond on Staten Island "without further molestation."[115]

His task accomplished by skirmishing with local militia and St. Clair's horse patrols, Simcoe later stated that he lost the one man killed early in the affray and suffered "a few wounded."[116] While Simcoe thought that "the enemy's loss" was much greater, St. Clair reported having only one man wounded. St. Clair added that "the party at Woodbridge committed no outrage of any kind upon either the persons or houses of the inhabitants, but carried off about thirty head of cattle."[117]

The more punishing blow was struck at Elizabethtown. St. Clair's guard of fifty men "were timely apprised" of the enemy's approach, and quickly retreated in the face of Stirling's and Skinner's overwhelming force. Skinner's advance raiders did manage to take some shots at a rearguard and wound one man.[118] With the town now unprotected, as was sometimes the case in the war following a victorious armed conflict by Loyalists, whose own property had often been seized by Patriots, the soldiers resorted to plunder and looting. There is no indication that General Skinner tried to stop it. "A number of houses in the town have been stripped of everything," St. Clair informed Washington the next day, "and ten or twelve of the inhabitants carried off." The *Pennsylvania Packet* reported sarcastically of the raiders, "After terrifying the *women and children*, they heroically marched off with their plunder and five or six prisoners."[119] Loyalist William Smith wrote in his diary from New York City the next day, "twenty men brought from Elizabethtown, mostly militia."[120]

As Stirling's and Skinner's troops began to evacuate Elizabethtown, St. Clair's guards and the local horse patrols reclaimed it, taking two stragglers left behind, but they turned out to be civilians from Staten Island who had followed Skinner's troops in order to plunder. The guards, horse patrols, and some local militia pursued Skinner's retreating raiders, and claimed to have wounded several, but there is no report of it in surviving British or Loyalist records.

A small, third force of British or Loyalists soldiers (their identity is not known) raided Rahway. St. Clair the next day reported to Washington that enemy troops "landed at Rahway, in a very obscure place, plundered two houses and carried off two men, and seem to have no other object."[121]

As for the main object, Birch's cavalrymen, accompanied by Captain Beckwith, reached Hackensack and regrouped there as planned. But after setting out from Hackensack for Morristown, the harsh weather stymied the mounted troops. "A body of cavalry passed into Jersey, but was obliged to return after a march of between five and six miles; the snow which fell on the 7th and 8th instant having rendered the roads impassable," Knyphausen reported.[122] Simcoe wrote that "Beckwith had found it impracticable to carry his attempt into execution, from an uncommon fall of rain, which encrusting the top of the snow, cut the fetlocks of his horses, and rendered it absolutely impossible for him to succeed."[123] Judge Thomas Jones railed in frustration about the failed attempt: "The guides got frightened, the party bewildered, they lost the road, and after a cold, tedious and fatiguing excursion of twenty-four hours, without ever seeing a Rebel, returned to New York, all frost-bitten."[124]

Before turning back, the commander of the main body of dragoons had five rockets fired into the night sky to signal Stirling to call off his raid of Elizabethtown. In turn, Stirling had five rockets fired to signal Simcoe to call off his raid and turn back to Staten Island.[125]

Loyalists in New York City quickly learned of the true purpose of the raid. Newspaper printer Hugh Gaine, showing less bitterness that Judge Jones, wrote in his journal, "The dragoons went out last night with an intent to take Washington, but the roads were so bad they could not proceed, so returned—ah well."[126] William Smith penned in his diary for February 11, with fair accuracy, "There went over the river last evening a party of 4 or 500 and 200 more from Staten Island, but they all returned on account of the depth of the snow. I suspect Washington was the chief object and the sallies from Staten Island feints."[127]

The smothering February 7–8 snowstorm had spoiled the British mission to kidnap Washington. While the bitterly cold winter that had iced over the Hudson River made the raid against Morristown possible, the same weather had ruined Beckwith's plan. When he penned it, the American commander-in-chief likely did not consider the significance of the following entry in his diary for February 8: "A fall of nine or ten inches of snow in the night from the northeast."[128] Ironically, the inability of Washington's Continentals to quickly clear the road of snow between Hackensack and Morristown had prevented the raid from being executed.

Later on February 11, General St. Clair sent Washington an account of the unsuccessful British raids. Somehow, the Scottish-born commander had planted a spy—the guide for Birch's dragoons. This man was likely a trader who plied his goods between the New Jersey shore and Manhattan, supplying British-held New York, but also obtaining key information. He could have also been one of the spies who participated in Washington's plan to capture the traitor Benedict Arnold, the story of which follows this one. This spy, whose identity is unknown, reported back to St. Clair, who explained to his superior:

> The party from Paulus Hook consisted of about three hundred horse, and landed at Hackensack.... They proceeded some distance into the country, and from the route they pursued, he [the spy] thinks, intended to have passed the Cedar Swamp, and were very particular in their inquiries about the situation of your quarters, and where I was quartered, and the guards that were posted between Hackensack and Morristown. He says particularly that, after marching some ways into the country, he heard an officer ask the commandant where they were going. He replied he could not tell him, but they had more than thirty miles to march that night. In a short time after this, finding the snow very deep and the roads not broken, they returned, and he [the spy] was dismissed.[129]

St. Clair warned the commander-in-chief. "If their design was an attempt on your Excellency's quarters.... I hope you will pardon me for hinting that there is not a sufficient body of troops near enough to render you secure. Had they designed to have fallen upon our rear, which they might have done, they had troops enough to have given us full occupation, and them the opportunity."[130]

Washington responded to St. Clair the next day, noting that he had just "taken precautions" to guard against an attempt by a party of dragoons "as might reasonably to be able to reach" his Morristown headquarters "in the course of a night." One precaution the commanding general took was to increase his guard around and inside the Ford Mansion. For example, Ensign Jeremiah Greenman recorded in his diary that starting on February 20 he and other soldiers of the Second Rhode Island Regiment of Continentals served "on his Excellency's picket guard" where at night a few guards were posted in each room in the Ford Mansion and "a sergeant and 6 men" guarded "the head of the stairs." Greenman's and his fellow Rhode Islanders' service inside the Ford house ended when they were relieved and replaced by other guards two days later.[131]

In his response to St. Clair, Washington added, "I hope that a short continuance of this weather will make the ice impassable by horse; from foot there is no danger at this distance."[132] In order to increase security against another raid on Morristown, he advised St. Clair to extend his horse patrols northward, at least until the ice across remained firm.[133] As temperatures warmed in late February, the ice in the bays melted, and the British shelved any further plans to kidnap Washington.

While the warmer weather melted the ice on the Hudson River, it also made the roads to Morristown passable by British dragoons. But Washington must have doubted that the British would plan a complicated amphibious operation, involving shipping dragoons and their horses across the Hudson River, to mount another raid against him at Morristown. He also realized that a raid by infantry was not a true threat to his personal safety. Still, he took no chances.

In March, Captain Beckwith kept himself informed of the American commander's security precautions, in case another attempt at Washington could be made. He had his own intelligence sources in and around Morristown. Those sources informed him of the impressive increased safeguards Washington had taken. On March 3, Beckwith received intelligence that "General Washington's bodyguard" at the Ford Mansion "is now augmented to 350 men … one-third of them lodge every night in the lower part of the house." On March 9, the intelligence captain received further information that "General Washington's guard is augmented to 400 men. The caution against being surprised is sentinels being posted on every road leading to headquarters. The discharge of a musket is the alarm."[134]

On March 16, a new storm dumped some nine inches of snow in and around Morristown.[135] Perhaps feeling vulnerable to a another raid attempt over the ice on the Hudson River, three days later Washington ordered two soldiers from each regiment and one sergeant from each brigade to join his Life Guard at the Ford Mansion.[136]

On May 16, 1780, Ensign Jeremiah Greenman wrote in his journal that he "went on his Excellency's Guard where there were four log houses built to post the Guard in case of an alarm."[137] The meaning of this entry is not clear, but it could mean that the log houses had been constructed to be used as defensive posts in the event of an attack on the Ford Mansion.

Even though he was frustrated by Washington's increased vigilance starting in March 1780, Beckwith continued to seek and receive reports of Washington's quarters, in hopes of seeing another opportunity to try to capture him. In July and August of 1781, for example, Washington's headquarters was sometimes located at Joseph Appleby's house, on the crossroad from Dobbs Ferry to White Plains in New York, about three-and-one-half miles from the ferry.[138] On July 28 a Hessian intelligence officer forwarded to Beckwith information obtained from a female spy who had gained access to Washington's headquarters, probably by performing chores such as laundry or cooking. "The woman is returned from Washington's quarters," wrote Lieutenant Carl Levin Marquard. "She saw him herself and says that Washington sleeps in the back bedroom; that there were two French sentries yesterday at his door; that his guard consists of French and Rebels, which she judged to be about 30 or 40 men; that she saw no horsemen there; that there was no camp in the rear of his quarters; ... that Appleby's was about half a mile back of the Rebel camps."[139] On August 11, Beckwith received information from a Continental army deserter that "Washington's house is about a quarter of a mile in the rear of the army at Appleby's house" and that "he has a guard of eighty men with him constantly."[140] Washington, unlike Lee on the night of December 12, 1776, took care to make sure he was well-guarded.

Interestingly, other than Lieutenant Colonel Simcoe, after the war none of the major participants on the British side wrote about the attempt to capture the Continental army's commander-in-chief. It may have been that they were too embarrassed to admit their role in kidnapping a man who had become revered in republican circles and elected to two terms as President of the United States.

Washington Attempts to Kidnap the Traitor Benedict Arnold in New York City

In the fall of 1780, General Washington authorized a kidnapping attempt against former Continental army major general Benedict Arnold, to this day the most infamous traitor in American history. Late on September 24, after learning of Arnold's unsuccessful attempt to turn fortifications at West Point over to the British, as well as his successful escape to a British vessel in the Hudson River, Washington brought the Marquis de Lafayette into a private room and said quietly, "Arnold had betrayed us. Whom can we trust now?" After showing the Frenchman the documents that damned Arnold, the famously composed Washington, Lafayette recalled, surrendered to "an ungovernable burst of feeling, fell on his friend's neck and sobbed aloud."[141]

Arnold had been arguably the Continental army's best fighting general. He first came to public notice when he claimed partial credit with Ethan Allen and his Green Mountain Boys for taking Fort Ticonderoga. He had commanded 2,000 Patriot soldiers who in the late fall and early winter of 1775 trekked from southern Maine through the northern Maine and Canadian wilderness, earning Arnold the sobriquet of the "American Hannibal." While his attack at the gates of Quebec in a snowstorm failed, leaving him wounded in the leg, no one questioned that he was an enterprising and courageous general. In late 1776, he showed amazing energy and skill in creating a makeshift fleet that stopped a British advance down Lake Champlain. The next fall he had probably played the key roles leading American troops to victory in two battles at Saratoga, forcing the surrender of British general John Burgoyne and his army. But suffering yet another grievous wound to his left leg in the last battle, Arnold became bitter that Congress promoted less able and junior generals in front of him. Given the command of Philadelphia, he was hounded by radicals led by Joseph Reed, who sought civilian control over the city. Upon being accused of fraud in connection with military contracts, the beleaguered Arnold felt that Washington had failed to support him. After falling under the spell of Peggy Shippen, the beautiful eighteen-year-old daughter of perhaps the wealthiest merchant in Philadelphia, Arnold began communicating with British secret service handlers. Soon Arnold had hatched a scheme to hand over to General Clinton West Point, one of the key fortifications in the north. But the plan fell apart, with one of Arnold's handlers, British major John André, being captured out of his uniform inside American lines and later hanged as a spy.

Washington wanted Arnold captured as soon as possible, charged with treason, and tried by a military tribunal, primarily to set an example for other potential traitors. Within a few weeks of Arnold's hasty departure, Washington learned that Arnold was in New York City recruiting a new cavalry force called the American Legion, which drew numerous Continental army deserters. Disgusted, Washington began to consider a plan to kidnap Arnold, have him court-martialed, and hanged.

On October 13, 1780, the commander-in-chief summoned Major Henry

"The escape of Sergeant Champe." Currier & Ives, 1876 (Anne S.K. Brown Military Collection, Brown University).

"Light Horse Harry" Lee to meet him the next morning to discuss "a particular piece of business."[142] The next day Lee, a brilliant, twenty-four-year-old cavalry officer from Virginia and commander of a mixed force of mounted and dismounted dragoons named Lee's Legion after him, found Washington at Lafayette's headquarters. "I have sent for you," said Washington, "in the expectation that you have in your corps individuals capable and willing to undertake an indispensable, delicate, and hazardous project. Whoever comes forward upon this occasion will lay me under great obligations personally, and in behalf of the United States, I will reward him amply."[143] Washington explained his desire for a special operation to capture Arnold.

Under no circumstances, he emphasized, was Arnold to be hurt or killed—even if that meant allowing him to escape. He wanted to "make a public example" of Arnold and feared the charge that "ruffians had been hired to assassinate him."[144] Washington personally gave Lee two letters of authorization and money to fund the operation.[145]

Lee fully supported the idea and, as he left Washington, began to ponder who would be the right man for this dangerous and delicate task. This man would have to have the skill set of a soldier, sailor and spy. He would need to be quick witted, as well as have a belief in the revolutionary cause so deep that he would risk his own reputation and life. Lee quickly focused on a broad-shouldered, twenty-three-year-old, four-year veteran from his regiment, the cavalryman Sergeant Major John Champe of Loudoun County, Virginia. Lee described Champe to his commander as "full of bone and muscle," and as "a very promising youth, of common taciturnity and inflexible perseverance. His connections, and his service in the army from the beginning of the war, assure me he will be faithful."[146] Washington likely recalled the recruit's father, Colonel John Champe, as they hailed from the same social circle in northern Virginia and Champe's daughter Jane became the first wife of Washington's younger brother Samuel. Washington expressed his enthusiastic support for the choice.

Major Lee knew his man. Lee explained the general plan and Champe's intended role to the young sergeant, who was not "deterred by the danger and difficulty" of the mission. But once Lee mentioned that Champe would be asked to pretend to desert Lee's Legion, Champe hesitated, due to the "ignominy" of leaving behind his fellow soldiers. Lee, however, explained that Washington, anticipating this concern, had informed him that "no act done by the soldier at the request of the commander-in-chief could be considered as desertion," and that Champe's "reputation would be protected by those who had induced him to undertake the enterprise, should he be unfortunate." Lee then offered Champe a promotion, and explained the shame that he would feel if a soldier from another unit accepted this important task in his stead. "Are you ready to earn immortal honor for yourself and your fellow soldiers, and do the most important services to your country, by carrying through this delicate and hazardous scheme for your General?" he asked his subordinate. Finally, the convinced Champe responded in the affirmative.[147]

Lee and Champe worked out a plan for the sergeant's desertion and making contact with two of Washington's invaluable New York City spies, neither of whom knew the other's name. Champe would also work with a trusted agent named Baldwin, from Newark, whom Lee would pay "one hundred guineas, five hundred acres of land, and three negroes."[148] (Virginians Washington and Lee were both slave owners, and New Jersey still held a substantial number of slaves.) Champe would "join General Arnold as a deserter from us, should engage in his corps now raising, and should contrive to insinuate himself" into a personal service or military position, putting him close to Arnold. In that role he would correspond or meet with Washington's two spies as often as possible.[149]

The most vexing question facing the American planners was how Champe and Baldwin would slip Arnold from the middle of British-held New York City, which was swarming with guards, soldiers, and sailors, across the Hudson River to Patriot-controlled New Jersey. Lee informed Washington that "when the favorable moment arrives," Champe and Baldwin would "seize the prize in the night, gag him, and bring him across" the river to an agreed location in the woods of Bergen.[150] "It was our purpose to seize Arnold unawares, to thrust the gag into his mouth, and placing each of us an arm within that of our prisoner, to hurry him through the least frequented of the streets toward the quay," Champe explained later. If anyone questioned why they were carrying a man through the streets, Champe would say that he was "a drunken soldier whom we were conveying to his quarters."[151] Lee agreed with the plan, but again stressed to the sergeant that "if you find that you cannot seize him unhurt, do not seize him at all; and if the choice is between his escape and his slaughter, let him go. To kill him would give the enemy an excuse for alleging all sorts of falsehoods against us."[152]

Wondering whether a mere gag would be sufficient to subdue Arnold, Champe must have considered knocking the traitor senseless. That would have made it easier to carry his prisoner through the back alleys of New York, but such a course of action would have been counter to his instructions. Champe and Baldwin might have considered coaxing Arnold into their small boat on some believable pretext and then springing their surprise on Arnold. That would have removed potential street difficulties from the equation, but it was not part of the agreed-upon plan.

On October 19, Lee passed on the plans for the special operation to Washington. Pleased, the commander-in-chief approved them the next day. In a note to Lee, he could not help but offer specific advice:

> The sergeant must be very circumspect; too much zeal may create suspicion, and too much precipitancy may defeat the project. The most inviolable secrecy must be observed on all hands. I send you five guineas, but I am not satisfied of the propriety of the sergeant's appearing with much specie. This circumstance may also lead to suspicion, as it is too well known to the enemy that we do not abound in this article.
>
> The interviews between the party in and out of the city should be managed with much caution and seeming indifference, or else the frequency of their meeting may betray the design.[153]

Finally, on the moonless night of October 20, 1780, at about 10:00 p.m. Sergeant Champe rode quickly past the Continental army guard post at Totowa, New Jersey, and headed southeast toward Bergen. He rode all night, racing ahead of any American patrol sent to capture the presumed deserter. About thirty minutes after Champe sped past the guard post, the camp watch officer rushed up to Lee, sputtering that an army patrol had come across a soldier on horseback headed away from camp. When challenged, the man had ignored it and galloped away. Lee did his best to stall any pursuit without giving away the secret mission. First, he asked if the man seen riding away was from the country. No, it was someone from the army, the officer insisted. Lee exclaimed that that was impossible, as his soldiers did not desert. The disappointed officer skulked away, but then on a hunch headed toward a stable and saw that Champe's horse was missing.

Next the officer went to Champe's tent and saw he was absent, and had taken his valise and orderly book. The officer raced back to Lee's tent and asked for permission to chase after Lee. Lee feigned disappointment and talked about the character of officers, wasting time. Finally, seeing he had no choice if he wanted to uphold the ruse, he agreed to send a party after the sergeant but then ordered another officer to command it, thus wasting more time. When the other officer arrived ten minutes later, Lee ordered him to "pursue as far as you can with safety Sergeant Champe, who is suspected of deserting to the enemy." "Bring him alive, that he may suffer in the presence of the army," Lee ordered the pursuers, "but kill him if he resists or escapes after being taken."[154]

The pursuit party left around midnight, just as rain began to fall. Champe had a one hour head start, but the wet ground gave the soldiers an advantage: Champe's horse wore a shoe that left a telltale mark. At each intersection of the road the pursuers stopped to examine the tracks for the telltale sign. Finally, as the sun rose in the morning, they could gallop at full speed without stopping.[155]

Champe was headed for Paulus Hook, where the British had armed galleys anchored to help defend against any boats crossing the Hudson River one mile to lower Manhattan, where British headquarters was located. When he reached a high point of land near the village of Bergen, he looked behind him and saw a dozen of Lee's Continentals a half-mile away. Desperate to elude them,

Champe remembered a shortcut as he raced by Bergen's Three Pigeons Inn—a side road that he had once taken with some of the very men chasing him now. Thinking that they too would take the shortcut, he feigned in that direction but then rode on another route to Paulus Hook. As Lee's men entered Bergen, confident that Champe would take the shortcut, they charged up the side road. But soon they realized their mistake and were again on Champe's trail.[156]

Two miles outside Bergen, with Lee's Continentals just 300 yards from him and British sentries patrolling the marshes in front of two armed galleys, a desperate Champe jumped from his horse, ran in between the sentries, and dove into Communipaw Bay. Now he deployed his second deception. He swam toward the nearby British galleys and called for help to sailors aboard them. Thinking the swimmer was yet another legitimate Continental deserter, the crews of the galleys fired cannon to scatter Lee's dragoons and fished Champe out of the water. Seeing that that they were outmanned, Lee's men gave up the chase and slinked back to camp, disappointed. After Champe spent a night on a galley, its British commander sent him to New York City, with a letter from an officer describing the circumstances of his desertion.[157] Lee, naturally, had to contain his joy at Champe's escape.[158]

Willard Sterne Randall, a recent biographer of Benedict Arnold, described Champe's subsequent adventure in New York City:

> [Champe] arrived in Manhattan on Saturday and was held at the Provost Jail until Monday, when he was taken to headquarters. He was interrogated for two hours, Sir Henry joining his staff officers toward the end. Champe told them what they wanted to hear: rations were scanty, the soldiers didn't like the French. Clinton tipped the man two gold guineas for his desertion and tried to enlist him in the British army. Champe said it would add to his risk of being hanged as a deserter: he would take his chances finding a job in New York City. In less than an hour, Champe "accidentally" ran into Arnold on the street. The sergeant was still wearing the uniform of his elite unit and was sure to catch Arnold's eye. Arnold liked the soft-spoken, earnest young man, especially after Champe told him that Arnold's desertion had inspired his own. Arnold took Champe to buy him a drink and offered him the same rank, that of highest-ranking noncommissioned officer in his American Legion. Champe signed up.
> As Arnold's senior noncom, Champe had access to the Arnolds' handsome townhouse, across from Bowling Green near the city's southern tip. On the north side of Arnold's house was a large, fenced-in garden running all the way down to the rocky Hudson shoreline. Rimming the north side of the garden, just across the fence, was a seldom-used alleyway which also ran down to the water's edge. Over the next several weeks, Champe frequently visited Arnold's house and observed his schedule, his habits. He discovered it was Benedict Arnold's invariable habit to end his day by taking a stroll at midnight before going to bed, ending it with a visit to the outhouse before going indoors. As he watched Arnold for several nights from the alley, Champe worked loose three or four fence palings and replaced them. Late at night, he and Baldwin could slip through the fence, down the alley, and around the dark-

ened headquarters to a waiting boat. They notified Major Lee that they would kidnap Arnold the night of December 11 and that his dragoons should be ready on the Jersey shore to take him to Washington.[159]

Champe's meetings with Generals Arnold and Clinton are supported by Lee's October 25, 1780, letter to Washington, which states in part: "My friend got safe into New York. He was before Sir Henry Clinton and passed all the forms of the garrison. He accidentally met Col. Arnold in the street which has paved a natural way for further acquaintance. The party entertains high hopes of success."[160] Through his conversations with Arnold and other British officers, Champe was able to conclude that rumors in Washington's camp that another high-ranking traitor was still in the Continental army's ranks were false and passed that important information to Washington's spy in New York City. With all of his direct contact with Arnold, as historian Michael Kranish has written, Champe "could have easily assassinated Arnold had Washington allowed it."[161] Instead, the former sergeant began to set in motion his plans to kidnap Arnold.

Champe first instructed one of his accomplices to bring a boat to a nearby landing on the Hudson River side of Manhattan. Champe would arrange for the man to be admitted into Arnold's garden, which the general had the habit of visiting every night. Champe himself would sneak into the garden under cover of darkness. While going off on his midnight stroll in the garden, the two men would grab Arnold, gag him, and carry him to the landing. Should someone stop them, as planned, Champe would say that they were assisting a drunken officer and taking him to headquarters.

Champe, however, had bad luck. Clinton had assigned Arnold to lead an expedition to the southward and with a squadron of ships ready to carry some 1,800 troops, the boarding of the soldiers was scheduled to begin the very night Champe was to seize Arnold. Clinton had given the traitor general his first chance to lead British troops in battle and hoped that other Americans would desert the Patriot cause.[162] Frustrated, Champe, still in his new uniform, had no choice but to accompany other American Legion troops in boarding their troop transports. "I was hurried on board the ship without having had time so much as to warn Major Lee that the whole arrangement was blown up," the sergeant recalled years later.[163]

Back on the Jersey shore, Major Lee and several of his men, along with horses held for Arnold, Champe, and Baldwin, waited in exasperation for several hours then finally gave up hope. A disappointed Lee returned to headquarters to inform Washington of the mission's failure. Washington was "chagrined" and worried that Champe had been "detected in the last scene of his tedious and difficult enterprise."[164]

Champe never again had an opportunity to capture Arnold. On board his troop transport, he did not find out until days after his December 21 departure from New York City that Arnold's force was destined to invade Champe's home state, Virginia. At the end of the month, the twenty-seven ships carrying Arnold's force sailed past the Virginia capes and headed for Norfolk. Champe decided he would desert a second time, this time from the British army.

Successfully deserting the British army at Petersburg, Virginia, the sergeant major rejoined Lee's Legion. Now a lieutenant colonel, Lee mustered the regiment and explained to the assembled dragoons Champe's true mission, informing them that Champe was no deserter, but a hero.

Washington deeply appreciated Champe's effort, but forced him to retire from service for his own safety. If the British ever captured the young Virginian, he would meet "certain death" and be hanged as a spy.[165] Champe returned to Loudoun County, married in 1783, and fathered seven children. He later moved his family to Romney, Virginia, in Hampshire County.[166]

In 1798, Washington made inquiries about Champe's whereabouts, hoping to appoint him to an army post. But the former sergeant had recently died.[167] Champe never received a promotion or reward for undertaking his dangerous mission, which remained a secret until 1812, when Lee's memoirs were published.[168] In 1847, Champe received a posthumous award of sorts: Congress granted his descendants funds equal to the commutation pay of an ensign in the Continental service.[169]

Washington's Second Attempt Against the British Commander-in-Chief in New York City

Despite Sergeant John Champe's failed attempt to nab Benedict Arnold in New York City, Washington never gave up the hope of capturing a senior British general within the enemy's main headquarters in the city. The commander-in-chief, after scrapping his March 1778 plan to abduct General Clinton in New York City, continued to look for other opportunities.

In early 1779, Washington approved and facilitated an unusual kidnapping plan that was the brainchild of Major General Alexander McDougall of the Continental army. While based with his army above New York City at West Point, he had conceived "a design of offering a reward for General Tryon and others."[170] McDougall's plan was to offer rewards for the capture of William Tryon and other high ranking leaders in New York City, with the hope that Loyalist soldiers in the crowded port would jump at the chance for riches and abduct them. Prior to the war, McDougall had been a radical Whig political leader operating

Lieutenant Colonel David Humphreys, who led the first attempt to capture General Clinton in 1778. From portrait by Gilbert Stuart, ca. 1810 (Humphreys, *Life of Humphreys*).

in New York City and often butted heads with then Governor William Tryon and New York City Mayor David Mathews, both of whom he despised.

To accomplish his plan, McDougall first needed Washington's approval and money from Congress for paying the rewards. He quickly received both. On February 22, 1779, Congress ordered the Paymaster of the Board of War

IV. *The War in the North* 105

View of Numbers 1 and 3 Broadway in Lower Manhattan, about 1830. Number 1, on the near corner, served as Clinton's headquarters, including when plans were made to kidnap him in 1779. Number 3, two doors down, was occupied by Benedict Arnold, when John Champe made plans to capture him in 1780 (Lossing, *Pictorial Field-Book of the Revolution*, Vol. II).

and Ordnance to issue "the sum of one thousand dollars in specie" to be forwarded "to the commander-in-chief for secret service."[171] In late February, Washington received the money from Congress and then immediately advanced "fifty guineas" from this amount to McDougall, which payment was described in Washington's ledger as "for Secret Services."[172] On March 3, Washington sent another one hundred and fifty guineas, which with the earlier delivery, he wrote to McDougall, would "nearly amount to the sum you requested from Congress."[173] Undoubtedly, this was the money McDougall intended to use to pay for rewards for kidnapping British leaders in New York City.

With the cash in hand, McDougall felt more was needed to lure Tory kidnappers. On March 10 then requested New York's Governor George Clinton to persuade the state legislature to pass a law that would pardon any Loyalist who assisted in kidnapping a British leader in response to McDougall's offer of a reward.[174] But Clinton was unable to advance the plan. "The legislature has adjourned," wrote Clinton to McDougall about a week later, "they had done nothing respecting the Robbers and Horse Thieves [i.e., the British leaders in

New York City], though it was a matter I had much at heart."[175] It appears that McDougall dropped his audacious plan at this point.

In September 1780, General Washington instructed his spies to determine the evening residences of Sir Henry Clinton and the highest-ranking German officer, Lieutenant General Knyphausen.[176] Obtaining the desired information, Washington assigned the task of organizing and leading a nighttime mission to seize one of the generals to Lieutenant Colonel David Humphreys of Derby, Connecticut. Recently appointed as one of Washington's aides-de-camp, the twenty-nine-year-old Yale graduate and aspiring poet was a good man for the job. Humphreys had participated in two successful land-sea raids already: one, as the second-in-command, against a British supply post at Sag Harbor in May 1777; and another as commander of a thirty-man force that crossed Long Island Sound to destroy three British vessels near Smithtown.[177]

Humphreys's request for the assistance of Captain Roger Welles of Colonel Samuel B. Webb's Additional Continental Regiment was approved. He also recruited a lieutenant and three ensigns, and hand-picked twenty-four non-commissioned officers and privates, many of them experienced boat hands familiar with the Hudson River.[178] The lieutenant colonel communicated his plans to Whig spies in New York City.

Washington must have delayed the date of Humphreys's special operation, once he committed in mid–October to the attempt to nab Benedict Arnold in New York City. But upon being informed on December 12 of the failure of Sergeant Major Champe's mission, Washington authorized Humphreys to execute his plan.

By December 23, 1780, Humphreys was ready. The whaleboats and guard boats required to transport his men had been gathered at Murder's Creek, south of West Point, under the care of Captain Welles.[179] Maintaining tight security, Humphreys, in order to reduce the risk of word of his plan leaking out, waited until the last minute to write out his orders, before Washington signed them. The commander-in-chief directed Humphreys to "take command of such of the detachments of water guards, now on the river, as you may think necessary" in order to "surprise and bring off General Knyphausen from Morris's house on York Island, or Sir Henry Clinton from Kennedy's house in the city," but only "if from the tide, weather, and other circumstances you shall judge the enterprise to be practicable."[180] Morris's house, known today as the Morris-Jumel Mansion, sat just south of what is now 162nd Street, overlooking the East River. The Kennedy house was, of course, located at the southern tip of Manhattan Island at Number One Broadway.[181] Washington was familiar with both houses, having stayed in each when his army occupied the island in 1776. He and Humphreys had no doubt discussed the mission's myriad challenges. Humphreys's small band would have to navigate, in small boats, the swirling Hudson River from Dobbs Ferry south to Manhattan Island; coordinate with Patriot spies and sympathizers in New York City; deal with British guards around the headquarters buildings; and, on their return, avoid any British warships and guard boats in the Hudson and East Rivers.

On Christmas Eve a barge and two whaleboats carried Humphreys's raiders out of Dobbs Ferry and on the start of the twenty-five mile journey to New York City. Soon, however, a strong northwest wind kicked up, making a landing on Manhattan Island impossible and dashing the men's hopes of success. "The wind was very fresh at north-west in the night, and the boats were forced past the city, and one of them almost down to Sandy Hook—one of the boats put in at Staten Island," recalled General William Heath. Unable to anticipate the change in weather, the lieutenant colonel's mission failed. Humphreys did successfully gather all of his half-frozen men in New Brunswick. Travelling back by land, Humphreys "and all the others returned to the army on the 1st of January."[182]

Not surprisingly, the kidnapping attempt soon became common knowledge in New York City, thanks to British spies in the American camp. Major Carl Leopold Baurmeister, a German officer on Knyphausen's staff, ended his accurate summary of the attempt by concluding, "As such incidents always do, it made us take more precautions."[183] The leaking of the news of the attempted raid had an undesired effect on future missions. "They say the Rebels intend taking off the commander-in-chief, who lives close on the North [Hudson] River—Sir Henry is a little alarmed on this occasion and keeps double guards at his house, which is within pistol shot of the North Battery," Lieutenant Thomas Hughes wrote on December 26.[184] "The accomplishment of the act would have been very extraordinary, if they could have succeeded in spite of the many sentries stationed about," noted Lieutenant John von Krafft. The Hessian officer added that "the row galleys which were usually there [in the Hudson River] had gone away and, of course, it had been immediately made known to the Rebels." General Clinton, Krafft continued in a more ominous tone, "formed the intention of revenging himself in a way which was before unknown."[185]

On February 4, 1781, an unidentified British spy wrote a letter in cipher to his British handler, offering precise details of how the Americans had planned to kidnap Clinton and Knyphausen. From near, or even within, Washington's headquarters in New Windsor, Connecticut, this snoop had gained his information by speaking with "no less" an authority than a loose-lipped "general officer." He wrote:

> A most daring enterprise had been lately concerted at the quarters of the chieftain here [meaning Washington's headquarters]. It was no less than an attempt to take

the commander-in-chief in his quarters in the city. A certain Colonel Humphreys, one of the chief's [Washington's] aides-de-camp, was to have gone down the river with a party, and land behind Kennedy's house, thence proceed up through the garden and secrete themselves behind the house, whilst some were to advance on each side of it, and seize the sentries in the street. Upon this a signal was to be given, and those on the back of the house were to crush in with crowbars, and take his Excellency [Clinton] with all his papers. Some traitors in the city were to know the night and hour of attack and were likewise to seize the adjacent sentries on receiving the signal. To facilitate this project, a captain's command was to land at Greenwich [village] and march to Knyphausen's quarters as well for the purpose of making an alarm as to take him. However romantic this may seem, yet I can assure you that it has been attempted to be put in execution. This Humphreys is quite sanguine in his expectations of succeeding at some convenient season.[186]

Knyphausen, who earlier in the year had backed an attempt to capture Washington, perhaps did not bear the American commander much ill will.

The Abduction and Dramatic Escape of General Peleg Wadsworth in Maine

By early 1781, the coast of northern Maine, then part of Massachusetts, had evolved into another battleground between Patriot and Loyalist irregular forces, similar to the "whaleboat war" along the Connecticut and Long Island coasts in Long Island Sound. Emboldened by the British outpost at Castine (then Bagaduce), where Fort George hosted British regular soldiers, Loyalists who had fled their homes in Boston and other coastal Masschusetts communities flocked for protection. From Castine, Loyalist privateers could harass American shipping and engage in plundering and pillaging of coastal homes and occasionally seize a local Patriot military leader. In July of 1780, for example, a displaced Loyalist named John Jones led a detachment of raiders to Pownalboro at night and kidnapped from their beds Brigadier General Charles Cushing and another brigadier general of the Massachusetts militia. The two generals were marched four miles in the woods, where a boat brought them to Fort George and prison. General Cushing was later paroled and exchanged, but he then resigned his various offices and departed the province of Maine. Fort George's commander, Colonel John Campbell of the British army, remained on the alert for more opportunities for abductions of high ranking Patriots.[187]

In the winter of 1780, Colonel Campbell gained intelligence from local Loyalists that the commander of American forces in the region, Brigadier General Peleg Wadsworth of the Massachusetts militia, was residing at an exposed house on the coast at Thomaston, and that he had requested to be discharged from his command. Wadsworth was a committed Patriot and effective Massachusetts officer. Born in Duxbury, Massachusetts, in 1748, and a graduate of Harvard College, he recruited a company of minutemen from Kingston and was chosen its captain. His company marched upon hearing of the Battle of Lexington and Concord. Wadsworth quickly rose in the ranks and was appointed to serve as second-in-command on the ill-fated Penobscot expedition. The object of this major invasion by Massachusetts in August of 1779 was to dislodge the British and Loyalists from Castine, but it turned into a disaster, with the Patriot forces losing an astounding forty-three vessels in the Penobscot River. While many of its commanders were court-martialed, including Paul Revere, Wadsworth was cleared and even heaped with accolades for effectively leading the safe retreat of the ground forces through the Maine frontier. In March of 1780, General Wadsworth was given command of all troops in the province of Maine and established his headquarters at Thomaston. But discouraged by the local response of Patriots and the lack of support from Boston, the thirty-three-year-old Wadsworth had become disenchanted with his post and sought to return to his home in Plymouth, Massachusetts.

Before Wadsworth could leave his command, on February 15, 1781, a raiding party was dispatched from Castine with the mission of kidnapping him. A Loyalist privateer commander, Captain Long, sailed his schooner *Argyll* along with eight of his men, plus Lieutenant Charles Witham Stockton of the King's American Rangers (also known as Rogers's Rangers) and one McNab from the British 74th Regiment stationed at Fort George who had volunteered for the raid. Stockton was the eldest son of Richard Witham Stockton, who had guided Lieutenant Colonel William Harcourt's party of dragoons in the capture of Charles Lee in December of 1776.[188] Two days after departing, early on the cold winter night of February 17, Captain Long guided his schooner up the Wessaweskeag River and anchored about four miles below Wadsworth's house in Thomaston, which also served as the general's headquarters. Captain Long left three of his men to guard his schooner, while, he, eight of his privateersmen, and Lieutenant Stockton landed on firm ground. Stockton, now in command, led the men on their trek towards Thomaston. The party rested and waited at the house of a Mr. Snow, presumably a Loyalist sympathizer, and then at about 11:00 p.m. proceeded up Wessaweskeag Pond toward the Mill River. When an unfortunate Maine farmer on an errand crossed the raiders' path, he was seized in order to prevent his delivering an alarm.

At Wadsworth's cramped three-room house that night were the general and his wife Elizabeth in one bedroom and his two young children and a family friend, a Miss Fenno, in a second bedroom. They were protected by a sentry standing guard at the door, and four (and possibly more) other soldiers stationed in the kitchen. Using the element of surprise, at about midnight, Stockton's party stormed the house. After overpowering the sole sentry, the raiders surrounded the house and fired their guns through the windows, wounding two of the guards. Other guards quickly grabbed their guns and returned fire, wounding three of Captain Long's men. In an adjacent bedroom, the British soldier McNab climbed through the window only to see just women and children, so he called off that attack. Meanwhile, in his nightshirt, Wadsworth barricaded himself in his bedroom and fired his pistol and a musket at the attackers, keeping them at bay. In the short but fierce firefight, Wadsworth was shot in his arm. With some of his men also wounded and others having fled, the general surrendered. Elizabeth draped a blanket around her husband's shoulders before the dispirited prisoner said his farewell and under a close guard began trudging in the cold darkness towards the waiting *Argyll*.

Elated but fatigued, Stockton, Long and their men, with their valued prisoner in tow, safely reached their schooner and sailed it back to Castine. At Fort George, Colonel Campbell was also happy for the successful mission. Campbell treated Wadsworth as a gentleman officer and had his wounds attended to by a physician. Though confined to a room, Wadsworth was allowed to eat in the officer's mess, was permitted books and writing paper, and was visited by his wife Elizabeth. As he recovered, he was joined in his imprisonment by Major Benjamin Burton of Cushing in Maine, who had been captured by a Loyalist privateer off Monhegan Island.

Fearing that they were not going to be paroled but instead shipped to England, Wadsworth and Burton began plotting their escape. It would not be easy. Not only were there sentries guarding all gates and other parts of the fort, two guards were constantly posted outside their room and could observe them through a grate. Still, Wadsworth and Burton bought a gimlet from a servant and the taller Burton began to use it to drill tiny holes into the ceiling, while the shorter and still sore Wadsworth stood watch. They used a paste from breadcrumbs to fill in the holes to hide their work. After three weeks, the captives were ready to make their escape. Choosing the stormy night of July 19, 1781, they punched through the weakened ceiling and crawled out along the joists above the ceiling. Avoiding detection in the stormy night, they were able to escape from the fort, taking separate routes. Finding a canoe on the banks of the Penobscot River, Wadsworth luckily met up again with Burton. They paddled across the river, successfully evading a search party. After travelling for three days in the wilderness, the exhausted men finally reached safety at Warren, Maine.

On June 22, waiting until it was clear that the escapees would not be caught, a glum Colonel Campbell wrote to General Henry Clinton in New York, leaving to the last paragraph the "sorry" news of Wadsworth's and Burton's escape. But if Stockton and Campbell had hoped to take a valuable general out of the war, they ultimately succeeded. After joining his family at Plymouth, Massachusetts, Wadsworth did not serve again in the military.[189]

There was one other prominent kidnapping in February 1781. On February 24, the British 16-gun sloop *Allegiance*, commanded by David Phips, ran up Frenchman's Bay and landed a party of Royal marines at Point Harbor, where they abducted Captain Daniel Sullivan, the brother of Major General John Sullivan of the Continental army and of James Sullivan, a future governor of Massachusetts. After seizing Captain Sullivan, the British marines burned down the victim's house, leaving his wife and children to spend the cold night in a fish shed. Taken to Fort George and imprisoned, Sullivan refused to take the oath of allegiance to the British government. He was then carried to Halifax and later was confined for four months on board the notorious *Jersey* prison ship off Brooklyn. Finally, he was permitted to visit his brother John in Philadelphia, then serving in the Continental Congress, ostensibly to persuade Congress to arrange for his exchange. But in reality, in order to get released from the *Jersey* and avoid the high risk of dying of disease there, Daniel had agreed to cooperate with the British secret service to try to persuade his brother that Congress should negotiate an end to the war and return America to Crown rule. The effort did not work and Daniel returned to New York City, whether back to prison is not known. Daniel reportedly died of illness on his way home and was buried on Long Island, where his family never discovered. When the area where his torched house was incorporated in 1792, the town was named Sullivan in his honor.[190]

After the war, in 1784, Peleg Wadsworth returned to Maine with his family, building Portland's first brick home, which is called today the Wadsworth-Longfellow House. While he later served as a member of the U.S. House of Representatives for seventeen years, he is perhaps best known today as the grandfather of, and responsible for, the Wadsworth in the name of noted poet Henry Wadsworth Longfellow.

V

The War in the South
(January 1781 to August 1781)

"This greatest of all traitors": Attempts to Kidnap Arnold in Virginia

With Benedict Arnold off to Virginia, American efforts to kidnap him shifted there. Arnold's expeditionary force, including his newly-formed American Legion and the Queen's Rangers under the command of Lieutenant Colonel John Graves Simcoe, reached Jamestown, Virginia, on January 1, 1781. Arnold sailed up the James River to William Byrd's sumptuous Westover estate and marched his men to Richmond, which he reached on January 5 without losing a man. After setting fire to military warehouses and foundries in the surrounding area and forcing Governor Thomas Jefferson and the state legislature to flee the state's capital, Arnold retreated back to Westover. From there his force travelled by water to the coastal town of Portsmouth on January 19.[1]

Arnold's movements were consistent with the main object of his

Benedict Arnold, in uniform after promotion to major general of the Continental army. Engraving by H.B. Hall, after a drawing by Swiss artist Pierre du Simitière in Philadelphia (National Archives).

112

mission to aid the operations of General Cornwallis in the Carolinas by engaging Virginia's troops and supplies and preventing their use to the south. In this, Arnold was so successful that not a single Continental or militiaman left the state until the end of February, while much of the state's resources were consumed by various bodies of militia called up to capture the despised invader.

The Virginia governor became enraged by both "the treasons of Arnold" and his depredations in and around Richmond. The drive for revenge within Jefferson burst forth in a plan "to drag" Arnold "from those under whose wing he is now sheltered." In a January 31, 1781, letter, the normally lofty-minded governor requested Brigadier General John Peter Muhlenberg of the Continental army to direct an effort to abduct the hated Arnold, and offered surprisingly detailed recommendations:

> Having peculiar confidence in the men from the western side of the mountains, I meant as soon as they should come down to get the enterprise proposed to a chosen number of them, such whose courage and whose fidelity would be above all doubt. Your perfect knowledge of those men personally, and my confidence in your discretion, induce me to ask you to pick from among them proper characters, in such number as you think best, to reveal to them our desire, and engage them [to] undertake to seize and bring off this greatest of all traitors. Whether this may be best effected by their going in as friends and awaiting their opportunity, or otherwise is left to themselves. The smaller the number the better, so that they may be sufficient to manage him. Every necessary caution must be used on their part to prevent a discovery of their design by the enemy, as should they be taken, the laws of war will justify against them the most rigorous sentence.[2]

Jefferson offered a reward of 5,000 guineas for bringing in Arnold alive. The governor wrote that while he would not be surprised if Arnold's captors "put him to death" before he could face proper justice (since Arnold merited the penalty "of death by his desertion"), a dead Arnold would carry an award of just 2,000 guineas. Like Washington, Jefferson wanted Arnold "exhibited as a public spectacle of infamy and of vengeance," through a widely publicized trial and subsequent hanging by military authorities.[3] He even went to the trouble of obtaining from Major General Baron von Steuben, the commander of Continental forces in Virginia, an order authorizing Muhlenberg "to call for and to dispose of any force you may think necessary to place in readiness for covering the enterprise and securing the retreat of the party." The author of the Declaration of Independence concluded his letter with the following advice: "You know how necessary profound secrecy is in this business, even if it be not undertaken."[4]

There is no evidence that Muhlenberg ever attempted to follow through with Jefferson's plan. An early biographer of General Steuben wrote in a book published in 1838, "The project unfortunately failed, owing to the extraordinary precautions which Arnold took for his own security. He remained close in his quarters while at Portsmouth, and never unguardedly exposed his person."[5] With Simcoe away from Portsmouth leading a raid in force, the German-Dutch general from Pennsylvania implemented a plan designed to draw Arnold out from behind the heavy fortifications protecting Portsmouth. On February 18, Muhlenberg, backed by more than 1,200 militiamen, ordered a cavalry unit to charge an inferior British picket guard within sight of the Portsmouth works. The raid resulted in the death of two enemy soldiers and the capture of the rest of them, without an American loss. But perhaps because his force was so weakened with the departure of Simcoe, Arnold refused to be drawn out into the ambush.[6] "We have waited for Mr. Arnold within one mile and a half of the town for three hours," wrote Muhlenberg to General Steuben, "but as he shows no inclination to turn out," the attempt was called off.[7]

Muhlenberg had another chance to take Arnold and his men by engaging in a joint operation with France, America's new ally. On January 26, Richard Henry Lee of Virginia had written to a friend in Congress arguing that if but one French ship-of-the-line and two frigates were sent to Virginia, "the militia now in arms are sufficient to smother these invaders in a moment."[8] At Congress's urging, this plan was forwarded by the French minister in Philadelphia to Captain Chevalier Destouches, the commander of the French fleet stationed at Newport, Rhode Island. This fleet, after transporting some 6,000 French regulars under General Rochambeau, had occupied Newport since July of 1781. The bored French were looking for an opportunity to use their powerful force to inflict a severe blow on the enemy, and the plan to capture Portsmouth at the time seemed like a good prospect. Perhaps thinking that it had been agreed to and supported by American military planners, which was not the case, Destouches agreed to cooperate with the plan to nab Arnold.

Wanting to speed their departure and not to allow local Rhode Island Tory spies to give intelligence to the enemy fleet at Gardiner's Bay off Long Island of French preparations for an expedition, Destouches ordered just four warships— only one of them a ship-of-the-line—under Captain Le Gardeur de Tilly to be dispatched to the Chesapeake Bay.[9] Slipping out of Newport on February 9 and benefitting from a favorable wind, Tilly arrived at Lynnhaven Bay in the Elizabeth River on February 13. The French captain was, however, not pleased with what he found. He was informed by local pilots that the depth of the river was too shallow for his 64-gun *L'Eveillé* to get close enough to Portsmouth to bombard it.[10] To storm a well fortified Portsmouth, Muhlenberg had only 1,200 men, with just 300 of them carrying bayonets, and two brass six-pound cannon. While thousands more Virginia militiamen had been ordered to march to support Muhlenberg, it would take time for them to arrive, and Tilly did not want to risk a Royal Navy force blocking his escape back out of the bay. With Muhlenberg's small February 18 demonstration failing to draw Arnold out, Tilly informed the American commander that he had no instructions to remain in the bay, and would sail "the moment the wind would permit him." The next day's "departure of the French vessels," wrote the commander of Continental forces in Virginia," Baron von Steuben, "has destroyed all hope of success in an attempt on Portsmouth."[11] On his way back to Newport, Tilly captured the 44-gun Royal Navy ship *Romulus*, which helped to assuage the bitter taste from the failed expedition.

Washington next persuaded his French allies to send an entire squadron of French warships from Newport, Rhode Island, this time with 1,100 French soldiers on board, to cooperate with an American force to trap Arnold in Portsmouth. The commander-in-chief also sent 1,200 men under the Marquis de Lafayette to reinforce General Steuben. Lafayette moved so quickly that he reached the Head of Elk (currently Elkton, Maryland) on March 3, three days ahead of Washington's calculation.[12]

Rather than bring Arnold back to the main army for a court-martial, Washington now ordered his French general to hang Arnold immediately when he captured him "due to his treason and desertion."[13] Perhaps because Arnold had led a destructive raid against his fellow countrymen in Virginia, Washington had moved to a harsher position.

With Destouches and Rochambeau making preparations for a major expedition at Newport harbor for all to see, Tory spies left Newport in time to warn the British navy commander off Long Island, Admiral Marriot Arbuthnot. On March 3, Arbuthnot wrote that "the blow meditating against General Arnold is of a deadly aspect" and that he was preparing for his fleet to follow that of the French.[14] Meanwhile, General Washington, after travelling by horseback with a small entourage along the back roads of southern New England, arrived at Newport on March 6 to meet with Rochambeau and to encourage Destouches's expedition. Destouches and his imposing French squadron, with Washington watching, sailed out of Newport at sunset on March 8 and headed on a southward course for Portsmouth. Two days later, learning from the commanders of two frigates sent to reconnoiter the French ships at Newport that Destouches had departed, Arbuthnot immediately dispatched his own fleet to the Chesapeake Bay.

The key to the contest was whether the French fleet could arrive at the Chesapeake Bay first, so that it could both establish a strong defensive perimeter in the bay and at the same time offload French soldiers to participate with the American allies in an attack on Arnold at Portsmouth. Destouches decided to take a relatively long route in order to avoid British spy ships, while Arbuthnot had his ships take the more direct route hugging the coast. With their copper-hulled ships making them faster than their counterparts, the Royal Navy ships actually arrived at the Chesapeake Bay ahead of Destouches. The two naval forces sparred with each other off Cape Henlopen on March 16. No ships were lost on either side, but with their plan of surprise foiled, the French sailed back to Newport.[15]

Outside Portsmouth, the eager Lafayette had arrived on March 19, with his reinforcements on the way. Later that same day, Muhlenberg and the Frenchmen went with some 300 men to test enemy defenses and have a look at Arnold's fortifications. "We drove in the pickets, killed 9, took some and wounded several, but were prevented from viewing the works, by want of cartridges, which rendered it imprudent to risk anything like a general action," wrote Muhlenberg.[16] The next day, when the two commanders received intelligence of the arrival of a fleet in the bay, news spread in the excited American camp.

At first, Arnold had a terrible fright when it was reported to him that it was the French fleet at anchor in Lynnhaven Bay. But by March 23 it was known that the ships belonged to the Royal Navy. After driving off the French, the British warships escorted their transports into Portsmouth. While in Lynnhaven Bay, Admiral Arbuthnot had ordered each of his warships to fly a French flag, in order to decoy and capture an American merchant vessel waiting for the arrival of Destouches in the bay. The ploy worked.[17] Arnold even went on board some of the British ships, so that, according to one British army officer, "all his apprehensions of danger are at an end."[18] The traitor Arnold thus remained secure in Portsmouth.

The two attempts to capture Portsmouth did take their toll on Arnold, as detailed in the diary of Captain Johann Ewald, an intelligent and resourceful German officer. Aware that Congress had condemned him to death, and that anyone lucky enough to seize him would be assured of receiving a large reward, Arnold feared the possibility of capture at every turn. At one point during his invasion of Virginia, Arnold asked a captive American captain, "What should be my fate, if I should be taken prisoner?" Looking at the leg that had been wounded during Arnold's heroic service as an American general, the captain reportedly said, "They will cut off that shortened leg of yours wounded at Quebec and Saratoga, and bury it with all the honors of war, and then hang the rest of you on a gibbet."[19]

Ewald, while conceding Arnold's courage and military prowess, did not appreciate the way his traitorous conduct had led to the hanging of his friend and fellow officer Major John André. Ewald, who saw much of Arnold at Portsmouth, wrote that the former Connecticut ship captain and small-time merchant "was a man of medium size, well built, with lively eyes and fine features. He could be very polite and agreeable, especially at the table [meaning in drinking, playing cards, and talking with fellow officers], but if one stayed too long in his company, then the apothecary and horse trader showed through the general. He spoke a great deal about his heroic deeds on the other side," with the American army at Quebec, Lake Champlain and Saratoga, and also "frequently mentioned his ingenious trick" to turn over West Point to the British army, using much "ridicule" and "wit" to enliven the story.[20]

Ewald noticed that while Arnold had demonstrated skill and courage leading British troops, at Portsmouth he showed "a cautious concern due to his fear of the gallows if he fell into the hands of his countrymen." According to Ewald, Arnold "always carried a pair of small pistols in his pocket as a last resource to escape being hanged." During the day of the March 19 attack against Portsmouth, Ewald found Arnold to be "very restless." "On that day," wrote Ewald in his diary, his commander "was not the American Hannibal," the title Arnold had earned as leader of a small American army that, in the late fall and early winter of 1775, had marched through the depths of the Maine and Canadian wilderness to the gates of Quebec.[21] After Ewald's jägers (German elite light infantry troops) had helped to repulse Muhlenberg's and Lafayette's foray on March 19, Arnold beckoned over Ewald. The commanding general "expressed his sorrow" at Ewald suffering an injury from a musket ball to his leg in the action, but then asked what he really wanted to know: "if the enemy would possibly take the post?" Arnold's question "annoyed" the wounded captain, for "he could see it all for himself." "No!" responded Ewald. "As long as one jäger lives, no damned American will come across the causeway."[22]

When Major General William Phillips, with 2,200 reinforcements, arrived in Virginia on March 26, 1781, he superseded Arnold as commander of British forces in Virginia. By letter of March 24, British commander-in-chief Henry Clinton, concerned about Arnold's safety, ordered Phillips to send Arnold to New York, "if you should not have particular occasion for his services." Arnold temporarily remained in Virginia after Phillips became ill and later died on May 13. On May 26, General Cornwallis, who took command of British forces in Virginia after arriving in Petersburg, wrote to Clinton that he had "consented to the request of Brig. Gen. Arnold to go to New York."[23] As late as April of 1781, Washington wrote of his continuing hope to take Arnold, but to his and Jefferson's regret, the Americans never could.[24] When French and American navy and army forces were finally able to coordinate a proper trap and siege at Yorktown, Virginia, later that fall, Arnold was safe in New York City.

Banastre Tarleton Almost Bags Thomas Jefferson

The next serious kidnapping attempt of the war fell to the British army in Virginia, which on June 4, 1781, targeted Thomas Jefferson himself. Two of the operation's main participants, General Charles Cornwallis and Lieutenant Colonel Banastre Tarleton, had played key roles in the capture of Charles Lee four-and-a-half years earlier. Just a mere cornet when he forced Lee's surrender at Basking Ridge in 1776, Tarleton by this time was one of the most feared cavalry commanders of the war and had a reputation for not taking prisoners, especially after his men destroyed the 11th Virginia Regiment at the Waxhaws in South Carolina in May of 1780. Tired of chasing General Nathanael Greene's army in the Carolinas, Cornwallis had decided to move his army north to support Benedict Arnold's invasion of Virginia. On his juncture with Arnold's force at Petersburg on May 20, 1781, all British troops in the state came under his command. The Virginia state assembly had opened its session in Richmond on May 7, 1781, in hopes of addressing how to cope with the British invasion of the state. But Cornwallis's advance on the state capital sent Jefferson, legislators, and most state officials scurrying for safety towards Charlottesville.

After seizing Richmond, Cornwallis on June 2 was camped on the North Anna River in Hanover County, along the main road to Fredericksburg. Here, he gained intelligence from an intercepted Patriot message that Jefferson and the General Assembly were headed to Charlottesville, where they planned to call out thousands more militia to help defend the state, and that Major General Baron von Steuben was at Point of Fork on the James River with only a small force to guard the military depot there. The British commander acted quickly, sending Lieutenant Colonel John Graves Simcoe and a combined force of 300 infantry, cavalry and artillerymen, including Simcoe's own mounted Queen's Rangers, off after the Baron at Point of Fork. (Simcoe later achieved a small triumph when Steuben abandoned his military stores there.)[25] Knowing that Tarleton, with some 180 of his leather-helmeted horsemen, were searching for Continental army units retreating east of Charlottesville through Louisa County, Cornwallis redirected him to "disturb the Assembly, then sitting at Charlottesville."[26] The British commander hoped to prevent the Virginia legislature from meeting and calling out more of the state's militia, and capture Govenor Jefferson.

Tarleton's force left Cornwallis's camp on June 3 in a steady rain. In addition to his 180 dragoons, he had with him 70 foot soldiers of the Royal Welch Fusiliers mounted on spare horses.[27] Historian Michael Kranish describes what happened next:

> The British force stopped at the crossroads, entering Cuckoo Tavern in Louisa, forty miles east of Charlottesville. As the soldiers ordered food and drink, they were observed by a young man who happened to be a member of the militia, Jack Jouett. Jouett stood six foot four and weighed 220 pounds, a flamboyant twenty-six-year-old

Opposite: Banastre Tarleton, who helped to capture Charles Lee and almost nabbed Thomas Jefferson. *Westminster Magazine,* London, 1782 (Library of Congress).

V. The War in the South

who wore a feathered hat and fancied himself one of the best riders of the Blue Ridge. Jouett's father ran the Swan Tavern in Charlottesville, where the legislators had been meeting and dining for several days, and was a commissary to the Continental army, selling beef from his farm. Jouett's older brother, Matthew, had been killed in 1777 in the Battle of Brandywine. Two younger brothers also served in the militia.

Jouett quickly guessed Tarleton's intentions and became concerned that the legislators might be targeted. The Jouett family knew Jefferson well, not just as the master of Monticello and governor but also from having served him at the Swan Tavern. Jouett was aware that Jefferson had returned to Monticello after hours of meetings in Charlottesville, while many of the legislators remained in the town. He decided to warn them, first going to Monticello and then heading to Charlottesville.[28]

On the way to Charlottesville the morning of June 4, Tarleton's men stopped at a handful of plantations in Albermarle County hoping to bag some state legislators and to prevent civilians from warning others of their approach. One of these plantations was Belvoir, the home of Colonel John Walker, a boyhood friend of Jefferson's who had previously served as an aide on General Washington's staff. Here, Tarleton captured his first prominent prisoners, including a South Carolina delegate to the Continental Congress, Francis Kinloch (who was, coincidentally, a cousin of one of Tarleton's officers). At another plantation to the north, Castle Hill, the estate of Dr. Thomas Walker, the father of Colonel Walker, Tarleton seized from their beds several visiting legislators, including Norman Brockenbrough. Then, just outside Charlottesville, Tarleton's troopers charged across the Rivanna River and scattered a small militia force intended to warn legislators if enemy troops were spotted. Tarleton later wrote that "as soon as one hundred cavalry had passed the water," he "directed them to charge into the town, to continue the confusion of the Americans, and to apprehend, if possible, the governor and the assembly."[29]

Meanwhile, Jack Jouett, winding up a moonlight ride on rarely used back roads he knew well, reached Monticello at 4:30 a.m., in time to warn Jefferson of Tarleton's approach. Jefferson later recalled that Jouett knew the "byways of the neighborhood, passed the enemy's encampment, rode all night, and before sunrise ... (on June 4) called at Monticello."[30] Unruffled, Jefferson loaded his wife and family into a carriage and sent them south, away from the enemy. But he tarried longer, collecting valuable papers to take with him. Jouett then rushed to Charlottesville, where he frantically implored state legislators staying at his father's tavern and other boardinghouses to flee immediately to the west or south. Without Jouett's nighttime ride and warnings, "not one man of those in town would have escaped the enemy," noted Benjamin Harrison, the Speaker of the Virginia House.[31]

As he neared Charlottesville, not sure if Jefferson was there with other legislators or at Monticello, Tarleton decided to send his main force into the village and at the same time to order Captain Kenneth McLeod to race up the winding road to Jefferson's plantation home. In Charlottesville, Jouett barely avoided capture, but several legislators and a former lieutenant governor were not so fortunate. Outside the town a young legislator from the west, frontiersman Daniel Boone, was also nabbed.[32]

Captain McLeod and his horsemen poured onto the grounds of Monticello and approached the main house. They had missed a fleeing Jefferson by a mere five minutes. After being again warned by Captain Christopher Hudson of the Virginia militia of the imminent arrival of Tarleton's troopers, Jefferson hopped onto his stallion Caractacus and sped down the mountain and along obscure forest paths. As he later wrote, "knowing that in the public road I should be liable to fall in with the enemy, I went through the woods."[33] Frustrated, a Loyalist dragoon seized Martin Hemings, one of Jefferson's slaves, and threatened to shoot him if he did not reveal Jefferson's whereabouts. Hemings refused to talk. Deciding against killing Hemings or searching for the governor, McLeod's men instead devoted their energies to polishing off some of Jefferson's finest wines. They then departed, empty handed, but without damaging the house or its belongings.[34] A relieved Jefferson later learned that Tarleton had specifically ordered "to suffer nothing to be injured" at Monticello.[35]

What Cornwallis would have done with Thomas Jefferson, had the state's governor fallen into his hands, is not known. Most likely, the high-value captive would have been bundled off to England, to join Henry Laurens of South Carolina locked up in the Tower of London. Laurens, a planter, merchant and slave trader who had become one of the richest men in the new United States, had succeeded John Hancock as President of the Continental Congress, serving in that capacity from November 1, 1777, to December 9, 1778. On August 13, 1780, he departed Philadelphia on the brig *Mercury*, to fulfill his appointment by Congress to negotiate a treaty of friendship and trade with Holland and to arrange for a $10 million loan. But the vessel that carried him was captured by a Royal Navy warship off Newfoundland on September 3. Despite throwing a bag containing his official papers overboard before his seizure, the bag floated and enemy seamen recovered them, and the British later used one of the documents as a pretext for declaring war on the Dutch.

After being examined by the Privy Council in London, on October 6, 1780, Laurens was confined in the Tower of London "on suspicion of high treason." Held there for almost fifteen months under severe conditions for a gentleman of his stature, his health seriously deteriorated. Laurens wrote in his diary on one occasion, "Maladies increasing upon me, my money expended, nothing to eat except what might be sent to me, which I accounted as nothing and which did not come every day." The governor of the Tower limited Laurens's access to physical exercise, pen and paper, and visits from his family and friends.

Still, Laurens twice refused a pardon offered to him in exchange for serving the British. In two petitions to British authorities, however, he justified his own role in the American Revolution in terms that some Patriots considered unduly subservient. Finally, on December 31, 1781, after news of the surrender of Cornwallis's army had arrived in England, and in part due the efforts of Benjamin Franklin and Parliament member Edmund Burke, Laurens was released from the Tower of London on heavy bail. Four months later, after staying at Bath to recover his health, he was exchanged for Cornwallis himself. Worn out by his imprisonment and racked by physical ailments, Laurens returned to South Carolina to find his plantation and home had been ravaged by enemy troops.[36]

As described earlier in this book, there is also the case of signer Richard Stockton, who, after being jailed for about one month, signed an oath of allegiance to the Crown. Paroled shortly thereafter, he never again participated in politics. It certainly would have been interesting to see how Jefferson would have reacted to the type of pressures put on Laurens and Stockton, had the Virginian been captured at Monticello and sent to the Tower of London.

Lower-level captives who had served in the Virginia General Assembly fared better than Laurens. But still, a pall of suspicion always hung over any military or civilian leader who was captured. Patriots could not be sure that the captive had not entered into some nefarious agreement with the hated enemy. These suspicions sometimes lingered for years after war's end.

The following excerpt was sent to Norman Brockenbrough, who was among the half-dozen or so Virginia legislators captured by Tarleton at Dr. Thomas Walker's residence at Castle Hill (which still stands today as a private residence near Monticello).[37] Written in 1784 and published in the *Virginia Gazette*, it was meant to clear Brockenbrough of charges that he had committed treason when a captive of Cornwallis. At the time in 1784, Brockenbrough was running for the office of sheriff. The letter was written by Judge Peter Lyons, who had been with him when they were both seized by Tarleton. Prior to their captures, they had been travelling to Charlottesville to serve in the General Assembly and had received conflicting reports about the location of the enemy. One report had British forces advancing on Charlottesville in their direction, but the men decided to listen to a later one that the enemy had not been heard from in the area.

The two delegates spent the night of Sunday, June 3, at Castle Hill. Lyons wrote:

> We therefore proceeded with more cheerfulness to Dr. Thomas Walker's, where we indulged the thought of being far from the enemy, and the pleasure of having a good night's repose. However, the salute in the morning was not so agreeable, for Dr. Walker came very early into our chamber [Lyons and Brockenbrough probably shared

the same bed, then a common practice], and told us the British were there, but desired us to lie still, and perhaps we might escape being discovered. On looking out the window, I saw the yard and house surrounded with soldiers, so that an attempt to get away was useless. I therefore lay down, but you proceeded to dress, so that when we were called down, which happened soon after. You went some time before I was ready, and what passed during that interval I know not. After I went down and had seen Colonel Tarleton, you asked me if I knew what they intended to do with me. I told you I did not, and inquired if you knew of your own fate. Your reply was that you had pressed to be discharged, urging your bad health, which was visible enough in your countenance; that you had applied to some of the officers to intercede with Tarleton to parole you, but that as you were a delegate [to the state assembly], he said he must carry you to camp, and I well remember when he was going off, he ordered an officer to take charge of you, and carry you on.... I heard no more of you until my son, who was likewise captured by that party, returned home, and told me you were paroled as soon as you got to camp, by order of Lord Cornwallis, who he understood expressed surprise that Colonel Tarleton should give any of the prisoners the trouble of going there, and I did not understand from him that you conversed with Lord Cornwallis, or was ever invited to his table. As to civility, we all received such more it than we expected; but we thought your treatment rather rigid, in being dragged so far to camp, when you were scarce able to ride, which good Mrs. Walker often mentioned and lamented during my short stay with her. This, Sir, is all I now recollect of that disagreeable affair, except that it was said a note had been sent to Dr. Walker by one of his neighbors to apprise him of Tarleton's approach, but came so late that it was intercepted by an officer, and delivered to Colonel Tarleton who kept it.[38]

In this matter at least, while Tarleton had acted with some "rigidity" in dealing with the ill Brockenbrough, overall he dealt with his captives in a humane manner. By war's end, however, Tarleton had gained such a bad reputation for ruthlessness that he was not invited by his own generals for the final dinner attended by British and American officers following the surrender at Yorktown.

Suspicions of questionable behavior even followed Daniel Boone, the first-time legislator from the backcountry Kentucky territory. When Fayette County was formed in the Kentucky territory as a new Virginia county, Boone had been elected a sheriff and delegate to the state assembly in January 1781. A friend described his dress in Richmond in the prior year as follows: "He was dressed in real backwoods style. He wore buckskin leggings neatly beaded of Indian manufacture" and silver buttons that had "his name engraved on them."[39] He had served as an officer of militia during Dunmore's War against the Indians in the West in 1774 and also was sometimes treated as a "captain" of scouting parties. On June 4, 1781, he and a young friend (either John Jouett from Kentucky or the omnipresent Jack Jouett) riding to Staunton where Boone would take his seat at the reconvened session of the legislature, were suddenly overtaken by a company of British dragoons. Unlike the bookish Jefferson, the frontiersman Boone had taken a public road and not the woods. Dressed in a hunting shirt and buckskin leggings, Boone was not suspected to be a potential legislator.

Rather than panic, the frontiersman and his friend struck up a conversation with the officer of the company as they rode on. Finally, coming to a fork in the road, Jouett, looking for an excuse for the pair to leave, turned to Boone and thoughtlessly said, "Wait a minute, Captain Boone, and I'll go with you." The officer now thought Boone was a Patriot militia colonel and took Boone into custody.[40]

Boone was taken to Tarleton's headquarters at Nicholas Lewis's plantation home less than one-half mile west of the Rivanna River, along with other Virginia state officials. Tarleton wrote that gentlemen prisoners were "treated with kindness and liberality," but "the lower class were secured as prisoners of war."[41] Boone was not identified as a gentleman and was therefore locked in a coal house. His son, Nathan Boone, later told an historian in an interview, "My father was conveyed to the British camp and put into a coal house.... He very probably explained his title of captain by referring to his old Dunmore commission."[42] Boone and other prisoners were then delivered to Cornwallis's headquarters on the James River. After several days' imprisonment, he was released. "Boone, who was with Lord Cornwallis, is since paroled," one Virginian wrote at the end of June, and records indicate that Boone returned to the Assembly, which reconvened in the town of Staunton in the Shenandoah Valley at the end of the month. According to one of Boone's biographers, James Mack Faragher, the frontiersman's children believed he had been released on his promise "not to take up arms anymore" against the British. "If so," concluded Faragher, "it was a pledge he did not keep, and there were those in Kentucky who pointed to this as further evidence that oaths meant nothing to Daniel Boone."[43]

When the Kidnapper Becomes the Hunted: The Case of Benjamin Cleveland

Kidnapping military and civilian leaders was not popular in the deep South, where a ferocious partisan war between Patriots and Loyalists broke out—outright murder of captives was more common. But occasional kidnappings of leaders did occur.

One theme of the kidnappings in the South was that on occasion the would-be kidnapper became the hunted. Two outstanding examples of a kidnapper subsequently finding the tables reversed occurred in the Carolinas, one in North Carolina and the other in South Carolina. In addition, another theme was captive leaders breaking their paroles and the associated consequences.

One Loyalist kidnapper made the mistake of capturing Benjamin Cleveland, a colonel of the North Carolina militia from what is today Wilkes County. As a child, Cleveland's family had moved to Albemarle County, Virginia, and thus Benjamin had grown up in a frontier border environment. After marrying Mary Graves, who hailed from a reputable family, Cleveland moved his new family to the even more undeveloped headwaters of the Yadkin in North Carolina, where he established a farm.

Residing in the crude and sometimes brutal North Carolina backcountry, with Daniel Boone as a neighbor, Cleveland rose to become a renowned Cherokee fighter and then Whig leader known for his burning hatred of Tories. Stories of his cruelty to Tories began to multiply.

In 1779, two Tories looted the home of Major George Wilfong, a Patriot and Cleveland's friend. The plunderers were later captured by Cleveland's men—the colonel had them hanged using Wilfong's clothes line they had stolen.[44] It was apparently for this act that Cleveland was indicted for murder in the superior court of Salisbury, but he was ultimately pardoned by the governor.[45]

One horrific story, told by North Carolina historian Lyman Draper, concerns two Tories taken from a jail cell, one of "whose crimes rendered him particularly obnoxious to the people." A mob placed the poor fellow on a log, threw a noose around his neck, threw the other end of the rope over a tree limb and fastened it, and then kicked the log out from under him. Cleveland then brought out the second Tory and, pointing to his dangling comrade, said, "You have your choice, either to take your place beside him, or cut your own ears off and leave the country forever." The second Tory, not risking arguing with Cleveland, called for a knife, "which he whetted for a moment on a brick, then gritting his teeth, he slashed off his own ears and left with the blood streaming down his cheeks, and was never heard of afterwards."[46]

Raising 350 men and commanding them at the tremendous American victory at King's Mountain on October 7, 1780, it is said that Cleveland was influential in the hanging of nine Tory captives after the battle.[47] Captain William Lenoir, who served directly under Cleveland and spent much of the war chasing Tory bands at the behest of Cleveland, in his post-war pension application, recalled that after the battle, thirty-two of the "most atrocious Tories" were selected to be hung. They were, according to the locals, assassins, house burners, and robbers, and deserved their punishments. According to Lenoir, three were hung at a time "until nine were executed, and the remainder respited." Lenoir also recalled another instance when Cleveland was trying to extract information of other Tories from a man named Williams, "who refused to give any, until Col. Cleveland adopted the expedient of hanging him for a while to the limb of a tree or a bent down sapling, but which did not produce the desired effect until the dose was repeated a second time with more severity than the first."[48] Anthony Allaire, a lieutenant in the Loyalist detachment that was crushed at the Battle of King's Mountain, was taken prisoner during the battle. He noted in his diary for October 14: "Twelve field officers were chosen to try the militia prisoners—particularly those who had the most influence in the country. They condemned thirty—in the evening they began to execute Lieut. Col. Mills, Capt. Wilson, Capt. Chitwood, and six others, who unfortunately fell a sacrifice to their infamous mock jury. Mills, Wilson and Chitwood died like Romans."[49] Allaire's account is consistent with that of Lenoir's; but neither man expressly stated whether or not Cleveland was a member of the court-martial. Most likely, Cleveland was on it.

Allaire did write two entries in his journal showing two sides of Cleveland's character. At the time, Cleveland was commanding an American contingent guarding a column of prisoners on the march. For October 30, 1780, Allaire reported, "a number of the inhabitants assembled at Bethabara [North Carolina] to see a poor Tory prisoner executed for a crime of the following nature. A Rebel soldier was passing the guard where the prisoners were confined, and like a brute addressed himself to those unhappy people in this style, 'Ah, d—n you, you'll all be hanged.' This man, with the spirit of a British subject, answered, 'Never mind that, it will be your turn next.' But Col. Cleveland's goodness extended so far as to reprieve him." Two days later, Allaire wrote, "My friend, Dr. Johnson, insulted and beaten by Col. Cleveland for attempting to dress a man whom they had cut on the march."[50]

John H. Wheeler, who published his recollections in 1851, recalled that a Patriot militia general once caught a Tory stealing a stirrup from his saddle and brought him to Cleveland. Wheeler wrote that Cleveland ordered the Tory "to place his two thumbs in a notch for that purpose in an arbor fork, and hold them there while he ordered him to receive fifteen lashes."[51] Clearly, Colonel Cleveland was not a man to cross.

On April 14, 1781, a small party of Loyalists led by Captain William Riddle, having crossed the Virginia border heading south, heard that Cleveland was nearby visiting and was lightly guarded. Riddle, responding to an offer of rewards for Patriot leaders brought to the British stronghold of Fort Ninety-Six in South Carolina, already had a Captain Ross in tow (possibly this was Captain James Ross of Granville County, North Carolina). Deciding to kidnap the despised but dangerous Cleveland and take him to Fort Ninety-Six as well, Riddle did not think his small party was sufficiently strong to rush the home where Cleveland was residing for the night. Instead, he decided on a ruse: he would steal the colonel's horses that evening, wait for Cleveland to join in a rescue party the next morning, and set an ambush at a vulnerable spot. Riddle also knew that, standing around six-feet tall and weighing close to 300 pounds, the North Carolina colonel could hardly run from his pursuers. Riddle's plan worked to perfection and they soon had Cleveland as a captive.

Riddle and his men, with their prisoner in hand, spent the rest of the day trekking fourteen miles into remote mountains and resting at a camp for the night near the Deep River, hoping to elude any rescue party. The next morning, Riddle ordered Cleveland to pen and sign passes, which could be presented to fool Whig soldiers manning checkpoints on the roads to Ninety-Six. Cleveland feared that once he completed this task, having lost his usefulness, he would be put to death. After taking as much time as he could writing the passes, just as he was finishing, a group of armed Wilkes County volunteers who had followed Riddle's trail, led by the captive's brother, Captain Robert Cleveland, burst into the camp and rescued Colonel Cleveland and Captain Ross.

Riddle and some of his men escaped in the confusion, but soon afterwards Riddle and two of his associates were captured. Upon the group's return to Wilkes County, a rump court-martial was immediately held, with the verdict condemning the three Tories to be hanged. Shortly afterwards, the men were hanged from an oak tree, with Riddle's wife witnessing the harsh frontier justice.[52]

After the war, Cleveland lost his farm due to a defective title and moved to Oconee County, South Carolina, the westernmost tip of the state, where he squatted on land that was still owned by local Indians. His days of terrorizing Tories were not over, even if the war was. When he captured the former Tory Henry Dinkins, who had also become a notorious horse thief and plunderer who had lived among the Cherokee, he hanged him on the spot. This made Cleveland popular in the district, where he was elected to be a judge, serving for many years, even if he spent much of his time on the bench snoozing while lawyers argued before him (according to a contemporary who knew him).[53]

The Execution of Isaac Hayne

In South Carolina, Whig resistance virtually collapsed following General Henry Clinton's capture of Charleston on May 12, 1780, as well as other British successes in the countryside. As a result, a number of Patriot officers from South Carolina, especially those who owned valuable plantations they wanted to protect, signed paroles—allowing them to return to their homes but not to provide any support against the British unless and until they were formally exchanged. Some even agreed to receive the protection of the British Crown by swearing allegiance to it.

One of the officers who apparently received the protection of the Crown was Brigadier General Andrew Williamson, a Scottish-born immigrant who, despite being illiterate, rose to own several plantations and to become one of the key leaders of the Patriot militia in South Carolina. Upon the fall of Charleston,

Williamson retired to his main plantation at White Hall, sold food to the nearby British garrison at Fort Ninety-Six, and even provided some assistance to the British war effort.[54]

Williamson became a marked man. In December 1780, Patriot General Benjamin Few of Georgia led troops in an invasion of the Fort Ninety-Six district and captured General Williamson at White Hall. Few's second-in-command, Colonel Samuel Hammond, tried to persuade Williamson to return to the Whig side, reasoning that British attempts to force parolees to take up arms against Patriot soldiers had violated their paroles, but Williamson kept to his parole and refused.

General Few made the mistake of keeping Williamson at White Hall for too long. On December 11, the commander of Fort Ninety-Six sent out a strong party to White Hall that drove off Few's men (killing fourteen and wounding seven of them) and rescued Williamson. Realizing that the backcountry had become too dangerous, and that once a kidnapping attempt had been made, other attempts could be expected, Williamson departed White Hall for the protection of Charleston. He then moved to a plantation, apparently one of his own, only a few miles outside of Charleston.[55]

Enter Lieutenant Colonel Isaac Hayne, a respected planter, horse breeder, state legislator, and militia officer from Colleton County, South Carolina, who had raised a company of volunteer cavalry that had operated in the rear of the British siege lines during General Clinton's successful siege of Charleston.[56] Hayne believed he was bound by a parole applicable to South Carolina militia and returned to his home to sit out the war at Hayne Hall, about four miles from Jacksonborough. However, Clinton's order of June 3, 1780, revoked all of the paroles of the militia, except those men who were actually within the Charleston garrison at the time of the surrender. Since Hayne was not actually in the garrison at that time, he was forced to declare his allegiance to the British Crown and receive its protection, or be subject to imprisonment by the British.

Hayne agreed to receive the protection of the Crown, but his motives are disputed. A contemporary British source claimed Hayne did so in order to sell provisions to the British garrison at Charleston, but this report is not supported by any other evidence.[57] In 1782, former South Carolina governor and then Congressional delegate John Rutledge wrote that Hayne swore an oath of allegiance to the king when the British commander in Charleston at the time refused to let Hayne leave the city unless he did so, and that Hayne complied because his wife and children were gravely ill with smallpox and this was the only way he could return to his plantation to care for them (his wife and a child later died of the disease).[58] In his memoirs, Major Henry "Light Horse Harry" Lee agreed with Rutledge on this point and added that Hayne's declaration of allegiance was made on the assurance that Hayne never would be asked to bear arms against his countrymen.⁵⁹

In April 1781, despite the increasing success of General Nathanael Greene and his Continental army in South Carolina, Hayne rejected a militia commission, understandably believing that accepting it would violate his oath. His refusal, however, hurt Patriot recruiting efforts in his home county and he was accused by Colonel William Harden, a local Whig militia leader, of "staying too much on formality."⁶⁰ When Colleton County later came under the control of the Americans, Hayne submitted to intense pressure to accept a position as colonel of the county militia regiment. He believed that he had been released from his parole, once the Americans had conquered the region of his residence.⁶¹ Hayne began encouraging men in Colleton County to rejoin his regiment, with some success.⁶²

On July 5, 1781, the thirty-five-year-old Hayne set his sights on kidnapping General Williamson. In a series of raids sweeping up several Loyalists, Hayne and a small party of mounted Colleton County militia also caught Williamson at his plantation near Charleston.⁶³ A Loyalist Charleston newspaper claimed that Hayne had carried away Williamson in his nightshirt "without allowing

This 1845 drawing depicts the capture of Isaac Hayne by Loyalist dragoons commanded by British Major Thomas Fraser, as well as the killing of Hayne's second-in-command, Lieutenant Colonel Thomas McLaughlin, who was cut to pieces when he tried to shoot Major Fraser with a pistol. From H. N. Moore, *The Life and Times of Gen. Francis Marion* (Philadelphia: John B. Perry, 1845), p. 120 (New York Public Library Collections).

him time to put on his clothes," which was considered to be a serious affront to a gentleman.[64]

Hayne's goal of kidnapping Williamson is unknown. British reports were that the Americans told Williamson "that the purpose in capturing him was to have been hanged in the camp of General Greene."[65] More likely, the Americans wanted to try again to persuade Williamson to return to the Whig side.[66]

The new commander of the British garrison of Charleston, Lieutenant Colonel Nisbet Balfour, worried that Williamson might indeed be hanged as a traitor and, angry about the affront to British honor since Williamson had been snatched so close to Charleston, immediately sent out a force of ninety dragoons under Major Thomas Fraser to rescue Williamson. Balfour later described what happened next in a letter to General Clinton:

> Major Fraser, with the mounted men of the South Carolina Rangers, was ordered to pursue, and, if possible, retake Brigadier Williamson, as it was feared his having reverted to British government might subject him to the worst treatment. By avoiding the main roads, Major Frazer was able to surprise Col. Hayne's camp, of Colleton County militia, where he was informed General Williamson then was, and coming upon it suddenly, killed a Lt. Col. [Thomas] McLaughlin, with ten or twelve others, made Col. Hayne a prisoner, and retook Gen. Williamson.[67]

At the time of Fraser's attack on July 8, Colonel Hayne was reportedly two miles from camp having breakfast at the house of a friend, and was further "unapprised of the enemy's approach until he saw them a few rods from the door" because his guard was negligently off in search of fruit. "Being very active and resolute, [Hayne] pushed for his horse, mounted, and forced his way through the foe." In attempting to leap a fence in his path, Hayne's horse fell, allowing his pursuers to capture him.[68] Williamson, in turn, returned himself to British custody, saying that he would be violating his loyalty oath if he fought again on the Whig side—the same oath that Hayne would be accused of breaking.

Hayne was imprisoned in a miserable cell in the basement of the Exchange Building in Charleston, while Balfour, and the commander of British forces in South Carolina, twenty-six-year-old Lieutenant Colonel Francis, Lord Rawdon, considered what to do with their prisoner. Both men were alarmed at the current state of affairs in the countryside outside Charleston. As early as July 7, 1780, Lord Rawdon wrote that "nine out of ten" Rebels were finding reasons not to honor their paroles.[69] On April 26, 1781, Balfour wrote to his superior, General Cornwallis, that the Rebels "have adopted the system of murdering every militia officer of ours as well as every man (although unarmed) who is known to be a Loyalist … the consequence will be … that we shall not have one Loyalist in the country, as they are crowding to town [Charleston] from all quarters."[70]

In May 1781, Balfour took steps to punish those who had taken oaths of allegiance and then had rejoined the Patriot army. He issued a proclamation, confirming one previously issued by Lord Cornwallis, announcing "the most fixed resolution of punishing, both in their persons and properties, all those who shall be found in arms against his Majesty's Government, after having claimed and obtained their Sovereign's most gracious protection."[71] While death was the accepted punishment for military parole violators, many parolees in the war who had been previously caught by the enemy were not executed. But the volatile circumstances of the war in the South made Hayne's situation tenuous.

Ultimately, the decision was made to hang Hayne. The primary rationale was to set an example to those in the future thinking about violating their paroles or oaths of allegiance. Another reason was to discourage Whig attempts to kidnap Loyalist officers at their homes.[72] Rawdon seemed particularly upset about reports that Hayne had carried away Williamson for the purpose of hanging him. The hanging by the Americans of Rawdon's friend, Major John André, also loomed over the proceedings.[73] On August 4, despite pleas for mercy from even some Loyalist leaders, Hayne was led to a gallows outside the main lines before a large crowd, allowed some last words with friends, and hanged.[74] Meanwhile, Williamson retreated to Charleston, where he remained until the British evacuated it near the end of the war.[75]

There is no record of anyone comparing Cleveland's hanging of Captain Riddle to Balfour's and Rawdon's hanging of Lieutenant Colonel Hayne (though as justification Nisbet did name several Loyalist officers who had been hanged by the Patriot side). Both condemned men were caught kidnapping an enemy officer; in addition, Hayne had arguably violated his oath of allegiance to the Crown. Regardless, the two hangings demonstrated the risks of attempting to kidnap an enemy officer or military leader.

Hayne's execution shocked and outraged Continental army officers. Their reaction confirms that officers on both sides during the war considered kidnapping to be an honorable military act, but executing the captive prisoner was not. Treating Hayne as a gentleman martyr, Lieutenant Colonel Henry Lee, in his memoirs, spoke of the dead officer as "a highly respectable citizen of South Carolina," who was primarily concerned with his "sick wife and children," and who, after being informed of his impending execution, "disdaining further discussion ... merely solicited a short respite, to enable him for the last time to see his children" and maintained a "dignified composure" even to his death.[76]

On August 12, upon hearing the news of Hayne's hanging, the commander of the Continental army in the south, Major General Nathanael Greene, immediately urged Lee and Colonel William Henderson that, should they take any British officers captive, to "keep them close prisoners until you hear further from me on the subject. I shall explain myself to you in a few days." His follow up letter to Henderson mentioned his desire to call a council of officers to discuss the possibility of retaliation. "If retaliation is not had," he wrote, "the militia will be all discouraged and quit the service." Recognizing the risks of this path, Greene also noted, "But if we retaliate ... its consequences may terminate finally in giving no quarter."[77] On August 20, the subordinate officers of the Southern Army handed Greene a petition that both rejected the British claim that as a parole violator Hayne was subject to be hanged and demanded that their commanding officer "retaliate in the most effectual manner" against a captive British officer, even at the risk of "additional dangers" to the lives of Continental officers held by the British.[78]

Perhaps trying to find a way out of his quandary, Greene wrote Lieutenant Colonel Balfour on August 26, informing him that he intended to carry out "immediate retaliation unless you can offer me something more to justify the measure." Greene threatened, "The objects I mean to retaliate upon ... are British officers and not Tory militia."[79] In response, Balfour argued that Greene would have to find an exact parity of circumstances, meaning he would have to have captive a British officer who had violated his parole. Leaving technical arguments aside, Balfour warned ominously, "I shall not tell you how many of the American officers ... are now in our power, nor remind you that Britain will loudly claim retribution for the blood of her officers, when carelessly shed."[80]

While Greene brushed aside Balfour's argument of parity of circumstances, and not having a British colonel as a captive, he still agonized over what course to take for some two months. Still, fellow Rhode Islander James Varnum, writing from Philadelphia, informed Greene of the continuing cries for revenge to be taken again British officers he heard in the halls of Congress.[81]

Because retaliation for Hayne's execution would have "necessarily" involved the "whole continent," Greene ultimately referred to the matter to Washington and Congress.[82] This may have been a delaying tactic, which allowed Greene to avoid inflicting retaliation and suffering from British retribution in kind, while he publicly continued to take a strong stand.[83] Finally, the commander-in-chief replied, "Of this I am convinced, that of all laws it is most difficult to execute, where you have not the transgressor himself in your possession. Humanity will ever interfere and plead strongly against the sacrifice of an innocent person for the guilt of another."[84] The Virginian's sage advice ended the matter, but Greene did refuse to permit a general exchange of prisoners.

It turned out that the French and American allies had an opportunity to retaliate against one of the perpetrators of Hayne's death. Rawdon, after sailing from Charleston for London, was captured by a French warship. There were cries to hang him in some quarters in the Continental army, but the British aristocrat remained safe in French hands. An unwilling witness to the surrender of Yorktown, Rawdon was soon joined in captivity by Lord Cornwallis.[85]

Back in London, on January 31, 1782, during debate in the House of Lords, the Duke of Richmond sought an inquiry into the matter of Hayne's hanging, stating that it had besmirched "the honor of the British name." On February 4, the Duke of Richmond continued his attack on Lord Rawdon in the House of Lords, calling the punishment "a piece of unwarrantable cruelty, and equally disgraceful to the nation and the profession of arms." Coming to Rawdon's defense, the Duke of Manchester countered that "an officer, who, after having broken his parole, should afterwards fall into the hands of the enemy, was deprived by his breach of faith of the advantage of a formal trial, and subjected to be executed *instanter*." Richmond lost his motion by a vote of 25 in favor and 75 against.[86]

This was all too much for Lord Rawdon, who by this time was free in London. In a February 21 letter, Rawdon challenged Richmond to a duel. Richmond tried to weasel out of it, but the younger Rawdon insisted that he "requires satisfaction for a gross injury offered."[87] After Richmond then apologized publicly, Rawdon withdrew his demand.

After learning of Richmond's charges against Rawdon for the death of Hayne, several South Carolina Loyalists wrote to King George III supporting the decision to hang Hayne, and enclosing a list of 299 South Carolina Loyalists that they claimed had been murdered by Patriot partisans.[88] In light of the brutal treatment of many Loyalists by Whig raiders in the South, historian Jim Piecuch accused Patriot leaders who denounced Hayne's hanging as "unabashed hypocrisy."[89]

VI

British Secret Service Operations in Upstate New York and Vermont (July 1781 to June 1782)

The British Attempt to Capture Major General Philip Schuyler at Albany

In 1781, British forces operating in Canada set their eyes on kidnapping prominent Americans in Vermont and upstate New York. These Whig leaders had stirred up opposition to English efforts to draw Vermont into British Canada. At the time, General Frederick Haldimand, the Governor of the Province of Quebec (which then included what is now Ontario), was engaged in negotiations with Ethan Allen and other political representatives of the Republic of Vermont, which had declared its independence from the state of New York in 1777. The British tended to view events as controlled by great men and so hoped that by removing these Patriot leaders their followers would become demoralized and the movement in Vermont to become a new province of British-held Canada would be energized.

In early May of 1781, Sir John Johnson, a prominent Loyalist leader who after the start of the war had fled from his vast estate in upstate New York, proposed to Governor Haldimand the abduction from his Albany home of Philip Schuyler, then a retired major general of the Continental army.[1] The Swiss-born general deferred.

In early July, Dr. George Smyth, a Loyalist doctor who had fled to Canada from Albany and had become deputy head of British secret service operations in upstate New York, suggested to Haldimand the kidnapping of a number of Whig leaders—those who were "the most obnoxious to the friends of government in the neighborhood of Albany." This time Haldimand consented, agreeing that the loss of Schuyler would be a significant blow to the "Rebel" cause. The governor immediately informed the head of British secret service operations in Canada, Captain Justus Sherwood, a Loyalist who had fled from Vermont and had once been imprisoned in the infamous subterranean dungeon called Simsbury Mines in Connecticut, before managing to escape. Haldimand urged Sherwood that he wanted the operations "to be carried into execution with all possible dispatch."[2] Smyth and Sherwood were based in St. Johns (now called Saint-Jean-sur-Richelieu), Canada, a major British outpost just south of Montreal.

By mid–July, Sherwood and his deputy, Smyth, had seven detachments ready to be sent from their base of operations, an island in Lake Champlain. Each party assigned to travel into New York State would consist of from four to six Loyalists and, at Haldimand's insistence, two British regulars—it appears that Haldimand did not trust Loyalists alone to complete the tasks and thought that the addition of regulars would make the operations more business-like. It was certainly a slap in the face of the leaders of the Loyalist kidnapping parties. Sherwood and Smyth chose the Loyalists, and Lieutenant Colonel Barry St. Leger of the British army selected the regulars.

Dr. Smyth instructed each of the parties to be close to its quarry by July 31, but none was to strike before then, allowing those with farther travel time to reach their destinations without alarms. Once each party had kidnapped its victim, the men were to withdraw as quickly as possible to Quebec. No one was to carry any identification or other written material that could be incriminating or that might give the enemy a clue about the multiple plots.[3]

The first and most important task of seizing Major General Schuyler fell to Captain John Walden Meyers. "Captain Meyers should carry off Schuyler. I trust him not to be in error," Haldimand instructed Dr. Smyth. "Failure would

Major General Philip Schuyler in his Continental army uniform. Engraving by T. Kelly in 1835 from a painting by John Trumbull in 1792 (reproduction by permission of the Society of the Cincinnati, Washington, D.C.).

render me much embarrassed," the general added.⁴ Why Haldimand felt that a successful kidnapping of his former officer-in-arms against the French during the French and Indian War would satisfy him, but a bungled one would not, is not clear. Perhaps he felt that a failed operation, coupled with conducting warfare in this arguably ungentlemanly way, would be a double blow to his reputation.

In July 1777 John Walden Meyers had given up his 200-acre Albany farm and had headed to join Burgoyne's army descending from Canada. He had subsequently acquired a reputation as an effective frontier raider. One story told of his trekking through the New York woods to join Burgoyne's force. When his faithful dog became fatigued, Meyers carried the pet, which drew a favorable comment from his brother-in-law, who had accompanied him. "We may have to eat him yet," Meyers responded in his thick, German accent.⁵

In Canada, in June of 1781, Meyers received command of his own unit, dubbed Meyers's Independent Company.⁶ But it was under strength, at times with only about twenty men.⁷ His company successfully raided Ballstown, New York, on June 13, 1781, netting several "rebel" prisoners. Meyers's party sent to abduct Schuyler consisted of only about twelve men, including two British regulars from the 34th Regiment, dressed in long smocks and buckskin breeches.⁸

Philip Schuyler had once been one of the highest-ranking generals of the Continental army. As the commander of the Northern Department, encompassing northern New York, Schuyler had the task in 1777 of trying to block the advance of General Burgoyne's British army travelling from Canada south in the Champlain Valley towards Albany, New York. Schuyler had done a creditable job, but on the eve of victory, Major General Horatio Gates used his political connections in Congress to get that body to relieve Schuyler of his command and to give it to Gates. An embittered Schuyler resigned from the Continental army, while Gates in October 1777 was showered with accolades after capturing Burgoyne's army following the battles at Saratoga.

While he had resigned his post as major general in the Continental army, Schuyler remained a prominent Patriot in political circles and a key military organizer in New York. General Washington himself continued to write to Schuyler with some frequency regarding military matters in northern New York. Furthermore, he was, along with Washington, one of the wealthiest and most socially prominent men in America. He was the head of one of a handful of landed patrician families—including the Livingstons, van Cortlands and van Rensselaers—that dominated the Hudson River Valley. Each owned huge manorial estates worked by hundreds of white tenant farmers, a rarity in the United States. Accustomed to the meek deference of his tenants and others in his socially stratified world, Schuyler was now the target of a kidnapping operation to be undertaken by a small band of common men.

Fortunately for the general, the Great Kidnap Caper of 1781 quickly went awry. First, a deserter from one of the parties forewarned Whig authorities. Next, Joseph Bettys, who led one of the raiding parties to nab a Patriot leader at Ballstown, New York, left his party in order to take a detour and successfully persuade a young woman to run off with him. The woman's father, Jellis Legrange, complained to the Albany County Commissioners for Detecting and Defeating Conspiracies, which on July 30 sent out search parties to find and arrest Bettys. This search effort posed a particular problem for Meyers, since he and his party were hiding in the area being searched. The next day, Legrange, with Loyalist connections, informed the Commissioners that Meyers was nearby with dispatches for some local Tories. The plot was revealed in greater detail when on the same day the commander of another of the raiding parties, Matthew Howard, targeting a Whig leader at Hoosick Falls, New York, was captured with written British secret service instructions in his possession.[9]

With all of these ominous signs, it was not difficult for Patriot authorities to deduce that the prominent General Schuyler was also targeted for kidnapping. On July 29, Schuyler was, as he wrote, "informed for the first time that parties were lurking about the place to carry me off." In the next week, after hearing more reports from local inhabitants, the Albany County Commissioners for Detecting and Defeating Conspiracies warned Schuyler that Captain Meyers and a small party were hiding in the woods near Albany, intending to capture him.[10]

Despite receiving this and other warnings, the American general had only a guard of four soldiers from the First New York Continental Regiment (also called Van Schaik's Regiment, after its commander, Colonel Gosen Van Schaik). "My gates and outward doors in the rear of my house were closed and secured at sunset, and four white men and two blacks were armed," Schuyler wrote later to the governor of New York, Brigadier General George Clinton.[11] Thus, it appears that the only extra precautions the general undertook for additional security in the face of an imminent threat to him and his family was to arm two black men he had on his estate and lock his two entry gates.

Schuyler remained at his commodious home, which he called The Pastures, and is now known as the Schuyler Mansion. With a splendid view of the surrounding countryside, it was a typical Georgian-designed brick house, except larger and more elegant than most. It had three stories, with the top floor occupied by the Schuyler's eleven children and their nurses, as well as by grandchildren when they visited, which was the case on August 7. The house's front door faced the Hudson River. Inside the front door on the first level was a large entrance hall, twenty-feet wide and running the entire length of the house. As was then the custom, this room was used for balls and banquets. On either side were two rooms, each twenty feet square, consisting of the dining room and library at the rear, and two drawing rooms at the front. The second floor, with another wide entrance hall, and four bedchambers off it, was reached by a curving stair case near the rear entrance door. Beyond the rear of the house were a host of barns, slave quarters, a cookhouse, and other outbuildings, with the whole enclosed by a wooden stockade with front and rear gates.[12]

The Pastures was located in an exposed position two miles south of the then Albany town limits. On the night of August 7, in addition to the general, The Pastures contained Schuyler's wife, Catherine, three adult female relatives (two of them pregnant), perhaps six children, at least six white and black servants, and just four guards.[13] Lieutenant Colonel Alexander Hamilton, who had married one of Schuyler's daughters, Elizabeth, on December 14, 1780, was marching with Washington's army, on its way to glory at Yorktown, Virginia.

After hiding his men in a friend's barn near The Pastures from July 29 until the search parties had exhausted themselves more than a week later, Meyers was finally ready to act. Showing courage and boldness, the shocking news brought to him of the failures of Bettys and Howard did not deter him. Meyers's twelve men, armed to the teeth, left the protection of the barn in the early evening of August 7, despite it still being light outside.

At about 8:00 p.m. Meyers and his raiders attempted to forcibly enter the rear door of Schuyler's home, as the general and his family dined on the main floor in the entrance hall, near the open front door, overlooking the Hudson River. In a letter to Washington penned the next day, Schuyler explained that Meyers and about twenty men had forced open the backyard gate. When some of them then broke into the house's back door, four servants "flew to their arms" to offer resistance. A Patriot newspaper added the following details: "two white men [soldiers] and a Negro [an armed servant], who discharged their muskets, and made several thrusts with the bayonet at them, whereby it is supposed some were wounded, as much blood was left on the place. This resistance delayed their proceedings, until they [the raiders] had secured the two white men, and wounded the Negro, who notwithstanding made his escape."[14]

With the attackers momentarily delayed, Schuyler took the opportunity to "retire out" of the entrance hall on the main floor to an upstairs bedroom, where he kept his weapons. The resistance of his servants and guards allowed the general time to rush unimpeded from the front of the entrance hall to its rear and then up the curved staircase. Some of the attackers had surrounded the house while others continued to try to force their way indoors. Meyers and his soldiers were able to push their way to the staircase and beyond. Meanwhile, Schuyler had run to pick up his pistols, which he fired from a window, even as Meyers's men "got into the salon [upper hallway] to attempt as I suppose [to barge into] the room I was in." Alarmed by Schuyler's firing, the attackers, according to the general, "retreated with precipitation as soon as they heard me call 'come on my lads, surround the house, the villains are in it.' This I did to make them believe that succor was at hand and it had the desired effects."[15] The raiders withdrew, carrying off two of Schuyler's defenders and some of his silverware from the dining room in the rear of the house. Local militia arrived too late to engage them.

Outside, Meyers and his men fled to the woods behind the stockade. There Meyers ordered the men to disperse in small groups and head for St. Johns. This was done, except for the local Loyalists, who slinked back to their homes. Meyers assumed the important task of guiding back to Canada the two British regulars, who had been slightly wounded.[16]

After Meyers's departure, an excited but safe Schuyler quickly scribbled a note to Assistant Quartermaster General Henry Glen of Schenectady, writing that "one of my people bravely defended the door which gave time for me to gain my room, where I remained without their attempting me. By firing I alarmed the town, which turned out with alacrity and expedition. The villains carried off one of my men, wounded another, and took some of my [silver] plate."[17] (In the rush of events, Schuyler did not realize that two of his guards had been captivated.) The former general requested that Glen send out parties of friendly Oneida and Tuscarora Indians to track the raiders through the forests along the Mohawk River, but it is not known if they were sent.[18]

Meeting the next day, the Albany County Commissioners for Detecting and Defeating Conspiracies ordered troops to scour the area and block nearby roads and likely Hudson River crossings, but to no avail. Next, the Commissioners issued warrants for suspected Loyalists who they thought had known that Meyers was lurking "in the woods" with a plan to try to snatch Schuyler, and brought them in for questioning.[19] On August 9, Governor Clinton increased the guard at Schuyler's residence.[20]

Meyers and his men made it back safely to St. Johns. Captain Meyers returned to St. Johns on the morning of August 17 and provided his superior officer, Lieutenant Colonel Barry St. Leger, with his version of the action. Meyers explained that his party had been "too small to effect his purpose, Schuyler's house being too large to be invested by a few men, by which means he [Schuyler] escaped by a back window."[21] Here, Meyers was relying on Schuyler's resourceful guards, who minutes after the attack had commenced had shouted that the general had jumped out of the window and was long gone[22]—they had fooled Meyers. Or Meyers did not want to admit to St. Leger that he had been tricked by Schuyler himself.

St. Leger subsequently wrote: "The attack and defense of the house was bloody and obstinate, on both sides. When the doors were forced, the servants fought till they were all wounded or disarmed. The uproar of Mrs. Schuyler and the cries of the children obliged them to retire with their two prisoners being the only persons that could be moved on account of their wounds. Two men of the 34th Regiment were slightly wounded."[23] It appears that the cries of the servants, women, and children in Schuyler's house helped as much as the general's gunfire to drive Meyers away.

According to Canadian historian Mary Beacock Fryer, a local man Meyers had recruited for the mission was killed in the attack.[24] Of Schuyler's four guards, the wounded man was Hans (John) Ward of the First New York Regiment, and Meyers's captives were Private John Cockley, and John Tubbs, an army courier assigned to Schuyler, both also of the First New York.[25] As was typical for the day, the name of Schuyler's slave who put up a courageous stand—despite not being a trained soldier and being wounded in the conflict—was not recorded.

If Meyers's party was only twelve men, and not eighteen or twenty as Schuyler thought, it probably was too small to accomplish the mission, once the element of surprise had been removed after Schuyler had been forewarned. Meyers ordered one or more men to watch outside in the event Schuyler tried to escape using another door or window, thus making the task of overpowering Schuyler's six defenders more difficult. One Patriot newspaper report indicated that Meyers had twelve or thirteen attackers, thus giving credence to Meyers's account.[26]

A newspaper report began to circulate in September of 1781, with an August 20 dateline. It contained a pretty accurate summary of the attack, and for that reason is worth quoting in its entirety. The details probably came from Schuyler himself.

> On the evening of the 7th instant, a certain Captain Meyer, formerly of Albany County, now of Roger's Rangers, at the head of 18 or 20 men, came to house of Gen. Schuyler, at Albany, and on being refused admittance at the back gate they forced it, entered the kitchen, and had proceeded to the back hall, before they were met by four white men and two blacks, who on discovering them, had been for their arms. The brave opposition made by these men and blacks afforded Gen. Schuyler time to gain his bedroom, where his arms were deposited. By this time the enemy had taken two of the men, wounded a third, and obliged the fourth, with the negroes, to seek shelter in the cellar. Some of the party then attempted to surround the house, whilst others entered. Those in the quarter exposed to General Schuyler's fire retired on the first discharge—though he repeated the fire frequently, to alarm the town. In the meantime, Meyer, with some of the party, had got upstairs, in the passage leading to the bedroom, but on their hearing the Gen. call to the citizens, to hasten up and surround the house, retired with precipitation. Though the citizens made all possible dispatch, and their approach was probably the means of the villains going off, yet they came too late. The party had carried off

the two prisoners, with some of the General's plate. General Clinton immediately on the alarm had ordered out a party of the regular troops, but as they were more remote than the citizens, they consequently could not arrive in season. Parties were immediately sent out, taking different routes, but by the last accounts, had not fallen in with them.[27]

When matters had settled down, General Schuyler sent Lieutenant Colonel St. Leger a letter requesting that the two men captured during the raid on his house be exchanged. Schuyler explained that one was an overseer on his estate who was still needed for that service, while the other was a militiaman to whom Schuyler said he owed his life and felt a strong obligation to help him return to his family. St. Leger forwarded the letter to General Haldimand, who ordered Schuyler's men exchanged as requested. But a search for them revealed that by mistake they had been put on a vessel headed for Salem, Massachusetts, for a prisoner exchange. Haldimand kindly wrote Schuyler a letter explaining the situation but assuring him that the men would eventually turn up in Albany (which they did).[28]

In his November 1 letter, Schuyler also asked St. Leger for a return of his silverware that had been purloined by Meyers and his men. In late October 1782, George Smyth sent a courier from St. Johns to return at least Schuyler's silver spoons.[29]

Not too long after the end of the war, a story arose that one of Meyers's men had hurled a tomahawk at young Margaret Schuyler, who was then running through the hall with her six month old sister, Catherine, in her arms. The tomahawk missed the intended target and became embedded in the main stair's banister, leaving a mark that tour guides to the Schuyler Mansion point out to this day. This story was told to historian William Leete Stone in about 1837 by Catherine herself; but, of course, Catherine was only an infant at the time of the raid. Catherine's recounting of the raid is a mix of fact and fiction, so it is impossible to verify the tomahawk story. The telling by authors became more elaborate afterwards, with an Indian throwing the tomahawk. The fact that neither Schuyler nor anyone else who wrote contemporaneously of the raid mentioned the presence of an Indian has undercut the creditability of the entire story.[30] The fact that the story has an Indian, and not a Tory, trying to kill a young woman carrying a baby tells more about the prejudice against Indians in Stone's day than anything else. Still, it is possible that one of Meyers's white raiders, with a background of fighting on the New York frontier and carrying a tomahawk, threw his tomahawk during the melee inside Schuyler's house at one of the general's guards. And, as historian Mary Beacock Fryer has persuasively argued, if the tomahawk landed perilously close to Catherine Schuyler, "it was by accident."[31]

The Great Kidnap Caper of 1781 Falls Apart

As noted above, British secret service officers George Smyth and Justice Sherwood sent off seven separate parties in July 1781 to kidnap leading northern New York Whigs. Each one consisted of at least four Loyalists and two British regular soldiers. Each party also hoped to pick up local militant Loyalists in their areas of operation. The keys to the grand scheme were maintaining secrecy and coordinated timing—if intelligence of the Great Kidnap Caper was kept secret and the raids happened all at once, potential targets would not be alerted to the danger. However, these twin goals were not met. Most damagingly, a deserter from a party headed by Lieutenant Israel Ferguson of the King's Rangers forewarned Whig authorities by July 29.[32]

Joseph Bettys of the King's Rangers turned out to be a complete disaster. Bettys, according to Loyalist historian Lorenzo Sabine, was "a shrewd, intelligent, daring and bad man," to whom "pity and mercy were emotions which he never felt." His service in the war, according to Sabine, "was marked by almost every enormity that can disgrace a human being. His very name struck terror, and a record of his enterprises and crimes would fill a book. He burned the dwellings of persons whom he hated, or took them off by murder. Fatigue, distance, or danger, were no obstacle in the accomplishment of his designs.... He fell upon his victims at noon as well as at midnight."[33]

Early in the war, Bettys had served under Benedict Arnold on Lake Champlain as mate of the galley *Philadelphia*, and in the course of a battle had performed such "feats of extraordinary valor" that Washington decided to pardon him when he was arrested later as a spy and condemned to death at West Point.[34] Yet Smyth and Sherwood trusted such a man to be involved in the Great Kidnap Caper of 1781, which depended on secrecy and coordinated timing.

After Bettys and his party separated from Meyers, Bettys was supposed to nab Dr. Samuel Stringer, a member of the Board of Commissioners, at Ballstown, New York. Instead, he took a detour to persuade a young woman to run off with him, despite his being married, with his wife (whom he called a "shrew") and child then residing at Ballstown. The woman's father, Jellis Legrange, even though a Loyalist, complained to the Albany County Commissioners for Detecting and Defeating Conspiracies, which on July 30 sent out search parties to find and arrest Bettys. Bettys's unauthorized detour risked exposing Meyers's operation, since Legrange's family lived in the area where Meyers and his party were hiding and waiting to raid Schuyler's estate. In addition, Legrange informed the Albany County Commissioners that he had seen "Hans Waltermeyer" the day before near Albany and that "Joe Bettys" was joining him. At least the angry father did not disclose the purpose of Meyers's visit to the Albany area.³⁵ Meanwhile, the rest of the men in Bettys's party, when their leader did not return in a timely manner, panicked and returned back to St. Johns.³⁶

After returning to St. Johns with Legrange's daughter but without Dr. Stringer, Bettys defied Lieutenant Colonel St. Leger's orders to give up the woman. Bettys had his paramour stashed in a hiding place and would not buckle under interrogation. The two lovebirds had been seen on the trail approaching St. Johns, so everyone in the town knew she was nearby.³⁷ As a consequence, Bettys was confined in the garrison, but Dr. Smyth conceded that "should this dame be sent back, I think he would not be long after her, which would ruin many of His Majesty's loyal subjects."³⁸

The commander of another of the raiding parties, young Matthew Howard, who was responsible for seizing Whig leader John Bleecker at Hoosick Falls, New York, also made a series of blunders. With a party of four Loyalists and two British regulars from Canada, as well as some other Loyalists picked up on the way, on August 4 Howard captured Bleecker, as well as a white man and a black man who had been assisting him working in his fields. On their return trip north to Canada, Howard and his party lost their way and spent the night in a clearing. At daybreak, they saw to their dismay that they had camped in a settled village. As was reported in Whig newspapers, Howard and his party,

> after passing two houses, and finding themselves observed, they began to run, whereby the inhabitants, being convinced they were enemies, immediately collected to the number of 15 or 16, and pursued them. Three of these, more alert than the rest, and having with them a dog trained to following a track, came up with them at the foot of the Green Mountains, and rushing them suddenly, secured their arms, and made them all prisoners before the rest of the party came up.³⁹

As previously mentioned, Howard had failed to follow Sherwood's orders and was captured with written instructions from Lieutenant Colonel St. Leger in his possession.⁴⁰ "I believe the Vermonters have or will hang Howard," wrote General Schuyler to Governor Clinton on August 9.⁴¹

Dr. George Smyth, in particular, worried about Howard's fate. Earlier in the war, after fleeing house arrest in New York and trying to make his way to Quebec, Smyth had been caught and locked up in Hoosick Falls. But then Matthew Howard had sprung him loose and guided him to St. Johns.⁴² Smyth was pleased when Howard limped into St. Johns in early August of 1781, after breaking jail at Bennington, Vermont. Howard informed his handlers how he was treated in an effort to force him to divulge more information. He was drawn up on a rope three times until he passed out, and then returned to his filthy cell to await the next development. Somehow, perhaps with the assistance of local friends, he escaped; the visible rope burns on his neck backed up his story.⁴³

In fact, none of the seven raids authorized by General Haldimand and launched by Sherwood and Smyth paid off. Owing to the uncoordinated attacks, Howard's mistake, and disclosures by the deserter, the rest of the kidnapping parties returned to Canada empty handed.

Without receiving authority from Sherwood, Smyth had sent an eighth group after General Jacob Bayley of Newbury, Vermont, who had lobbied against American participation in peace negotiations that had been initiated by Haldimand. Smyth gave the assignment to Captain Azariah Pritchard, who had already captured Bayley's protégé, Thomas Johnson (see the next subchapter). Pritchard "had orders to take Gen. Bayley and bring him in, but if he was not able to walk, to kill him and bring his papers."[44] Justin Sherwood, however, had a pact with Vermonters to stay neutral and did not want a high-profile kidnapping to upset the arrangement. Once Sherwood, at the last minute, discovered the plan to nab Bayley, it was called off.

Thus did the Great Kidnap Caper of 1781 fail in ignominy. Not one of the high-profile Whigs targeted by the British secret service was captured. A few low-level soldiers and government officials were taken back to Canada as prisoners; at least they could be used to exchange for prisoners of the same rank held by the Americans. But the British also suffered a public relations blow. American newspaper editors who got wind of the plot reported, "It appears that the British are not ashamed to employ their adherents, thus to steal away inhabitants of our country" and "even condescend to offer rewards for the encouragement of this low unmanly business."[45]

In the spring of 1782, Bettys, back in the good graces of Sherwood and Smyth, had sloppily allowed himself to be captured while visiting friends in New York. Smyth feared that Bettys would be hanged as a spy, but Haldimand insisted that Sherwood arrange for Bettys to be exchanged, on the grounds that Bettys was an officer in a Loyalist regiment and that Haldimand had never executed any of the American spies he had captured in Canada. But the Commissioners in Albany ignored Sherwood's pleas, and Bettys was hanged in the town. According to a Loyalist observer, the former kidnapper jumped from the scaffold, ensuring that he would quickly break his neck rather than suffer a slow strangulation.[46]

Born in Albany, Peter Gansevoort was also targeted for kidnapping. In April 1777, as a twenty-eight-year-old colonel, he successfully defended Fort Stanwix at Rome, New York, against an attacking British force led by Lieutenant Colonel Barry St. Leger, to whom Smyth and Sherwood reported. This signal victory helped lead to the great victory at Saratoga later in the year. In 1778 and 1779 Colonel Gansevoort commanded Fort Schuyler in upstate New York during General John Sullivan's campaign against New York's Five Nations tribes.

On March 26, 1781, the New York legislature appointed him brigadier general of the state's militia. Gansevoort was clearly a high-value target for Smyth and Sherwood, as well as for the revenge-seeking St. Leger.

According to early New York historian William Leete Stone:

> A scheme was devised to seize him [Gansevoort] at one of the ferries which he was about to cross, the execution of which was intrusted to a hostile partisan named Tanckrey. By some means, however, Colonel Henry van Rensselaer, at Halfmoon [in Saratoga County], obtained information of the project, and lost no time in admonishing the general of his danger by letter. Having also heard of the rendezvous of Tanckrey and his gang, van Rensselaer dispatched a detachment of troops, under Major Schermerhorn, for their apprehension. They were found at the house of a Mr. Douglass; but before Schermerhorn's troops had surrounded the house, their approach was discovered, and they were fired upon by the marauders, all of whom, with a single exception, succeeded in getting off through the rear of the house. Two of the Schermerhorn's militia were wounded.[47]

Governor George Clinton, like his counterpart in New Jersey, was a fierce Patriot and the target of a number of kidnapping plots, particularly in 1781. Prior to becoming the governor of New York, Clinton had been appointed as a brigadier general in the Continental army and still held the post. On August 10, the day after the attempt on Schuyler, General Washington penned a letter to Clinton providing details of a separate plot to kidnap him. Because Governor Clinton was based in the lower part of the state, this particular plot emanated out of British-held New York City. In an August 14 letter to Schuyler congratulating the general on beating back Meyers's kidnapping attempt and disclosing the recent plan to nab him, the governor added that this was the third plot to kidnap him "in the course of the Spring and Summer" of 1781.[48] The details of this last plot were fleshed out on November 8, 1781, when a Loyalist who had been detained, and in an effort to avoid being hanged, confessed that "Governor Clinton is to be taken and delivered into New York by George Harden, James Riley and two others from Dutchess County whose names I have forgot, for which they are to receive 200 guineas."[49] Fortunately for Governor Clinton, none of the plots against him came to fruition.

Thomas Johnson: British Agent or Double Agent?

In the spring of 1781, Captain Azariah Pritchard of the King's American Rangers, a Loyalist unit led by renowned frontier fighter Robert Rogers, took advantage of an opportunity to kidnap militia officer Lieutenant Colonel Thomas Johnson of Newbury, Vermont. A miller by trade, before the war Pritchard had lived in Derby, Connecticut. He had subsequently fled with his family to Quebec and become a secret agent for the British army, carrying out numerous missions in Connecticut and Vermont.[50] On the night of March 8, 1781, Pritchard and ten of his men surprised and abducted Johnson and four others from Peacham, Vermont, and then marched them through the northern woods to the British fort at St. Johns.[51]

Lieutenant Colonel Johnson, a Vermont militia officer, first gained notice by taking care of the prisoners of Fort Ticonderoga captured by Ethan Allen and his Green Mountain men in 1775. He also co-commanded a fierce but ultimately unsuccessful American attack on fortified British positions on Mount Independence on September 18, 1777. At the time in March 1781, Johnson had a contract to build a grist mill at Peacham, Vermont, and it became known that he would be arriving there with stones in early March. A little after midnight on March 8, Pritchard's men surrounded the house at which Johnson was staying, broke into it, and took prisoner Johnson and four other men. "To my great surprise," Johnson wrote in his journal, he knew several of the men in the raiding party.[52]

Johnson was a protégé of General Jacob Bayley, a firm Patriot leader of Vermont who opposed any connection of Vermont to Canada. But Johnson's wife, Abigail, was also related to the former British governor-general of Canada, Sir Guy Carleton. Thus British secret service officers in St. Johns saw a good opportunity.

On the march to St. Johns, Johnson was well treated. As they marched north in the woods through four feet of snow towards St. Johns, Johnson wrote in his journal for March 10, "The Captain [Pritchard] and men were very kind to us." Two days later, the commandant of a fort sent Johnson "a good dinner and a bottle of wine." Arriving at St. Johns the next day, its commander, Lieutenant Colonel Barry St. Leger, according to Johnson, "took me to his home and gave me a nice shirt" as well as "some refreshments, which I needed." That evening, St. Leger had Johnson at his table for dinner, with Lieutenant Colonel Robert Rogers as another guest. In addition, Johnson was allowed to roam within St. Johns, which, he wrote was "the first instance of a prisoner having his parole in this fort without some confinement."[53]

It soon became clear why British and Loyalist officers were treating him so kindly: they hoped to turn him to their cause as part of the British effort to influence Vermonters to join Canada. They put pressure on Johnson to be a spy by refusing his requests to be exchanged formally, as he had a right to expect. At first, Loyalist officers thought that Johnson could be turned, but then they changed their minds. Captain Sherwood wrote that Johnson "can't bear to hear of American losses in men or money, but will dispute anything of that nature as warmly as I ever heard a Rebel."[54]

On May 3, 1780, Ira Allen, accompanied by a lieutenant and fourteen privates from the Vermont militia, arrived at Isle aux Noix under a flag of truce to negotiate with Justus Sherwood about Vermont allying itself with King George III. But even though Johnson was at Isle aux Noix, he complained, "I had no liberty to speak to those of my acquaintance who came in with the Flag." Johnson was shortly thereafter moved to St. Johns, away from the delicate discussions, which later ended with no agreements.[55]

Finally giving in, as a condition for his release in October of 1780, Johnson agreed to provide the British with intelligence, to assist Loyalist scouts, and to return to Montreal if requested. His handler, Captain Sherwood, hoping that Johnson would use his strong influence to persuade Vermonters to ally with Britain, allowed him to return to his home in Newbury, Vermont, shortly thereafter.[56]

In August 1781, as previously described, one of the eight parties sent out by Haldimand was Captain Pritchard's with the assignment to capture General Jacob Bayley of Newbury, Vermont. Bayley had lobbied against American participation in peace negotiations that had been initiated by Haldimand; Johnson was Bayley's protégé. This plan, however, was called off at the last minute.

After returning to his home in Vermont, on May 30, 1782, Johnson wrote a letter to George Washington, claiming that during his captivity in Canada he had been gathering intelligence for the Americans and that soon after his arrival in Canada he had "contracted an intimate acquaintance and conversation with leading men in that quarter." Johnson further informed Washington that he had learned that the British and Vermonters at Isle aux Noix had discussed Vermont's raising 600 troops, plus enough men for a twenty-gun ship, to be commissioned by the king.[57]

Despite the British realization after Yorktown that the war to bring America back to the British fold was lost, Canadian rulers still hoped to nab Vermont. In June 1782, the British secret service plan to kidnap General Bayley was revived. Captain Azariah Pritchard and his party of eight men from St. Johns were ordered to trek to Newbury, Vermont, and meet with Johnson, who would advise them on the best way to capture Bayley. Pritchard and members of his party met on June 15 at an agreed rendezvous point with Johnson, who tried unsuccessfully to dissuade Pritchard from making the attempt. Pritchard did refuse to try to nab Bayley while the latter was farming "in the Great Meadow, at day time," but instead agreed to make the attempt that night just after dusk. On his return trip home, Johnson claimed to have dispatched a note to Bayley warning him of the danger.[58]

Joseph White, one of Pritchard's party and a former resident of Newbury, later wrote that after sneaking up to Bayley's house late that same day, "we went as nigh to the house as we could and watched until the dusk of the evening, then pressed into the house. Several men ran out of the other door. Two guns were shot at them. One Continental soldier [Ezra Gates] was wounded in his arm." But the raiders found that Bayley was not home—he had fled across the Connecticut River into New Hampshire after being warned of the plot to kidnap him. White continued: "as the alarm guns began to be fired very thick all around, we got off as quick as we could."[59] Pritchard and his men managed to capture three of Bayley's guards and James Bayley, one of the general's adult sons. A local force of about thirty men could not catch up or find Pritchard's party.[60]

Thomas Johnson fell under the suspicion of both sides. A friend of Pritchard's from Newbury accused Johnson of alerting Bayley, while Joseph White reported that Johnson was "kind and true."[61] In Canada, Sherwood believed Johnson was guilty of "treachery," but his colleague, Dr. Smyth, was persuaded that the lieutenant colonel was not to blame for the failure to catch Bayley.[62] In Vermont, Johnson's neighbors wondered if Johnson was an agent who was part of the plot to kidnap Bayley.[63]

Still claiming to be a strong Whig, Johnson explained his predicament to General Washington, stating that he could only obtain his freedom by agreeing to be an agent for his British handlers, but that he had intended all along to serve as a double-agent for the Patriot cause. Washington understood and exonerated Johnson.[64] The Vermont Historical Society, which stores Johnson's papers, wrote of him:

> Johnson had to defend his reputation in Newbury for many years. The nature of his capture, his lenient treatment in captivity, the nature of his parole, and that his wealth had grown during the war caused suspicion. The fact that his wife, Abigail Carleton, was related to Sir Guy Carleton, Governor General of Canada, and the suspicion that he aided the British in an unsuccessful attempt to capture General Jacob Bayley in 1782 also caused distrust of Johnson. Some said he was a British agent, some said a double agent. After the war Johnson seems to have earned the trust of the people of Newbury. He served as Newbury's first postmaster, 1785–1800, and served as town representative to the Vermont General Assembly for eight years. His business interests and land acquisitions prospered. Thomas Johnson died January 4, 1819 in Newbury, Vermont.[65]

Still, years after Johnson's death, local feelings continued to run high—the lieutenant colonel's grave stone was marred by the word "Tory" scratched onto it.[66] Johnson's experience highlights one of the dangers of being successfully kidnapped: the risk of being accused of being a spy for the enemy.

Two historians who have closely studied that matter believe that Johnson gave the British useless or misleading information and that he was a double agent supporting the American cause.[67] I agree with them.

VII

Yorktown and Beyond (September 1781 to September 1783)

David Fanning Captures North Carolina's Governor

After the British had seized Charleston, South Carolina, in May of 1780, General Charles, Earl Cornwallis, commander of the southern forces, had sought to extend British control to North Carolina and to encourage Loyalists there. His first step was to try to take possession of Wilmington, then a town of about 1,000 residents. On January 21, 1781, a British expeditionary force of 300 British soldiers departed Charleston and arrived at the Cape Fear River in North Carolina four days later. Commanded by Major James Henry Craig of the British 82nd Regiment, a veteran of the Battle of Bunker Hill described by a contemporary as "hot, peremptory and pompous," Craig captured Wilmington on January 28, taking 200 "Rebels" as prisoners.[1]

One Loyalist who had been relatively quiet during the war up to then but who was emboldened by the British seizure of Wilmington was David Fanning. Originally from Raeburn's Creek, South Carolina, Fanning had been arrested and jailed on numerous occasions by Patriot authorities for his Tory beliefs. He finally fled his home and hid in the woods, before moving to Chatham County in North Carolina. With Wilmington in Major Craig's hands, Fanning sought an active role in the fighting. Clad in "a long white hunting shirt and mounted on a common draft horse," Fanning began his career of raiding with a small band of eight to ten men, who were based at John Reins's house at Bushy Creek. In July of 1781, recognizing Fanning's value as a leader, Major Craig bestowed upon Fanning a British red coat, a sword and pistols and made him a colonel of the Loyalist militia. One of his men gave him a fast mare called Red Doe, whose blood lines were traced for many years afterwards in North Carolina.[2]

Fanning soon began to make a name for himself as an effective raider, which can be gleaned from his autobiography: "I burnt Capt. Coxe's house, and his father's. I had also two skirmishes and killed two of the Rebel party. On my return to Little River, I heard of a Capt. Golson, who had been distressing the Loyalists; and went in search of him myself, but unfortunately I did not meet him, but fell in with one of his men who had been very assiduous in assisting the Rebels. I killed him."[3] After a surprise raid or ambush, often under cover of night, Colonel Fanning could move his small party quickly toward Wilmington and the protection of Major Craig's troops. Fanning quickly gained an infamous reputation among Whigs.

After receiving his red coat and sword from Craig, in July of 1781, Fanning captured Colonel Ambrose Ramsey, Judge John Williams, and several other Chatham County militia officers at Chatham Courthouse. Fanning and his men lay in wait at the courthouse early in the morning while the unknowing Whig militia officers entered the building for a scheduled court-martial, reportedly to try local Tories and possibly hang them. Rather than execute his prisoners, Fanning paroled most of them but used Ramsey and other high-ranking captives to outline Loyalist grievances. Fanning's party, Ramsey wrote, "consisted of persons who complained of the greatest cruelties, either to their persons or their property. Some had been unlawfully drafted, others had been whipped and ill-treated, without trial; others had their houses burned, and all their property plundered and barbarous and cruel murders had been committed in their neighborhoods." Fanning's men demanded "an immediate stop ... to such inhuman practices" or else "the whole country will be deluged in blood, and the innocent will suffer for the guilty."[4] The plea, however, did not work.

Fanning moved on to capture Colonel Phillip Alston of Chatham County at his house, after a vicious firefight. Despite reportedly losing two of his men in the skirmish, the Tory leader agreed to parole Alston as well.[5] At this time, Fanning was willing to capture and parole Whig leaders, and not to execute them.

While despairing of the British presence in Wilmington and the rise of Loyalists raiders in the eastern part of the state, North Carolina Patriots were hopeful after the state General Assembly elected Dr. Thomas Burke as their new governor on June 25. A native of Ireland, the one-eyed Burke had served four years as the state's delegate to the Continental Congress. An enterprising and intelligent man, Burke seemed on his way to lead Patriots in retaking the state and forcing their enemies to withdraw. Burke caught the attention of General Nathanael Greene, commander of the American armies in the South, who noted that the new governor had provided "energy and a new turn to affairs" in the state.[6] To curb Fanning and other Loyalists, in July Governor Burke had ordered General John Butler's force of state militia to patrol the country between the Cape Fear and the Neuse River.

In early September of 1781, with the Continental army focusing on surrounding and capturing Cornwallis's army at Yorktown, Virginia, Fanning put out a call for armed Loyalists to collect at Coxe's Mill. He was soon joined by 200 Scottish Highlanders from Cumberland County and 70 from Bladen County, increasing his force to an impressive 1,200 men, although some of them did not carry weapons.

On September 7, Governor Burke left Halifax and set out for Hillsborough, where he had rented a house and had arranged to meet his wife. From there he hoped to organize a new campaign against armed Loyalists. Although advised by his friends to take a military escort and despite being warned in mid-August that Fanning had his sights on him, Burke scorned the advice. After arriving at Hillsborough, on September 10 Burke wrote General Butler, alerting him of the gathering threat from Fanning's force. The governor, still careless of his own safety, believed that Fanning would strike at Butler rather than attack Hillsborough. "They will make a rapid movement on horseback and if possible surprise you," he warned his general.[7]

Prior to September, according to Fanning, he had "previously determined within myself to take the Rebel, Governor Burke of North Carolina and I had a conversation with Major Craig on the subject. I now thought it a favorable opportunity."[8] Major Craig approved; he had already instituted a program of capturing prominent Patriots around Wilmington, including Cornelius Harnett and John Ashe, who had died from maltreatment.[9] Craig approved of Fanning's goal, describing Burke as "by far the man of the greatest abilities and one of the most violent in this Province."[10]

Informing only his second-in-command of his prominent target, Fanning moved a force of about 600 to 700 picked men towards Butler's force, encamped on the Cape Fear River some forty miles away. After marching sixteen miles to Rocky River and obtaining intelligence of the situation in Hillsborough from a nearby friend, Fanning finally had to disclose to his men his plan to capture Governor Burke. This news energized Fanning's soldiers, who marched for two days towards Hillsborough.

At 7:00 a.m. on September 12, Fanning's Loyalists appeared on the outskirts of Hillsborough. A dark night and early morning fog had permitted the Tory columns to elude patrols and almost encircle the town. Attacking the town from three directions, Fanning's men met little resistance. Scattered fire from individual houses did not stop the attackers, and soon they had the governor's house in their sights. Trying their best to resist, the governor's party was reluctant to surrender in light of the "savage manners and appearance" of

Fanning's men. At length, Burke's aide-de-camp, John Reid, left the house and returned with "a gentleman in the uniform of a British officer." This officer presumably was Fanning. Assured of fair treatment, Burke surrendered his sword.[11]

Not only had Fanning captured the state's Patriot governor, he had bagged some 200 prisoners, including members of the state Council, several Continental officers, and seventy Continental soldiers holed up in a church. He had also freed thirty Loyalists and British soldiers, including one who was scheduled to hang that day. Suffering only one man wounded, Fanning claimed to have "killed fifteen of the Rebels and wounded twenty."[12] After a period of looting—brought on in part by the discovery of a supply of whiskey—at 12 noon Fanning's men, with prisoners and booty in tow, set out for the safety of Wilmington.

During the confusion of the attack, Robert Mebane, a Patriot militia colonel, escaped Hillsborough and was able to inform Butler of what had transpired. Butler hurriedly marched from 300 to 400 militiamen to Lindley's Mill in Alamance County, where a large plateau provided an ideal location for an ambush. Perhaps careless from their success, Fanning's advance guard was surprised in the ambush. The enterprising Fanning led a column around the rear of Butler's men, who, though surprised at first, regained their composure and put up a stiff defense. After four hours of fierce fighting, Butler's force retreated, having failed to rescue Governor Burke or any of the other prisoners. Both sides suffered casualties, with Fanning suffering twenty-seven killed and sixty so seriously wounded that they were left on the field. Fanning himself was shot in the arm and, unable to travel with his column, hid in the woods, guarded by only three of his men.[13] Butler in turn lost twenty-four killed, ninety wounded and ten prisoners.[14]

With Butler's men still in pursuit, the Tories and their prisoners continued their march towards Wilmington. Learning of the affray, Major Craig marched out with a detachment of the 82nd Regiment to meet them, making contact with the Loyalist column on September 23. Craig dispatched a force of his regulars for a night attack on advance elements of Butler's pursuing force, which retreated in confusion, leaving behind twenty dead and twenty-five more prisoners. Assuming custody of a dejected Governor Burke, Craig brought him and the other captives into Wilmington.[15]

Refusing Patriot requests to exchange Governor Burke, Craig held on to him, in case the Whigs captured Fanning and wanted to execute him. Craig ultimately sent Burke to Charleston, with the admonition not to permit his parole. After a period of close confinement on Sullivan's Island, Burke was paroled to James's Island on November 6. Matters went smoothly until a party of Tories was permitted to camp on the island; the newcomers hailed from North Carolina and they despised Burke. One night Burke's residence was fired upon, killing one man and wounding another. Burke requested that Major General Alexander Leslie of the British army agree to parole Burke and allow him behind American lines, but the request was not granted. Fearing for his life, and reasoning that because General Leslie had ignored his complaints of his personal danger his parole was therefore terminated, Burke decided to escape. The day after he did so, a man was shot in the doorway of his quarters on the assumption that the man was Burke.[16]

On January 20, Burke arrived at General Greene's camp. Breaking parole was considered a serious charge by the Patriots; gentlemen did not break their word. Burke claimed that he was exchanged, while General Leslie insisted that he be returned to British custody immediately. Burke resumed his governorship on February 1 under a cloud of suspicion from which he never recovered. Officers in Greene's Continental army, for one, considered Burke's conduct "highly reprehensible" and "dishonorable to the State" of North Carolina.[17] Burke was finally formally exchanged on October 23, 1782, but it was too late to save his political career. After an illness at his residence in Hillsborough, Burke died at the age of just thirty-six on December 2, 1783.[18]

Fanning, in turn, was disappointed that his capture of Burke had not ended Patriot resistance in eastern North Carolina. Still, he could be proud that he had led one of the most successful raids of the war undertaken by Loyalists. Even Major Craig, in Wilmington, was impressed, writing that the Loyalists in his region had displayed "a degree of spirit in our cause that has never been shown in any other part of America."[19]

Murder in North Carolina and Georgia

The surrender of Cornwallis's army at Yorktown on October 19, 1781, did not end the war immediately. While the opposing armies generally stayed in place, awaiting peace negotiations, small-scale military conflicts, particularly in the South, continued to occur. The risk of a military leader being kidnapped continued to exist.

By the start of 1782, even David Fanning recognized that the course of the war had turned against his cause, but he nonetheless continued his marauding. Now, however, he turned to killing his Whig victims or burning their houses. This bloody new path was not taken out of general frustration. Instead it was in specific retaliation for Whig authorities in North Carolina in early February 1782 hanging three of Fanning's men, Captain Thomas Dark and two privates.[20] In a February 26, 1782, letter to Governor Burke, an outraged Fanning mentioned the three of his men who had been hanged, as well as six others under a sentence of death. He warned the governor,

"I will retaliate blood for blood, and tenfold for one, and there shall never be an officer or private of the Rebel party escape that falls into my hands hereafter, but what shall suffer the pain and punishment of instant death."[21] Fanning kept his word. In his own memoirs, Fanning admitted that he had killed certain Whigs in direct retaliation for the cold-blooded killings of other Loyalists.[22] Fanning saw no distinction between state sanctioned hangings and murder.

Alexander Gray, a former North Carolina state legislator, in 1847 interviewed surviving county residents who remembered Fanning's rampage through Randolph County, North Carolina, in March of 1782, as well as other depredations committed by Fanning and his men. For example, Gray was informed, "On one occasion Fanning and his troop called at a smithshop to get their horse shoes repaired, where he met with a young man of the name of Bland, who had for a time served under him, but had withdrawn himself with a hope that he would be permitted to live at home in peace; Fanning charged him with being a deserter, stabbed him several times with his sword, and then shot him, and after turning him over with his foot to see that he was dead, said the d—d rascal would never deceive him again." Another time, a traveler on his way to Cross Creek spent a night at the house of Captain William Bell, a Whig, "when he fell into Fanning's hands he was hung, stripped of his clothing, horse, baggage, &c., and left lying naked in the road." Bell later identified the corpse.

On Sunday morning March 10, 1782, Gray was told, Whig Colonel Andrew Balfour "was sitting in his door reading his Bible" when "one of Fanning's company shot him through the shoulder, his wife and sister seized him in their arms, and while in this position Fanning with a pistol shot him through the head." Then Fanning and his men plundered the house before going on to the house of William Millikin, a Whig whom Fanning "no doubt intended to treat in the same way; but Millikin being away from home (for in those days no man thought himself safe in his own house) Fanning burnt the house, and proceeded three miles further to the house of Col. Colvin [Collier], a man whom he [Fanning] dreaded, and had frequently seen in his rear when on a retreat." Fanning "turned his wife and children out of doors, and burnt the house."[23]

There are several contemporary references to Fanning's murder of Colonel Balfour. A Major A. Tatom, later a state legislator, wrote to Governor Burke, in a letter dated March 20, 1782: "On Sunday the 11th instant, Col. Balfour, of Randolph, was murdered in the most inhumane manner, by Fanning and his party, also, a Captain [John] Bryant and a Mr. King were murdered the night of the same day, by them. Colonel Collier's and two other houses were burned by the same party."[24] Colonel Balfour's sister, Margaret Balfour, wrote to her sister on September 24, 1782:

On the 10th of March, about twenty-five armed ruffians came to house with the intention to kill my brother. Tibby and I endeavored to prevent them; but it was all in vain. The wretches cut and bruised us both a great deal, and dragged us from the dear man then before our eyes. The worthless, base, horrible Fanning shot a bullet into his head.... The sight was so shocking that it is impossible for the tongue to express anything like our feelings; but the barbarians, not in the least touched with our anguish, drove us out of the house, and took everything they could carry off except the Negroes who happened to be all from the home at the time.... We remained only a few days at our own plantation, after the dreadful disaster, having been informed that Fanning was coming to burn the house and take the Negroes.[25]

After describing more brutal raids committed by Fanning, Alexander Gray told the already famous story of the escape of Colonel Andrew Hunter of Randolph County. In May of 1782, Hunter was overtaken on a road and captured by Fanning and his band, and informed that he would be immediately hanged as a parole violator. Fanning dismounted from his mare, Red Doe, to oversee the hanging. Hunter then broke free from his captors and jumped onto Red Doe and quickly rode away, taking with him Fanning's saddle and the pistols Major Craig had presented to Fanning. Hunter escaped his pursuers on the fast steed, but not before being wounded twice by musket shots fired by Fanning's men. According to Fanning's own narrative, Hunter later promised to return the mare to Fanning, if Fanning would not harm his wife and children, whom Fanning had taken hostage.[26] Fanning reportedly took Hunter's pregnant wife and all of his slaves to a remote location in Moore County on Bear Creek awaiting Hunter's response.[27] Fanning did not harm Hunter's wife, but he did gain revenge by abducting Hunter's slaves and, as Gray was informed, "by plundering his [Hunter's] property and burning his house."[28]

Meanwhile, Major General Nathanael Greene faced problems maintaining discipline in his poorly clad, fed and paid Southern Army. The May 25, 1782, edition of the *Virginia Gazette* reported the following kidnapping threat against Greene, then with his army on the Ashley River in South Carolina:

> Our latest accounts from the southward mention a conspiracy against General Greene. The enemy, it seems, had bribed one of his servants; and measures were concerted for carrying the General off prisoner. The plot, however, was found out and the traitor executed.

"Light Horse" Harry Lee thought that mutineers had engaged in "continued correspondance with the enemy" and that "Greene himself was to be seized and delivered to the enemy." The plot's ringleader, a sergeant in the Pennsylvania line, was hanged on April 22, 1782, and the mutiny was "crushed."[29]

As late at September 1783, there were rumors of Colonel David Fanning, then holed up in British-held Charleston, trying to obtain permission from the commander of the garrison, General Alexander Leslie, to enter the countryside and attempt to kidnap Patriot leaders. In a September 9 letter, a South Carolinian warned General Greene that Fanning had "long" been soliciting Leslie to offer "a handsome reward" to him to bring in "the head to Gen. Leslie of yourself, General Marion or any other person he might require." Greene's friend further reported that according to the latest intelligence, Fanning came "out of town last Thursday or Friday with only a Negro to endeavor to accomplish some vile purpose." The letter writer wondered whether General Francis Marion, the Swamp Fox, "should have a hint of this."[30]

In his memoirs, Fanning never mentioned going after either Greene or Marion. Instead, according to Fanning, he departed Charleston on September 5 with "two men and my negro" to try again to retrieve Red Doe, the highly valued mare of his on which Andrew Hunter had escaped from Fanning's grasp in May. Fanning's effort was unsuccessful and he returned to Charleston on September 28. There a ship was ready to take him and a group of 250 Loyalists to St. Augustine, Florida, where Fanning planned to lead a settlement.[31] When that venture failed, he wound up in New Brunswick in Canada. In 1801 he was convicted of rape and sentenced to death, but was pardoned by the provincial governor. Fanning then moved to Nova Scotia, where he built and owned several merchant ships and passed away peacefully in 1825.

In Georgia, a small British army under Lieutenant Colonel Archibald Campbell had captured Savannah in 1779, leading to a fierce struggle for power in the hinterlands between Patriots and Loyalists. When a Patriot government was finally restored at Augusta in September of 1781, it was weak. That same month, a group of armed Tories tried to capture the new governor, Nathan Brownson, as well as his Executive Council, but did not succeed. Another unsuccessful attempt was made by Tories in March of 1782, this time against the new governor, John Martin.[32]

In early December of 1781, a strong force under General John Twiggs defeated a party of Cherokee. The December 20, 1781, edition of the *Royal Georgia Gazette*, published in Savannah, had a different take, explaining that Twiggs's force had "plundered and murdered several traders and Cherokee Indians (not even sparing women and children) who were on their way to Savannah." According to Georgia historian Hugh McCall, writing soon after the war, while returning from this mission, the President of the Executive Council, Myrick Davis, and two other members of the Executive Council, Thomas Lewis and Major David Emmanuel, had "carelessly fallen in the rear" of Twiggs's main force, more than one mile behind. Suddenly, the small group was overtaken by a party of Loyalists commanded by Captain Benjamin Brantley. "Lewis and Emanuel escaped by the speed of their horses," wrote McCall, "but Davis was taken prisoner, and afterward murdered."[33]

Governor Brownson, in a December 15 letter to Nathanael Greene, had a different version of what had happened. Brownson wrote that "a party of outlying Tories" had captured Davis, Lewis and Emmanuel, "took & carried them some miles & then attempted to butcher them. The other two [Lewis and Emmanuel] made their escape, one with a bullet through his body, the other unhurt, but Mr. Davis fell a victim to their more than savage cruelty." Brownson noted that Georgia had "suffered a great loss," for Davis was "truly a Patriot and much esteemed, both in his private and public character." His "assassination," added Brownson, would be sure to "increase the horrors of war, already too horrible, in this part of the Continent."[34]

Washington Plans to Abduct a Future King of Great Britain from New York City

By late March of 1782, after the stunning American victory at Yorktown, the tide of war had turned in favor of the Americans (and the French), and military operations were winding down. Nevertheless, Washington approved an operation to kidnap King George III's son, Prince William Henry, and Admiral Robert Digby, both of whom were visiting British-occupied New York City. The prince, third in line to the British throne when he arrived in New York City on September 26, 1781, was the "first of royal lineage" to visit America.[35]

It is not clear what the American commander-in-chief intended to do with the young prince. Normally, a high-ranking officer was exchanged for someone of equal rank, but obviously the Americans did not have a royal counterpart being held captive by the British who could be exchanged on a one-for-one basis. Washington might have thought that capturing the Prince would have struck at British morale and forced George III to finally agree to peace terms recognizing American independence and ending the war, which had dragged on despite the great French and American victory at Yorktown. Or perhaps the commander-in-chief had less grand motives in mind, thinking that William Henry could be exchanged for numerous American captive prisoners still suffering in fetid conditions on board the notorious *Jersey* British prison ship off of Brooklyn.

Born at Buckingham Palace on August 21, 1765, despite being fawned over and flattered, William Henry tried to lead the life of a normal boy. When a young friend appeared tongue tied in his presence, he begged his playmate to reflect that they were both boys and therefore likely to want to think and behave in the same way.[36]

Thomas Byam Martin, the son of a baronet, recalled many years later that the first time he met the Prince he was eight and William Henry was sixteen. The Prince was, said Martin, "a fair-looking youth" with a florid complexion, light hair and a pleasing countenance, but a squat form." Young Martin could not understand the "respect, ceremony and submission" shown towards Prince William Henry by his father and other officials, "almost doubting if the youth could be of the same flesh and blood as ourselves." The Prince, thought Martin then, talked too much and too assertively, and it was high time that he experience "the wholesome check of a little man-of-war discipline." A few days later Martin and his ten-year-old brother Joe picked a quarrel with William Henry in the garden of Buckingham Palace. Eagerly stooping to their levels, William Henry cuffed their heads, which started a brawl that only stopped when some adults arrived.[37] Martin, who would as an adult be promoted to Admiral of the Fleet, and William Henry, later became life-long friends.

When he was a lad of thirteen, his father decided that William Henry should be sent to North America as a sailor on a Royal Navy ship, presumably with the goal of improving the morale of the British army and navy stationed, and the disappointed Loyalists residing, there. Given that the war was now a world war against both France and Spain, and that efforts to subdue the rebellion among the former thirteen colonies was not proceeding as hoped, King George III looked for any edge to better his position. As young William was unlikely to succeed to the throne, being third in line, he could still serve his country and perhaps as well become a positive influence on his two older brothers.

The King conferred with then Captain Digby, soon to be promoted to admiral, about the idea of William Henry serving on board his ship. Digby was delighted at the prospect. A tough, handsome officer of forty-six years, Digby was well connected socially and was considered to be an efficient, ambitious officer, well suited to this unusual task.[38] His sovereign instructed Digby: "You will direct him to be treated with civility but no visible marks of respect." He advised that his son "should be obliged to perform most rigidly every duty of the station in which he is placed on board the Admiral's ship" and that he be "taught obedience and to conduct himself with politeness." The father further instructed that "a Lieutenant be always on watch when it is his turn of duty, who must report very exactly how he has behaved" and that "a proper officer to go with him at such times as the Admiral may think it right to send him to sail in small vessels and also when he goes to swim."[39]

On June 15, 1779, William Henry was brought to Portsmouth in England and appointed a lowly midshipman on the *Prince George*, Admiral Digby's 98-gun flagship. To the Prince's chagrin, he was accompanied by the Reverend Henry Majendie, who would tutor him on his voyages. The Prince carried with him a letter from his father containing advice such as "You are now launching

Prince William Henry, the future King William IV of Great Britain, when he was 16 years old. This drawing shows him as a midshipman on board the HMS *Prince George*, which carried him to New York City, where he arrived in September 1781. From a painting by Benjamin West (Anne S.K. Military Collection, Brown University).

into a scene of life, where you may either prove an honor or a disgrace to your family" and "Though when at home a Prince, on board the *Prince George* you are only a boy learning the naval profession; but the Prince so far accompanies you that what other boys might do, you must not."[40]

William Henry took to his new life with gusto. Life on board a Royal

Navy ship was harsh by any standard, but as the King's son, he was resented by other boys who lacked his privileged upbringing and were on the lookout for any evidence that one of the boys was not working his fair share. Trying to fit in, the Prince asked the other boys to call him William Guelph, one of his father's family names, and he had at least one epic fight over a sea chest and also became involved in a tavern brawl. Soon William Henry would participate in several fleet actions against the Spanish navy, and when a 64-gun ship was captured by a British crew, it was renamed the *Prince William*, "in respect to his Royal Highness, in whose presence she had the honor to be taken."[41]

When Admiral Digby in the *Prince George* was given command of the American station, the King decided to allow his son to go along. When the sixteen-year-old Prince arrived in New York City at 6:00 p.m. on September 26, 1781, he was, according to Loyalist William Smith, "received by Sir Henry Clinton, the Governor, and a crowd behind Kennedy's house on the North [Hudson] River."[42] Archibald Kennedy's house, at Number One Broadway at the southern tip of Manhattan Island, still served as the headquarters of General Clinton, commander-in-chief of British forces in North America. "I was received by an immense concourse of people, who appeared very loyal, continually crying out, 'God Bless King George,'" wrote the Prince to his father the next day.[43] One Quaker supporter even came up to William Henry and exclaimed, "It is not for want of respect that I do not take my hat off, but because my religion requires it."[44] The Prince remarked that he "had the pleasure of seeing the famous General Arnold," not too long after the man who was once the Patriot's best field general had turned traitor.

But William Henry was not too impressed by war-time New York City. "The town is built in the Dutch way, with trees before the houses," he informed his father. "The streets are in general narrow and very ill paved. There is but one church, all the others being converted into magazines or barracks." With a military eye, he added, "The inhabitants of the town are in number 25,000. They have 3,000 militia, besides which there are about 1,000 men raised at their own expense and clothed and armed."[45] He was taken to Bowling Green to the pedestal of his father's statue, which in July 1776 had been toppled by the Rebels and the statue's head paraded about town on pike-staffs.

Soon word arrived in New York City that the British army under Lord Cornwallis had surrendered to a joint French and American force at Yorktown, Virginia. Despite this catastrophic news, the Prince assured his father, "All the British, both seamen and soldiers, and Hessians behaved with the greatest spirit and resolution."[46] Still, there would be no further major expeditions by British forces to try to retake America.

Meanwhile, the Prince settled into his routine. He and Admiral Digby resided at the fine Gerardus Beekman mansion, at the northwest corner of Sloat Lane and Hanover Square, which had been commandeered by Royal Navy senior officers.[47] (Hanover Square, then the heart of the downtown district, is where the current Pearl Street and Wall Street meet.) In the mornings, he would study under the Reverend Majendie, and in the afternoons he often took strolls in the city, worrying some officials about his safety.

The Prince quickly endeared himself to locals with his boyish charm. "He is an amiable young Prince and gave satisfaction to all who saw him," wrote one Dutch-American Loyalist observer.[48] Another New Yorker described him as a "fine, bluff boy of sixteen; frank, cheery and affable."[49] A London magazine later recalled of his visit:

> One of his favorite resorts was a fresh-water lake in the vicinity of the city, which presented a frozen sheet of many acres, and was thronged by the younger part of the population for the amusement of skating. As the Prince was unskilled in that exercise, he would sit in a chair fixed on runners, which was pushed forward with great velocity by a skating attendant, while a crowd of officers environed him, and the youthful multitude made the air ring with their shouts for Prince William Henry.[50]

New York City newspapers ran poems and ballads to celebrate the royal personage in their midst, including the following:

> Rising o'er the Atlantic main,
> William the Star of Morn appears;
> Night with all her grisly train
> Of dangers and fears
> Is flying fast away!
> Soon shall the Royal Sun arise,
> And give the long-expected day![51]

Perhaps weary of reading such plaudits, Colonel Matthias Ogden of the 1st New Jersey Continentals, whose regiment was then based in New Jersey, proposed a plan to kidnap Prince William Henry, Admiral Digby, and other notables in late March of 1782.[52] Ogden, who was raised in the same Elizabethtown household as Aaron Burr and had attended the College of New Jersey (now Princeton University), had demonstrated his courage during the failed assault on lower Quebec on December 31, 1775.

Ogden's plan immediately captivated the commander-in-chief. "The spirit and enterprise so conspicuous in your plan for surprising in their quarters, and bringing off, Prince William Henry and Admiral Digby merits applause, and you have my authority to make the attempt in any manner, and at such a time, as your own judgment should direct," Washington wrote on March 28.[53] The general did warn "against offering insult or indignity to the persons of the Prince, or Admiral, should you be so fortunate as to capture them," and recommended

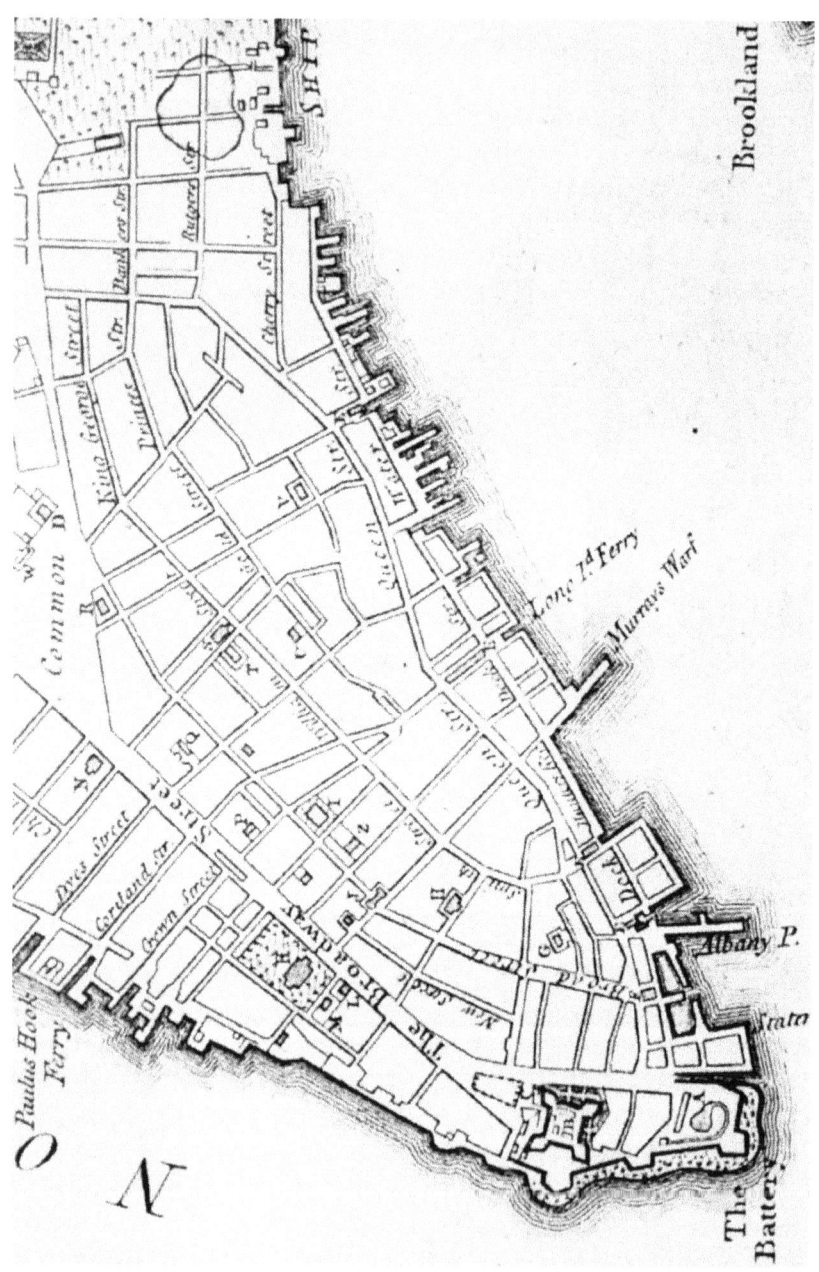

Map of New York City, including Lower Broadway, location of the residences of Henry Clinton and Benedict Arnold. Detail from "A Plan of the City and its Environs of New York in North America," published in London in November 1776 (Library of Congress).

that Ogden "impress the propriety of such conduct upon the party you command." Once captured and safely secured, Ogden was "to delay no time in conveying them to Congress and reporting your proceedings, with a copy of these orders."[54]

Colonel Ogden was fully aware, of course, that the powerful Royal Navy controlled the waters of the East River and the Hudson River. But perhaps a party of men in small boats could avoid the warships in the rivers and slip onto Manhattan Island under the cover of a dark and rainy night.

Ogden's plan called for him to surprise both the Prince and the Admiral in their city quarters and quickly hustle them off Manhattan Island. His force would include a captain, a subaltern, three sergeants, and thirty-six other soldiers. In four whaleboats equipped with muffled oars, Ogden's well-armed men would embark from the New Jersey shore on a rainy night, pass around the tip of Manhattan to enter the East River, and land on the east side of lower Manhattan (near the current South Street Seaport) at about 9:30 p.m. at a spot not far from Hanover Square, the location of their targets' quarters.

The operation's leader had solid intelligence about several guard posts that his party wanted to avoid, but might have to confront, as he explained to Washington:

> The Prince's quarters are in Hanover Square in the large house of Bateman's [should be Beekman's]. It has two sentinels from the British 40th Regiment quartered in Lord Stirling's house on Broad Street, 200 yards from the scene of the action. The main guard, consisting of a captain and forty men, is posted at City Hall; a sergeant and twelve men, at the head of the old slip; and a sergeant and twelve men, opposite the Coffee House. These are the nearest men in arms and must be guarded against. The place of landing to be at Coenties Market, which is between the two sergeants' guards.[55]

Ogden did not reveal to his commander one important fact, probably because Washington was already aware of it: at this time, downtown New York City was packed with more than 1,500 British and Hessian regular soldiers, in addition to the 3,000 Loyalist militiamen mentioned by William Henry in his letter to his father, as well as multitudes of rough sailors on temporary leave in the port.[56]

Ogden drew up a detailed plan and sent it to Washington for his approval. Leaving some men to guard the boats, Colonel Ogden and the balance of his force would proceed to the Prince's house at Hanover Square, take out the sentinels guarding the house, force its doors, and secure the prince and the admiral, as well as any other notables who were present. Ogden's plan of seizing the Prince included the following details:

> The order of debarkation to agree with the mode of attack as follows:

> First, two men with guide, seconded by two others, for the purpose of seizing the sentinels—these men to be armed with bayonets and clad in sailors' habit. They are to proceed immediately on their landing and execute their orders.
> Second, eight men, preceded by four with two axes and two crow bars, for the purpose of forcing the doors should they be fast—these men likewise in sailors' dress, followed by four men with guns and bayonets, who are to secure the entry and cut off all communication of servants. The eight men are to be armed with pistols and cartridges, whose duty it will be to seize the persons of the young Prince, the young nobleman, the Admiral, etc…, with their papers if to be seen, and to bring them off as soon as possible.
> Third, a captain and 18 men to follow briskly, forming at the house and defending it until the business is finished.

In instructing the lead two soldiers who were to disable the sentinels guarding the Prince's residence at Hanover Square to be "clad in sailors' habit," presumably Ogden meant garb typically worn by sailors on private commercial vessels or privateers, and not the regulation clothing of Royal Navy sailors. Any man in disguise would risk being hanged as a spy if caught by the British.

Ogden then detailed the equally hazardous task of returning with his quarry back to his small boats:

> Fourth, the subaltern, with the remainder of the soldiers and one-half of the remainder of the oarsmen, to be formed on the right and left of the boats and to defend them until our return. The remainder of the oarsmen to keep the boats for the best position for embarking.
> The manner of return as follows:
> Six men from the captain, with those unemployed in carrying off the prisoners, to precede those engaged in that business, followed by the captain and his party, joined by the four men from the entry. At half-gunshot distance, covering the embarkation in the following order:
> First, the prisoners, and their attendants.
> Second, the boatmen.
> Third, the subaltern—then himself and party.
> Two or three dark lanterns will be wanting, with the sailors' clothing and the pair of pistols.[57]

In the end, it did not matter. The operation to kidnap the prince and the admiral was never attempted. After March 28, the date that Washington approved Ogden's plan, he received the following report, dated March 23, 1782, from one of his spies in New York City:

> Great seems to be their apprehensions here. About a fortnight ago a number of flatboats were discovered by a sentinel from the bank of the river [Hudson], which are said to have been intended to fire the suburbs, and in the height of the conflagration to make a descent on the lower part of the city, and wrest from our embraces his Excellency Sir H. Clinton, Prince William Henry, and several other illustrious personages—since which great precautions have been taken for the security of those gentlemen, by augmenting the guards, and to render their persons as little exposed as possible.[58]

Washington warned Ogden on April 2: "I received information that the sentries at the doors of Sir Henry Clinton's quarters were doubled at eight o'clock every night from the apprehension of an attempt to surprise him in them." "If this be true," added the commander-in-chief, "it is more than probable the same precaution extends to *other* personages in the City of New York, a circumstance I thought it proper for you to be advertised of."[59] The precautions taken by British forces probably convinced Ogden to scuttle his operation.

It is not known whether the flatboats discovered on the banks of the Hudson River by the British were ones Ogden planned to use. It could well have been the case that they were not. They could have been those of Washington's spies, surreptitiously used for going back and forth between Manhattan and the New Jersey mainland. Already aware of prior attempts to kidnap him at his headquarters at Number One Broadway, Clinton was likely already on edge against any inkling of an attempt to kidnap his important charge, the King's third son.

After his promising start in New York, the Prince became bored during the winter, allowing his studies to slacken, and engaging in certain activities that did not please his parents, such as some heavy drinking, gambling and sex. It was thought best to send him out on more cruises against the French, which was done. On November 4, 1782, he sailed in a small schooner to join the HMS *Balfour*, then lying off Staten Island. A short time later, he was able to meet a thin, twenty-four-year-old engaging captain, Horatio Nelson. Captain Nelson wrote to one of his lieutenants on shore in New York, "I had the honor of an introduction to the Prince on board the *Balfour* by my Lord Hood, was very much pleased with him, he will make a good sailor, or I am much mistaken."[60]

A half-century later, in 1831, Louis McLane, then the U.S. ambassador to Great Britain, showed a copy of Washington's March 28, 1782, letter addressed to Colonel Ogden to King William IV. The former Prince William Henry had been crowned king of Great Britain in the prior year. "I am obliged to General Washington for his humanity, but I'm damned glad I did not give him an opportunity of exercising it towards me," the king reportedly remarked.[61] Washington's and Ogden's correspondence, copies of which were provided by Ogden's son, was published in England's *Athenaeum* magazine in May of 1831 and created quite a stir among His Royal Highness's subjects.

An early and sympathetic British biographer of the king was not so charitable, writing of Washington, "The part in which he took in the kidnapping of Prince William will always stand in record against him, as one of the most despicable acts of his life."[62] But as noted above, it was probably the case that Washington wanted to use Prince William Henry to barter for the release of American prisoners. In June of 1782, apparently trying an alternative, softer approach, Washington sent a note to Admiral Digby, asking him to do what he could to help relieve the sufferings of American captives held on British prison ships.[63]

Still, if the attempt to abduct Prince William Henry had succeeded, one wonders if it might have backfired. Washington might have thought that capturing the Prince would have forced George III to agree to peace terms recognizing American independence. But the outrage in London might have led to a groundswell of support for continuing the war and a renewed effort to subdue or punish Washington's army. (Thus, Washington's gamble was risky.) As it turned out, the attempt was not made, and an August 2, 1782, letter sent by Admiral Digby and Sir Guy Carleton to Washington contained the first news that Great Britain had commenced negotiations in Paris for ending the war.[64]

A British biographer of King William IV wondered if Washington wanted to make Prince William Henry the king of America. By doing so, he argued, King George III would have reconciled himself to the outcome and the war would have ended.[65] But there is no foundation in the record for the biographer's outrageous suggestion.

While he charmed as a prince, King William IV did not have a distinguished or a long reign. While important reforms took place during his reign, they likely would have occurred in any event. He had ten children outside of his marriage. But he performed his royal duties diligently and became somewhat popular.[66] He reigned from 1830 until 1837, when he died at the age of seventy-six and his eighteen-year-old niece, Victoria, became queen.

Living with the Risk of Kidnappings

Abduction attempts could naturally cause the target considerable apprehension and stress. The wife of Hessian Lieutenant General Friedrich Riedesel, Frederika Charlotte Louise von Massow, afterwards Baroness Riedesel, described the psychological effects that repeated efforts had on her husband in the spring of 1781. A young and attractive woman, Frederika had seen the horrors of war as wounded and dying officers from General John Burgoyne's army were brought back from the front lines at Saratoga in upstate New York. Both she and her husband had been captured with Burgoyne's army after the Battles of Saratoga and subsequently released in a prisoner exchange. General Riedesel was then assigned to command British-controlled Long Island, where the low-level whaleboat and kidnapping war continued. His wife recalled:

> The Americans constantly attempted surprises in order to take prisoners. Major Maybaum was drawn out of his bed; and we knew they aimed to do the same thing

VII. Yorktown and Beyond 167

with my husband. Our house was situated close to the shore and was perfectly isolated, so that if they [the Rebels] had overcome the watch they could easily have carried him away. Everyone was therefore constantly on the watch. Throughout the entire night, at the slightest noise, he [General Riedesel] would wake up and place himself in readiness for an attack; and thus he lost considerable sleep. I also became so accustomed to watching, that daylight would often surprise me, when I would lie down and catch a few hours of sleep; for it was only when my husband believed that I was wide awake and on guard, that he would allow himself to sleep—so terrible was it to him the thought that he might again be taken prisoner.[67]

The multiple attempts to capture Governor William Livingston of New Jersey must have worn him down as well. In August of 1782, Ralph Macnair, a New York City resident and probably a Tory, requested from Livingston a travel pass to Philadelphia to collect debts owed to him by once-captive American officers. Macnair suggested that the two meet at Livingston's Liberty Hall residence. "Your seeing me at my own house is impracticable," the governor complained, "as I have not for some years past been able to live under my own roof, on account of the particular passion that your countrymen [i.e., Tories] had for making prisoner of an old fellow who in General Clinton's opinion was not worth the trouble, though to my certain knowledge he spared no pains to effect it."[68]

General Washington summed up the sacrifice that Patriot leaders had to bear. In a February 2, 1778, letter to Governor Livingston, the commander-in-chief wrote that threats of capture and assassination were "a tax, however severe, which all those must pay who are called to eminent stations of trust, not only to be held up as conspicuous marks to the enmity of the public adversaries to their country; but to the malice of secret traitors and *envious intrigues* of false friends and factions."[69]

Frederika Riedesel, Baroness Riedesel, wrote of the worries of her husband, a senior general of German forces, of being kidnapped while sleeping at night at a house on Long Island (Huddleston, *Gentleman Jonny Burgoyne*).

Appendix A

Letter from Colonel James Abeel Summarizing Information Regarding the Raid Intended to Capture Washington in February 1780

The author of this letter, James Abeel, Deputy Quartermaster General, from Albany, was a lieutenant colonel in the quartermasters corps, and became one of Nathanael Greene's most trusted and diligent deputies.[1] In this letter, Abeel summarizes his conversation with a resident of Elizabethtown, who had some accurate information regarding the February 1780 raid intended to capture Washington at Morristown, but who probably exaggerated the number of cavalry and infantry involved. Because this letter has only been reprinted, to my knowledge, in the *History of Chatham*, its contents in relevant part are set forth below.

> The following intelligence was given to me this day by a person from Elizabethtown and I believe may be depended on as a fact. That a party of between 4 and 500 horse and three-thousand foot under the command of General [Charles] Grey crossed Paulus Hook on Thursday and marched as far as the west end of Colonel Schuyler's swamp and intended to march on to Morristown by way of the Notch. The light horse were to endeavor to bring off his Excellency, and the foot to take the route towards Chatham to support the horse if they succeeded in their enterprise and to bring off a number of cattle belonging to the public in their route, which are at Horse Neck. General Skinner and Colonel Stirling to cross with about 2,000 men at Elizabethtown and Colonel Simcoe with 300 horse and some foot to cross at Rahway to draw our attention that way. But the snow being so deep in the swamp that General Grey could not advance, a signal by 5 rockets was given to General Skinner that it was not possible to advance and by Skinner with 5 rockets from the bridge at Elizabethtown to Simcoe, which occasioned their return to Staten Island and the other places they crossed…. The river was passable on the ice from Paulus Hook to Long Island. Most or all of the British troops came from Long Island to New York and Staten Island…. I make no doubt that his Excellency has long ago had the intelligence, but if he should not, I now send it.[2]

Appendix B

Colonel Matthias Ogden's Plans for Capturing Prince William Henry in New York City in March 1782

The following, undated plan, never previously published in its entirety, was written by Colonel Matthias Ogden of the 1st New Jersey Continentals on or about March 26, 1782, and was submitted to General Washington, who approved it on March 28. It details Ogden's scheme to capture Prince William Henry, Admiral Robert Digby, and other valuable British visitors to New York City.

Col. Ogden's Plan for Surprising Characters in New York
Plan

It will be necessary to have four whaleboats well manned by good oarsmen, with their officers and crews, including guides. Besides these a captain, a subaltern, 3 sergeants and 36 chosen men who can row the boats with ease.

It is known where the boats are and they may be collected without suspicion, along with the oarsmen. It is taken for granted that the oarsmen will not object to the boats going, though for fear of giving cause of suspecting the design, nothing has as yet been said to them.

The time of embarkation must be the first wet night after we are in readiness. The place is not yet agreed upon, as it will be necessary to consult those who have a perfect knowledge of what *boats can do, the passage, tides,* etc.... Lest they might draw inferences from such inquiries, this matter must be put off as long as possible. We must, however, embark at such part of the Jersey shore as will give time to land in the City by half-past nine [at night].

The men must be embarked in the order of their debarkation.

The Prince's quarters are in Hanover Square in the large house of Bateman's. It has two sentinels from the British 40th Regiment quartered in Lord

Stirling's house on Broad Street, 200 yards from the scene of the action. The main guard, consisting of a captain and 40 men posted at City Hall; a sergeant and 12 men at the head of the Old Slip; and a sergeant and 12 men facing the Coffee House. These are the nearest men in arms and must be guarded against.

The place of landing to be at Coenties Market, which is between the two sergeants' guards.

The order of debarkation to agree with the mode of attack as follows:

First, two men with guide, seconded by two others, for the purpose of seizing the sentinels—these men to be armed with bayonets and clad in sailors' habit. They are to proceed immediately on their landing and execute their orders.

Second, eight men, preceded by four with two axes and two crow bars, for the purpose of forcing the doors should they be fast—these men likewise in sailors' dress, followed by four men with guns and bayonets, who are to secure the entry and cut off all communication of servants. The eight men are to be armed with pistols and cartridges, whose duty it will be to seize the persons of the young Prince, the young nobleman, the Admiral, etc...., with their papers if to be seen, and to bring them off as soon as possible.

Third, a captain and 18 men to follow briskly, forming at the house and defending it until the business is finished.

Fourth, the subaltern, with the remainder of the soldiers and one-half of the remainder of the oarsmen, to be formed on the right and left of the boats and to defend them until our return. The remainder of the oarsmen to keep the boats for the best position for embarking.

The manner of return as follows:

Six men from the captain, with those unemployed in carrying off the prisoners, to precede those engaged in that business, followed by the captain and his party, joined by the four men from the entry. At half-gunshot distance, covering the embarkation in the following order:

First, the prisoners, and their attendants.

Second, the boatmen.

Third, the subaltern—then himself and party.

Two or three dark lanterns will be wanting, with the sailors' clothing and the pair of pistols.[1]

Chapter Notes

Preface

1. At Dictionary.com, the online dictionary at www.dictionary.com.
2. Tacitus, *The Histories*, book 3, section 65. The remainder of the quote is "and that evil words and deeds should fear an infamous reputation with posterity."
3. G. Washington to S. Parsons, March 5, 1778, in Twohig et al. (eds.), *Washington Papers* 14:72.

Chapter I

1. Fischer, *Paul Revere's Ride*, 182 and 110–11; Philbrick, *Bunker Hill*, 119–23; Hallahan, *The Day the American Revolution Began*, 12–14, 24–26 and 28–29; Brooks, *The Boston Campaign*, 49. It is sometimes reported that Gerry fell face down in the cornfield. Historian David Hackett Fischer wrote, "Details of this incident must be read with caution. It was used as an electioneering weapon against Gerry when he ran as a Jeffersonian candidate for governor." Fischer, *Paul Revere's Ride*, 391, n. 23. Hancock and Adams, before departing Lexington, concluded that such a large expedition probably did not have their capture as their primary mission, and correctly surmised that the British troops "were ordered to seize and destroy the stores belonging to the Colony, then deposited at Concord." Jonas Clarke Recollection, quoted in Fischer, *Paul Revere's Ride*, 111.
2. Fischer, *Paul Revere's Ride*, 182.
3. Ibid., 84–85; see also Philbrick, *Bunker Hill*, 113–15; Brooks, *The Boston Campaign*, 38–39. J. L. Bell, an expert in the history of revolutionary Boston, wrote that if Hancock had insisted on staying at the Lexington parsonage, "the British troops would have passed right through town on their way to Concord. That's because Gen. Thomas Gage did not order his officers to search for Hancock and Adams. Gage's intelligence files and orders were entirely focused on the weapons that the Massachusetts Provincial Congress had amassed in Concord and elsewhere. No British soldiers went near the parsonage. Revere's original warning to Hancock and Adams was unnecessary." Bell, "Did Paul Revere's Ride Really Matter," April 21, 2014, in the online *Journal of the American Revolution*, at www.allthingsliberty.com (citing Thomas Gage Papers, American Series, Clements Library, University of Michigan).
4. Lee, "The Lee Family of Marblehead," in *Essex Institute Historical Collections* 52:336 (1916).
5. Dunmore's small fleet operated off Norfolk, Virginia, for most of the fall. See letters dated Sept. 30, 1775, Oct. 21, 1775, and Nov. 24, 1775, in Clark, Morgan & Crawford (eds.), *Naval Documents of the American Revolution* 2:259–60, 659–64, and 1120.
6. G. Washington to L. Washington, Aug. 20, 1775, in Twohig et al. (eds.), *Washington Papers* 1:335. On October 5, Lund wrote back:

> T'is true many people have made a stir about Mrs. Washington's continuing at Mount Vernon, but I cannot think her in any sort of danger. The thought I believe first originated in Alexandria—from thence it got to Loudoun. I am told the people of Loudoun talked of sending a guard to conduct her up into Berkeley [now West Virginia] with some of their principal men to persuade her to leave this [place] and accept their offer. Mr. John Augustine Washington wrote to her pressing her to leave Mt. Vernon. She does not believe herself in danger, nor do I. If they attempted to take her in the dead of night they would fail, for 10 minutes' notice would be sufficient for her to get out of the way. Lord Dunmore will hardly venture himself

174 Notes—Chapter I

up this river [Potomac River] ... I have never advised her to stay nor indeed to go. Col. Bassett thinks her in no danger. You may depend on it I will be watchful, and upon the least alarm persuade her to move.

L. Washington to G. Washington, Oct. 5, 1775, in ibid., 2:116. The plucky Martha refused to panic. No British vessel seriously threatened Mount Vernon until the spring of 1781, when the British war sloop *Savage* dropped its anchor in the Potomac River, with its captain demanding provisions and making the implicit threat of burning Mount Vernon if he was refused. To Washington's chagrin, Lund Washington stepped aboard the *Savage* and agreed to provide the British sailors with some foodstuffs, thus saving Mount Vernon. Chernow, *Washington: A Life*, 399–400; Kranish, *Flight from Monticello*, 232–33.

7. T. Jefferson to F. Eppes, Nov. 21, 1775, in Boyd (ed.), *Jefferson Papers* 1:264.

8. Advertisement for the play "The Fall of British Tyranny," in *Continental Journal*, Sept. 5, 1776.

9. Traugott Bagge's Narrative of Events in North Carolina, June 1, 1775, in Clark, Morgan & Crawford (eds.), *Naval Documents of the American Revolution* 2:591.

10. C. Harnett to New Bern Committee, June 13, 1775 in *ibid.*, 675; Journal of His Majesty's Sloop *Cruizer*, June 2, 1775, in *ibid.*, 599 (Martin comes aboard briefly and is given a thirteen-gun salute).

11. J. Martin to S. Graves, July 8, 1775, in *ibid.*, 843; J. Martin to the People, July 18, 1775, in *ibid.*, 918; J. Martin to Lord Dartmouth, Aug. 28, 1775, in *ibid.*, 1251; Powell (ed.), *Dictionary of North Carolina Biography* 3:218; O'Kelley, *Military Operations ... in the Carolinas* 1:37–38. The Wikipedia webpage for "Robert Howe" states that this raid had as its intent "kidnapping Governor Martin," but the author did not find any support for that position in the North Carolina books he reviewed.

12. Quotations in Brooking, "The Arrest of Georgia's Royal Governor Sir James Wright," May 9, 2014, in the online Journal of the American Revolution, at www.allthingsliberty.com.

13. *Ibid.*; Information to the Town of Savannah from Governor James Wright, Jan. 18, 1776, in Clark, Morgan & Crawford (eds.), *Naval Documents of the American Revolution* 3:852.

14. Journal of the Georgia Council of Safety, Jan. 18, 1776, in Clark, Morgan & Crawford (eds.), *Naval Documents of the American Revolution* 3:853.

15. Quoted in Brooking, "The Arrest of Georgia's Royal Governor Sir James Wright," May 9, 2014, in the online Journal of the American Revolution, at www.allthingsliberty.com; see also Journal of the Georgia Council of Safety, Jan. 19, 1776, in Clark, Morgan & Crawford (eds.), *Naval Documents of the American Revolution* 3:867.

16. Brooking, "The Arrest of Georgia's Royal Governor Sir James Wright," May 9, 2014, in the online Journal of the American Revolution, at www.allthingsliberty.com; Jones, *History of Georgia* 2:211–12.

17. Journal of the H.M.S. *Scarborough*, Feb. 12, 1776, in Clark, Morgan & Crawford (eds.), *Naval Documents of the American Revolution* 3:1239; Journal of the H.M.S. *Raven*, Feb. 12, 1776, in *ibid.*

18. H. Laurens to Georgia Provincial Congress, Feb. 16, 1776, in *ibid.*, 1325.

19. J. Hancock to J. Witherspoon, June 19, 1776, in Smith (ed.), *Letters of Delegates to Congress* 4:270 and n. 1; J. Hancock to J. Trumbull, Sr., June 24, 1776, in *ibid.*, 309; J. Hancock to J. Trumbull, Sr., April 23, 1777, in *ibid.*, 6:639 and n. 1; Continental Congress Resolution, June 24, 1776, in Ford (ed.), *Journals of the Continental Congress* 5:473; New Jersey Provincial Congress Resolutions, June 16, 1776, in Force (ed.), *American Archives*, Series 4, 6:1621.

20. Flavell, *When London was Capital of America*, 159; Lander, "A Tale of Two Hoaxes in Britain and France in 1775," *Historical Journal* 49:4, 1013–14 (2006). Lander's article provides the most details of the alleged plot.

21. O'Shaughnessy, *The Men Who Lost America*, 320–21.

22. Lander, "A Tale of Two Hoaxes in Britain and France in 1775," *Historical Journal* 49:4, 998 (2006).

23. Flavell, *When London was Capital of America*, 160–61.

24. Quoted in *ibid.*

25. Quoted in *ibid.*, 161.

26. Lander, "A Tale of Two Hoaxes in Britain and France in 1775," *Historical Journal* 49:4, 1000 (2006).

27. Flavell, *When London was Capital of America*, 162.

28. *Ibid.*, 162–63; Lander, "A Tale of Two Hoaxes in Britain and France in 1775," *Historical Journal* 49:4, 1019 (2006).

29. C. Lee to A. McDougall, Oct. 26, 1775, in *Lee Papers*, 1:215.

30. G. Washington to J. Hancock, June 10,

1776, in Twohig et al. (eds.), *Washington Papers* 4:487–89.

31. David Mathews Loyalist Claim Submission, summarized in Egerton, *Royal Commission*, 168.

32. Return by General Greene of the Arrest of Mr. Mathews, June 22, 1778, in Force (ed.), *American Archives*, Series 4, Volume 6, 1158 (quoted in Shattuck, "Plotting the 'Sacricide' of George Washington," July 25, 2014, in the online Journal of the American Revolution, at www.allthingsliberty.com).

33. Twohig et al. (eds.), *Washington Papers* 4:72–74, n. 1.

34. Shattuck, "Plotting the 'Sacricide' of George Washington," July 25, 2014, in the online Journal of the American Revolution, at www.allthingsliberty.com.

35. Quoted in *ibid*.

36. *Ibid*.

37. *Ibid*. For more on Washington's Life Guard, see Ward, *George Washington's Enforcers*, chapter 5.

38. Quoted in Shattuck, "Plotting the 'Sacricide' of George Washington," July 25, 2014, in the online Journal of the American Revolution, at www.allthingsliberty.com.

39. Quoted in After Orders, June 28, 1776, in Fitzpatrick, *Washington Writings* 5:182.

40. Court-Martial Record for the Trial of Thomas Hickey and Others, June 26, 1778, in Force (ed.), *American Archives* 4:6, 1084. Hickey's court-martial record is also in the George Washington Papers at the Library of Congress.

41. Quoted in After Orders, June 28, 1776, in Fitzpatrick, *Washington Writings* 5:182.

42. Sol. Drowne to Sally Drowne, June 24, 1776, Henry Russell Drowne Collection, Fraunces Tavern. Some histories contain only one or two citations to contemporary letters mentioning the plot against Washington; the author has found five contemporary letters and one diary entry that refer to the purported assassination attempt. In addition to Solomon Drowne's letter, see Peter T. Curtenius to Richard Varick, June 22, 1776 (New York), quoted in Hughes, *George Washington*, 392; William Henshaw to his wife Johnston, June 22, 1776, quoted in Wade and Lively (eds.), *This Glorious Cause*, 69 (the plan of the Tories "was to murder General Washington, seize on the person of the other general officers, and blow up our magazines, at the instant of time the King's troops should land"); William Eustis to David Townshend, June 28, 1776, in Slafter (ed.), "Letters of Governor Eustis," *New England Hist. and Genealogical Reg.* 23:207–08 (1869); Joseph Hewes to Samuel Johnson, July 8, 1776 (Philadelphia), in Powell (ed.), *Tryon Correspondence* 2:862; Diary Entry, June 22, 1776, in Bushnell (ed.), *Journal of Solomon Nash*, 21 ("Yesterday several Tories were taken up and confined who were contriving a plot to kill General Washington") (Solomon Nash was an artilleryman from Abington, Massachusetts); W. Eustis to D. Townshend, June 28, 1776, in Slafter (ed.), "Letters of Governor Eustis," *New England Hist. and Genealogical Reg.* 23:208 (1869) (quoted in the main text).

43. McCullough, *1776*, 133; Chernow, *Washington*, 233.

44. Quoted in After Orders, June 27, 1776, in Fitzpatrick, *Washington Writings* 5:182; see also *ibid.*, n. 26.

45. *Constitutional Gazette* (New York), June 29, 1776; see also Ward, *George Washington's Enforcers*, 62; General Orders, June 28, 1776, in Twohig et al. (eds.), *Washington Papers* 4:129–30 and n. 1; Sol. Drowne to William Drowne, July 13, 1776, Henry Russell Drowne Collection, Fraunces Tavern ("I suppose you have heard of the execution of one of the General's Guards, concerned in ye hellish plot, discovered here some time past. There was a vast concourse of people to see the poor fellow hanged.").

46. W. Eustis to D. Townshend, June 28, 1776, in Slafter (ed.), "Letters of Governor Eustis," *New England Hist. and Genealogical Reg.* 23:208 (1869).

47. J. Hodgkins to his wife Sarah Hodgkins, July 17, 1776, in Ward and Lively (eds.), *This Glorious Cause*, 209.

48. Shattuck, "Plotting the 'Sacricide' of George Washington," July 25, 2014, in the online Journal of the American Revolution, at www.allthingsliberty.com.

49. W. Eustis to D. Townshend, June 28, 1776, in Slafter (ed.), "Letters of Governor Eustis," *New England Hist. and Genealogical Reg.* 23:208 (1869).

50. G. Washington to J. Hancock, June 28, 1776, in Twohig et al. (eds.), *Washington Papers* 4:134–35.

51. Chernow, *Washington*, 233. For more on the plot, see Hughes, *George Washington*, 392–405.

52. General Orders, June 28, 1776, in Fitzpatrick, *Washington Writings* 5:195.

Chapter II

1. Quoted in Smith, *Benjamin Harrison*, 42.
2. B. Rush to J. Adams, July 20, 1811, in Butterfield (ed.), *Letters of Benjamin Rush* 2:1089–90.
3. Quoted in Bill, *A House Called Morven*, 38.
4. Smith (ed.), *Letters of Delegates* 5:256, n. 4.
5. Id., 465, n. 4.
6. The December 29, 1776 orders issued by Lieutenant Colonel James Webster, cited in the main text accompanying note 11 below, indicate that Stockton's captors were from the New Jersey Volunteers.
7. Extract of a letter from Philadelphia, Dec. 30, 1776, in *Massachusetts Spy*, Jan. 30, 1777, and *Norwich Packet*, Feb. 3, 1777.
8. W. Smith Diary Entry, Jan. 16, 1777, in Sabine (ed.), *Historical Memoirs of William Smith*, 2: 66. Most sources state that Stockton was captured on November 29 or 30, and a few state it occurred as late as December 1; but given Stockton's dating a letter December 2, the author has selected December 2 as the date of his capture. The December date is supported by the July 8, 1778 edition of *The New Jersey Gazette*, which reported that Richard Stockton and John Covenhoven were seized in "the month of December, 1776." For the most complete discussion of Richard Stockton's capture, release, and taking General Howe's protection, see a series of 2008 and 2009 stories by J. L. Bell in his online website at boston1775.blog spot.com (search for "Richard Stockton").
9. Bill, *A House Called Morven*, 40.
10. B. Rush to R. H. Lee, Dec. 30, 1776, in Smith (ed.), *Letters of Delegates* 5:706.
11. New Jersey State Archives, Dept. of Defense Manuscripts, Loyalist Mss. No. 192-L (found by Todd Braisted and set forth in J. L. Bell, "Richard Stockton's Release Date," July 28, 2009, at boston1775.blogspot.com (search for "Richard Stockton")).
12. Ford (ed.), *Journals of the Continental Congress* 7:12–13.
13. J. Hancock to G. Washington, Jan. 6, 1777, in Smith (ed.), *Letters of Delegates* 6:40.
14. Bell, "Primary Sources on Richard Stockton," Sept. 8, 2008, in Bell's online website at boston1775.blogspot.com (search "Richard Stockton").
15. Quoted in Burrows, *Forgotten Patriots*, 82.
16. Burrows, *Forgotten Patriots*, 82–87.
17. B. Rush to R. H. Lee, Jan. 7, 1777, in Butterfield (ed.), *Letters of Benjamin Rush* 1:126.
18. E. Boudinot to G. Carlton, Oct. 2, 1783, in Smith (ed.), *Letters of Delegates* 21:10; see also Bill, *A House Called Morven*, 40.
19. E. Gerry to J. Warren, Dec. 23, 1776, in Smith (ed.), *Letters of Delegates* 5:641.
20. A. Clark to J. Hart, Feb. 8, 1777, in *ibid.*, 6:240.
21. J. Hancock to R. T. Paine, Feb. 9, 1777, in *ibid.*, 247.
22. J. Witherspoon to D. Witherspoon, March 17, 1777, in *ibid.*, 6:454–56.
23. *Minutes of the Council of Safety*, 178.
24. W. Smith Diary Entry, July 10, 1779, in Sabine (ed.), *Historical Memoirs of William Smith*, 2:130.
25. Benjamin Rush Recollection, in Rush, *Autobiography*, 147.
26. B. Rush to G. Morgan, Nov. 8, 1779, in Butterfield (ed.), *Letters of Benjamin Rush* 1:245.
27. B. Rush to J. Rush, April 21, 1784, in *ibid.*, 327; see also *ibid.*, 245, n. 3.
28. Bell, "Richard Stockton and the Creation of a Legend," Sept. 18, 2008, in Bell's online website at boston1775.blogspot.com (search "Richard Stockton").
29. See online list of statues in The National Statuary Hall Collection at www.aoc.gov/the-national-statuary-hall-collection and search for Richard Stockton.
30. See Public Law 106–554, Section 311; see also "Procedure and Guidelines for Replacement of Statues in the National Statuary Hall Collection," obtained by going to www.aoc.gov/the-national-statuary-hall-collection, clicking on "About the National Statutory Hall Collection," and clicking on the PDF at the bottom of the webpage where state's deciding to replace a statute is discussed. Accessed March 23, 2016.
31. Hammond, *John Hart*, 61–62; Boatner, *Encyclopedia of the A.R.*, 493; Maring, *Baptists in New Jersey*, 73; Benjamin Rush Recollections in Rush, *Autobiography of Benjamin Rush*, 148.
32. F. Lewis to S. Sayre, Sept. 4, 1779, in Smith (ed.), *Letters to Delegates* 13;451 (this was the same Stephen Sayre who was involved in the alleged plot to kidnap King George III); Twohig (ed.), *Washington Papers* 7:115, n. 1; Boatner, *Encyclopedia of the A.R.*, 2619.
33. Ferris (ed.), *Signers of the Declaration of Independence*, 95–96.
34. John Fell Diary Entry, April 23, 1777,

Memorandum in the Provost Jail, in Onderdonk, *Revolutionary Incidents of Suffolk and Kings Counties,* 219.

35. Stephen Kemble Diary Entry, April 23–24, 1777, in *Kemble Papers* 1:114 (1883).

36. W. Livingston to G. Washington, April 30, 1777, in Twohig et al. (eds.), *Washington Papers* 9:308–09. Washington informed Livingston that he would try to exchange some Tories for Fell, but his effort did not succeed. See G. Washington to W. Livingston, May 11, 1777, in *ibid.,* 387–88.

37. W. Livingston to the Assembly, May 9, 1777, in Prince et al. (eds.), *Livingston Papers* 1:326.

38. See, e.g., *Minutes of the Provincial Congress and the Council of Safety,* 115, 169, 183 375.

39. For more on Abraham Buskirk and his experience in the Revolutionary War, see Braisted, "How George Washington Saved the Life of Abraham Van Buskirk's Son," in the online Journal of the American Revolution, at www.allthingsliberty.com.

40. This story is told in several biographies of John Fell and other New Jersey works. It was probably originally told by John Pintard, who during the war assisted his father, Lewis Pintard, in attempting to alleviate the plight of American captives in British jails in New York City, and wrote of his recollections of the experiences of the prisoners. See John Pintard Recollections, quoted in Pasko (ed.), *Old New York,* 307–08. John Pintard's recollections may have first appeared in the September 10, 1831, edition of *The New York Mirror.*

41. Burrows, *Forgotten Patriots,* xi & 247. One historian who closely studied the matter, Larry Bowman, argued that the British were "not guilty of excessive disregard of the welfare of prisoners." Bowman, *Captive Americans,* 126. He further argued that while prisoners suffered through neglect, the motivations behind the failure to provide for the captives "were not evil or vindictive in nature," but rather "stemmed from the complicated issues surrounding what was then a unique war. The limitations of the eighteenth century also contributed to the lack of care of the captives …." Id., 132–33. While Bowman makes some decent points, the author believes that Burrows has the stronger argument. For more on this topic, McBurney, *Kidnapping the Enemy,* 81–84.

42. See McBurney, *Kidnapping the Enemy,* 84–90.

43. L. Pintard to Gen. Jones, undated [probably around January 10, 1778], in Onderdonk, *Revolutionary Incidents of Suffolk and Kings Counties,* 219.

44. John Fell Diary Entries, Sept. 26–29, 1777, Memorandum in the Provost Jail, in Onderdonk, *Revolutionary Incidents of Suffolk and Kings Counties,* 222.

45. John Pintard Recollections, quoted in Pasko (ed.), *Old New York,* 306–07. John Pintard's recollections may have first appeared in the September 10, 1831, edition of *The New York Mirror.*

46. Burrows, *Forgotten Patriots,* 88 and 90; John Fell Diary Entries, May 27, June 3, Aug. 14, and Nov. 19, 1777, Memorandum in the Provost Jail, in Onderdonk, *Revolutionary Incidents of Suffolk and Kings Counties,* 219, 221 and 223.

47. See W. Livingston to E. Boudinot, Aug. 29, 1777, in Prince et al. (eds.), *Livingston Papers* 2:48–49 and 49, n. 1.

48. *Pennsylvania Evening Post,* Aug. 26, 1777, in Stryker (ed.), *Documents Relating to the Revolutionary History of the State of New Jersey* 1:454–47 and accompanying notes.

49. John Fell Diary Entries, May 20 to Dec. 8, 1777, Memorandum in the Provost Jail, in Onderdonk, *Revolutionary Incidents of Suffolk and Kings Counties,* 219–224.

50. Ward, *Between the Lines,* 87–88; Israel Abner Pension Application, New Jersey, National Archives Building; Moody, *Memoirs,* 8–9.

51. J. Roberston to W. Livingston, Jan. 4, 1778, in Prince et al. (eds.), *Livingston Papers* 2:159–60.

52. W. Livingston to J. Robertson, Jan. 7, 1778, in *ibid.,* 161.

53. *New York Gazette,* Dec. 8, 1777, in Stryker (ed.), *Documents Relating to the Revolutionary History of the State of New Jersey* 1:505.

54. Stryker (ed.), *Documents Relating to the Revolutionary History of the State of New Jersey* 1:55, n. 1.

55. Unless otherwise stated, the part of the capture of Charles Lee is based on the first three chapters of McBurney, *Kidnapping the Enemy.*

56. Quoted in *The American Museum,* 452 (May 1789).

57. Quoted in McBurney, *Kidnapping the Enemy,* 4.

58. *Ibid.,* 5.

59. *Ibid.,* 6.

60. N. Greene to N. Cooke, Dec. 4, 1776, in Conrad et al. (eds.), *Greene Papers* 1:362.

61. C. Lee to H. Gates, Dec. 13, 1776, in *Lee Papers* 2:348.

62. Quoted in McBurney, *Kidnapping the Enemy*, 45.
63. James Wilkinson Recollections, in Wilkinson, *Memoirs* 1:105.
64. *Ibid.*
65. Extract of a Letter from Verplanck's Point, Dec. 21, 1776, in *Connecticut Gazette*, Jan. 9, 1777.
66. William Bradford's Recollections, Diary Entry, Jan. 1, 1777, in Dexter (ed.), *Stiles Diary* 2:106.
67. B. Tarleton to J. Tarleton, Dec. 18, 1776, quoted in McBurney, *Kidnapping the Enemy*, 45.
68. Quoted in *ibid.*, 46.
69. William Bradford's Recollections, Diary Entry, Jan. 1, 1777, in Dexter (ed.), *Stiles Diary* 2:106.
70. *Ibid.* This short description of the raid omits accounts of the raid by other participants, and does not include descriptions of the raid prior to the arrival of Harcourt at Widow White's Tavern or the trip back to Pennington.
71. Quoted in Barber and Howe, *Historical Collections of New Jersey*, 444, n.
72. Quoted in McBurney, *Kidnapping the Enemy*, 67.
73. Diary Entry, Aug. 28, 1781, in Acomb (ed.), *Journal of von Closen*, 114. Closen called Widow White's Tavern "Bullion Tavern" and its proprietor, "Mademoiselle Bullion," and complained about "a rather mediocre dish" he ate there. *Ibid.* Bullion's Tavern was located south of Basking Ridge at Liberty Corner. Accordingly, it is possible that Closen never made it to Basking Ridge and Widow White's Tavern. The alternative is that Closen did visit Widow White's Tavern but misidentified it as Bullion's Tavern.
74. John Trumbull, Jr., to Jonathan Trumbull, Dec. 16, 1776, in Force (ed.), *American Archives*, 5th Series, 3:1247.
75. G. Washington to L. Washington, Dec. 10–17, 1776, in Twohig (ed.), *Washington Papers* 7:290.
76. Quoted in Burrows, *Forgotten Patriots*, 71.
77. Extract of a Letter from an Officer of the 64th Regiment, in York Island, to his Friend in London, Dec. 30, 1776, New York, in Force (ed.), *American Archives*, 5th Series, 3:1294.
78. Quoted in McBurney, *Kidnapping the Enemy*, 85.
79. *Ibid.*, 98.
80. T. Nelson to T. Jefferson, Jan. 2, 1777, in Boyd et al. (eds.), *Jefferson Papers* 2:4.

81. Cortland Skinner Submission in Support of Richard Witham Stockton's Memorial, Feb. 28, 1783, British National Archives, AO 13/112A, 262. Stockton's Memorial is dated January 28, 1783. *Ibid.*, 260–61. Skinner's mention of Stockton's role as guide in the capture of Lee was not mentioned in Richard Witham Stockton's Loyalist Revolutionary War Claim summarized in Coldham (ed.), *American Migrations*, 434.
82. Letters in support of Richard Witham Stockton's Memorial, each dated 1782 or 1783, by William Harcourt, Earl Cornwallis, James Grant, and Banastre Tarleton, in British National Archives, AO 13/112A, 263–66.
83. Cortland Skinner Submission in Support of Richard Witham Stockton's Memorial, Feb. 28, 1783, in *ibid.*, 262. A copy of this letter was discovered and supplied to descendants of Richard Witham Stockton by Loyalist historian Todd Braisted. In turn, a copy of this letter, and other copies of many other related documents, were provided to me by Chris Hay of Maple Ridge, British Columbia, Canada, one of Stockton's descendants (a fifth great grandson). (Skinner stated that he promoted Stockton on December 10, but that was not possible, as the capture of Lee occurred on December 13; it is likely Skinner promoted Stockton around December 15). In my book focusing on the capture of General Charles Lee, and in the best biography of Lee by John Alden, the authors concluded (wrongly) that Stockton was likely not the main guide for Harcourt's party. McBurney, *Kidnapping the Enemy*, 60–61 and 233–34, n. 59; Alden, *General Charles Lee*, 332–33, n. 2.
84. Dornfest, *Military Loyalists of the A.R.*, 326. The image of Richard Witham Stockton used in this book is based an original portrait painted by American painter Henry Benbridge in about 1770. A photograph of the original portrait appeared on page 107 in Frederic Fairchild Sherman's *Early American Painting*, published in 1932. At the time, the book indicated the painting was in the collection of John Hill Morgan of New York City. The Smithsonian Institution also mentioned the painting in a publication about Henry Benbridge in 1971. According to Chris Hay, who has studied the matter, the current location of the painting is not known. If the reader becomes aware of the owner and location of the original painting, the author would appreciate being informed about it.
85. I. Putnam to Pennsylvania Council of Safety, Feb. 18, 1777 (from Princeton), in Livingston, *Israel Putnam*, 342 (Putnam described

Stockton as the enemy's "renowned land pilot"); Jones, *Loyalists of New Jersey*, 212 ("Double Dick").

86. Asher Dunham Memorial, March 7, 1786, in British National Archives, AO 13/21, 154. Cortland Skinner's letter in support of Dunham's memorial did not mention Dunham's role serving as a guide in the capture of General Lee, and Dunham's role in the abduction of Lee was not mentioned in any contemporary newspaper articles either. This is in contrast to the mentions from those sources of Stockton's role. Accordingly, there is less proof that Dunham participated in Lee's capture than in Stockton's case. William Robins, born in 1759 and at the outbreak of the war residing in Quibbletown (now New Market) in Somerset County, New Jersey, stated that he joined British forces in 1776 and that initially "he served as a guide under Lord Cornwallis" and that he had been "a principal guide at the capture of General Lee." Quoted in Jones, *Loyalists of New Jersey in the Revolution* (summarizing official Loyalist claims for reimbursement). Given that Robins is not mentioned in any other record as associated with Harcourt's capture of Lee, and that he was only eighteen years old at the time of Lee's abduction, it is doubtful that he was "a principal guide" for Harcourt.

87. For the size of Stockton's force, see his Application for Reimbursement of Losses, March 23, 1784, in British National Archives, AO 13/3, MC 493.

88. I. Putnam to G. Washington, Feb. 18, 1777, in Twohig et al. (eds.), *Washington Papers* 8:362; T. Lowery to G. Washington, Feb. 19, 1777, in *ibid.*, 371; G. Washington to New York Convention, Feb. 20, 1777, in *ibid.*, 387; I Putnam to W. Livingston, Feb. 18, 1777, in Prince et al. (eds.), *Livingston Papers* 1:241–42; John Neilson Obituary, in *The New England Magazine* 4:432 (1833).

89. Extract of a letter from an officer of distinction, dated Princeton, February 18, 1777, in *Pennsylvania Evening Post*, Feb. 20, 1777 (This letter is nearly identical to Putnam's letters of the same date to Washington and Livingston; in this letter, Putnam ended with the postscript, "Since writing the above, the whole of the prisoners have arrived here").

90. G. Washington to J. Hancock, Feb. 20, 1777, in Twohig et al. (eds.), *Washington Papers* 8:382.

91. H. Hughes to Joshua Huntington, March 2, 1777, in "Huntington Papers," *Connecticut Hist. Soc. Coll.* 20:53 (1923).

92. Extract of a Letter from an Officer at Morristown, Feb. 21, 1777, in *Connecticut Courant* (Hartford), March 3, 1777 and *Independent Chronicle* (Boston), March 6, 1777.

93. Quoted in Livingston, *Israel Putnam*, 342.

94. W. Howe to G. Washington, Nov. 26, 1777, in Twohig et al. (eds.), *Washington Papers* 12:413. Washington conceded this treatment. G. Washington to W. Howe, Nov. 28, 1777, in *ibid.*, 438 ("When Major Stockton was first captured, I believe that he and one or two officers taken with him suffered the treatment which you mention"). See also Richard Witham Stockton Application for Reimbursement of Losses, March 23, 1784, in British National Archives, AO 13/3, MC 493 (Stockton was "handcuffed and in that manner marched to Philadelphia where he was kept in close confinement for near eighteen months in different gaols ...."); Asher Dunham Memorial, March 7, 1786, in British National Archives, AO 13/21, 154 (Dunham was "marched in irons from Princeton to the Philadelphia gaol").

95. Extract of a Letter from Philadelphia, Feb. 24, 1777, Philadelphia, in *The Royal American Gazette* (New York), March 6, 1777 and *Scots Magazine* 39:248 (1777).

96. *Pennsylvania Packet* (Philadelphia), Feb. 25, 1777; *Pennsylvania Evening Post* (Philadelphia), Feb. 22, 1777; Richard Witham Stockton Application for Reimbursement of Losses, March 23, 1784, in British National Archives, AO 13/3, MC 493 ("closely confined"). For Lieutenant Frances Fraser being captured at Bennett's Island with Stockton and Dunham, and imprisoned with them at Philadelphia, see Miscellaneous Loyalist Muster Rolls, 1778–1782, Accession No. 5066, Library of Congress.

97. G. Washington to H. Gates, March 10, 1777, in Twohig et al. (eds.), *Washington Papers* 8:548.

98. R. W. Stockton, A. Dunham, et al. to Continental Congress, Oct. 1777, in Papers of the Continental Congress, m247, r100, i78, vol. 18, p. 117, National Archives Building. Stockton subsequently wrote another letter complaining about conditions in the Carlisle jail to Thomas Peters, a deputy to Elias Boudinot. Stockton wrote, in part, that the plight of the captive officers "really surpasses everything that was ever heard of in a Christian land. We are mixed with ruffians and criminals ... sick and well all together ...." In other handwriting, probably by Peters, is written the following: "The officers at

180 Notes—Chapter II

Carlisle are in a room the best the gaol will afford, but it is not a good one & though prisoners of different character are confined under the same roof, they are not together, so that it is not the whole truth which is equal to a falsehood as to the idea Mr. S [Stockton] means to convey." R. W. Stockton to T. Peters, undated [probably about February 1778], Society of the Cincinnati.

99. John Connolly, Richard Wm Stockton, Charles Harrison, Asher Dunham, Robert Morris and Francis Fraser to H. Laurens, May 17, 1778, in Connolly, *Narrative*, 34–35.

100. R. W. Stockton to T. Peters, undated [probably about February 1778], Society of the Cincinnati.

101. Dornfest, *Military Loyalists of the A.R.*, 326.

102. Sabine, *Biographical Sketches of Loyalists*, 334–35; Jones, *Loyalists of New Jersey*, 34.

103. Unless otherwise stated, the part of the capture of Richard Prescott is based on the fifth and sixth chapters of McBurney, *Kidnapping the Enemy*.

104. *Ibid.*, 134–37 (citations omitted). Of course, this quotation omits Barton's meticulous planning, the first part of the raid, and the arrival of Barton's party at Warwick Neck, with their prisoners in tow.

105. G. Washington to J. Spencer, July 17, 1777, in Twohig et al. (eds.), *Washington Papers* 10:313.

106. I found the following information after the publication of my *Kidnapping the Enemy* book. In his pension application submitted in 1832, Timothy Anderson of East Windsor, Connecticut, wrote the following: "he entered the service of the United States in August of 1777 as a volunteer in a guard commanded by Lieutenant Allen in said East Windsor. When General Prescott was taken prisoner at Rhode Island in 1777 he was sent to Connecticut for safekeeping under the superintendence of General Erastus Wolcott of East Windsor. A military company was raised by General Wolcott, placed under the charge of Lieutenant Allen and the guard did vigilant duty day and night. Five sentries were placed all around the house where he was kept, viz. at the house of Capt. Grant in said East Windsor." Timothy Anderson Pension Application, 1832, National Archives Building. For more on Prescott's stay at East Windsor, see McBurney, *Kidnapping the Enemy*, 150–51.

107. Diary Entry, July 11, 1777, in Mackenzie, *Diary* 1:148.

108. See *ibid.* and McBurney, *Kidnapping the Enemy*, 145.

109. Burrows, *Forgotten Patriots*, 70. Burrows wrote during the U.S.-Iraq war, when many questioned the usefulness of information extracted under torture.

110. See chapter 8 of McBurney, *Kidnapping the Enemy*.

111. See chapter 9 of *ibid.*

112. G. Washington to J. Spencer, Sept. 2, 1777, in Twohig et al. (eds.), *Washington Papers* 11:130.

113. James Wilkinson Recollections, in Wilkinson, *Memoirs* 1:852 (spies informing Washington in what room Clinton slept); Stephen Kemble Diary Entry, July 20, 1776, in *Kemble Papers* 1:82 (1883) ("Col. Patterson, the Adjutant General, went on a flag-of-truce to New York and was received with great pomp by a guard, and was conducted to Capt. Kennedy's house, where he saw a great court, gentlemen well dressed, etc.... He had an audience of Mr. Washington ...."); *Connecticut Courant*, Oct. 7, 1776 (after a devastating fire, Captain Kennedy's house was one of the only buildings left standing on the west side of Broadway). Clinton moved into the Kennedy house on November 9, 1777. Stephen Kemble Diary Entry, Nov. 9, 1777, in *Kemble Papers* 143 (1883). Archibald Kennedy, later known as the Earl of Cassilis, built his mansion at Number One Broadway in 1760. Trask, *Bowling Green*, 41; Brown, *Valentine's Manual of Old New York*, 107. General Charles Lee, when he assumed command of defending New York City in the winter of 1776, had been the first war-time general to use the Kennedy house as his headquarters. Lossing, *Pictorial Field-Book of the Rev.* 2:798; Trask, *Bowling Green*, 42.

114. G. Washington to S. Parsons, March 5, 1778, in Twohig et al. (eds.), *Washington Papers* 14:72.

115. G. Washington to S. Parsons, March 8, 1778, in *ibid.*, 104.

116. W. Smith Diary Entry, Feb. 2, 1780, in Sabine (ed.), *Historical Memoirs of William Smith*, 2:222; Trask, *Bowling Green*, 42.

117. James Wilkinson Recollections, in Wilkinson, *Memoirs* 1:852.

118. T. Mifflin to S. Webb, June 28, 1777, in Ford (ed.), *Webb Correspondence* 1:216; Leftkowitz, *George Washington's Indispensable Men*, 102–03.

119. G. Washington to S. Parsons, March 8, 1778, in Twohig et al. (eds.), *Washington Papers* 14:104.

120. James Wilkinson Recollections, in Wilkinson, *Memoirs* 1:852–53.

Chapter III

1. G. Washington to W. Maxwell, September 5, 1777, in Twohig et al. (eds.), *Washington Papers* 14:154. Fisher's house was owned by mill-owner Andrew Fisher and was located on the Christina River immediately north of Iron Hill and one-and-a-half miles upstream from Cooch's Bridge. *Ibid.*, n. 2. Cooch's Bridge was south of Newark, Delaware, and about five miles northeast of Elkton, Maryland. The Battle of Cooch's Bridge, also called the Battle of Iron Hill, was a skirmish between American militia under Maxwell and German forces on September 3, 1777. Boatner, *Encyclopedia of the A.R.*, 283.
2. J. McKinly to H. Laurens, Aug. 20, 1778, in *Delaware Archives* 3:1416; Scharf, *History of Delaware* 1:477–78 and n. 2. "John McKinly … lived on the north side of Third Street, between French and King, in a house furnished rather pretentiously, as a set of seven Chippendale chairs, now in the possession of the Historical Society of Delaware, indicate." Lincoln, *Wilmington, Delaware, Three Centuries Under Four Flags*, 94.
3. Captain Andrew Snape Hammond Orders, Sept. 20, 1777, in Clark, Morgan & Crawford (eds.), *Naval Documents of the American Revolution* 9:946.
4. J. McKinly to Jenny McKinly, Oct. 21, 1777, in Evans (ed.), "Letters of Dr. John McKinly to His Wife," *Pennsylvania Magazine of History and Biography* 34:1, 12 (1910).
5. Ryden (ed.), *Letters to and From Caesar Rodney*, 282, n. 1; Evans (ed.), "Letters of Dr. John McKinly to His Wife," *Pennsylvania Magazine of History and Biography* 34:1, 9–20 (1910).
6. Thomas Kean quoted in Rowe, "The Travail of John McKinly," *Delaware History* 17:24 (Spring-Summer 1976).
7. T. McKean to G. Read, Feb. 12, 1778, in Thompson (ed.), *Life and Correspondence of George Read*, 299 and quoted in Ryden (ed.), *Letters to and From Caesar Rodney*, 254, n. 1.
8. Ryden (ed.), *Letters to and From Caesar Rodney*, 254, n. 2; see also Rowe, "The Travail of John McKinly," *Delaware History* 17:30 (Spring-Summer 1976).
9. C. Rodney to T. McKean, March 9, 1778, in Ryden (ed.), *Letters to and From Caesar Rodney*, 254.
10. J. McKinley to Jenny McKinly, Oct. 21, 1777, in Evans (ed.), "Letters of Dr. John McKinly to His Wife," *Pennsylvania Magazine of History and Biography* 34:1, 16 (1910).
11. Quoted in Coleman, *Thomas McKean*, 219.
12. C. Rodney to H. Laurens, Aug. 24, 1778, in *ibid.*, 281.
13. Ford (ed.), *Journals of the Continental Congress* 11:816–18; 12:898 and 908–912.
14. Quoted in Coleman, *Thomas McKean*, 228.
15. J. Lovell to R. T. Paine, September 24, 1777, in Smith (ed.), *Letters of Delegates* 8:14.
16. Quoted in Thompson (ed.), *Life and Correspondence of George Read*, 334.
17. J. Kirkbride to T. Wharton, Feb. 14, 1778, in Hazard (ed.), *Pennsylvania Archives*, Series 1, 6:261.
18. G. Washington to T. Wharton, Feb. 23, 1778, in Twohig et al. (eds.), *Washington Papers* 13:651. For more detail on this raid, see J. Lacey to G. Washington, Feb. 19, 1778, in *ibid.*, 592 and 593, n. 1; J. Ewald Diary Entry, in Tustin (ed.), *Diary of the American War*, 120.
19. Committee at Camp (signed by Joseph Reed) to J. Lawrence, Feb. 18, 1778, in Smith (ed.), *Letters of Delegates to Congress* 9:125. Reed later reported to a friend that one man had been hanged for the kidnapping of Justice Knox. *Ibid.*, n. 1.
20. Committee at Camp (written in Joseph Reed's hand and signed by Francis Dana) to H. Laurens, Feb. 25, 1778, in *ibid.*, 174.
21. Congressional Resolution, Feb. 27, 1778, in Ford (ed.), *Journals of the Continental Congress* 10:204–05.
22. G. Washington to W. Smallwood, May 19, 1778, in Twohig et al. (eds.), *Washington Papers* 15:168–69.
23. Article in *Pennsylvania Ledger*, March 18, 1778, in Lee (ed.), *Documents Relating to the Rev. History of N.J.* 2:126–27.
24. *Ibid.*; see also Berger, *Broadsides and Bayonets*, 165; Prince et al. (eds.), *Livingston Papers* 3:15, nn. 1–9 and 16. The *Pennsylvania Ledger* article did not name the two American officers who were captured and described the house in which they were seized as "Benjamin Vanleer's" in New Jersey. Benjamin Vanleer was a physician residing prior to the war in Haddonfield, New Jersey, and who after the war moved his practice to Philadelphia. Wickes, *A History of Medicine in N.J.*, 430.
25. J. C. Symmes to W. Livingston, Jan. 7, 1779, in Prince et al. (eds.), *Livingston Papers* 3:12–15.

26. Quoted in Fowler, "'Loyalty is Now Bleeding in New Jersey,'" in Tiedemann et al. (eds.), *The Other Loyalists*, 56.
27. Court-Martial Record of William Crossing, Dec. 17, 1779, Documents of the Continental Congress, M332, R178, i160, f228–31, National Archives.
28. J. Sullivan to H. Laurens, Dec. 20, 1778, in Hammond (ed.), *Sullivan Letters* 2:464.
29. J. Garzia to J. Sullivan, Feb. 19, 1779, in *ibid.*, 517–18.
30. Papas, *Staten Island and the American Revolution*, 97–98; Schama, *Rough Crossings*, 114–16.
31. Blanco (ed.), *The American Revolution* 1:79–80; Boatner, *Encyclopedia of the American Revolution*, 45 and 529–30.
32. David Fanning Recollections, in Fanning, *Fanning's Narrative*, 105.
33. J. P. Jones to Lady Selkirk, May 8, 1778, in Clark, Morgan & Crawford (ed.), *Naval Documents of the American Revolution* 12:675.
34. Sequel of the Proceedings of Captain Paul Jones and His Crew at Whitehaven, April 24, 1778, in *ibid.*, 597–99; Examination of David Freeman, April 24, 1778, in *ibid.*, 596 (Freeman was the deserter and gave evidence to two Whitehaven justices of the peace); J. P. Jones to American Commissioners in France, May 27, 1778, in *ibid.*, 755–56.
35. Thomas, *John Paul Jones*, 113–14 and 125–27; for the number of the raiders being twelve, see Diary Entry, April 24, 1778, in Green (ed.), *Diary of Ezra Green*, 23.
36. Extract of a letter from Dumfries, April 24, 1778, *The Gazetteer and New Daily Advertiser* (London), May 1, 1778, in Clark, Morgan & Crawford (ed.), *Naval Documents of the American Revolution* 12:643.
37. Quoted in Thomas, *John Paul Jones*, 127.
38. Tonsetic, *Special Operations during the American Revolution*, 130.
39. J. P. Jones to Lady Selkirk, May 8, 1778, in Clark, Morgan & Crawford (ed.), *Naval Documents of the American Revolution* 12:675–76; see also J. P. Jones to American Commissioners in France, May 27, 1778, in *ibid.*, 755–56.
40. For the death of Wallingford, see Log of the *Ranger*, April 25, 1778, in *ibid.*, 846; Diary Entry, April 24, 1778, in Green (ed.), *Diary of Ezra Green*, 23.
41. Comte d'Orvilliers to G. Sartine, May 8, 1778, in *ibid.*, 676–78.
42. Coggins, *Ships and Seamen of the A.R.*, 111.
43. Quoted in Weintraub, *Iron Tears*, 196–97.
44. Thomas, *John Paul Jones*, 133.
45. J. P. Jones to Lady Selkirk, May 8, 1778, in Clark, Morgan & Crawford (eds.), *Naval Documents of the American Revolution* 12:675.
46. M Schweighauser to B. Franklin, Feb. 10, 1779, in Oberg (ed.), *Franklin Papers* 28:500 and n. 4.
47. B. Franklin to J. P. Jones, March 14, 1779, in *ibid.*, 29:119.
48. Thomas, *John Paul Jones*, 140.

Chapter IV

1. W. Livingston to G. Washington, Oct. 5, 1777, in Prince et al. (eds.), *Livingston Papers* 2:85.
2. W. Livingston to G. Washington, Jan. 13, 1778, in *ibid.*, 177. Washington wrote in response, "I hope as you have got notice of a design against you that you will be able to counter plot your enemies and that they may fall into the snare which they intend for you." G. Washington to W. Livingston, Jan. 20, 1778, in Twohig et al. (eds.), *Washington Papers* 13:296.
3. W. Livingston to G. Washington, Jan. 26, 1778, in Prince et al. (eds.), *Livingston Papers* 2:193.
4. *Ibid.*, 288, n. 2 (citing General Assembly and Legislative Council Acts). It does not appear that Livingston called on these troops very often, in part out of a desire not to remove them from what he considered more important services, and also perhaps because he did not want the expense of supplementing their food allowances. To avoid the exposure of residing at Liberty Hall, Livingston rented a farm in Parsippany, belonging to Lemuel Bowers, a tavern keeper and merchant, from 1777 to 1780. The house, known as the Benedict House, located at 25 Parsippany Road, not far from the intersection of Interstate Route 80 and Route 46, survives to the present day. See email from Eric Olsen of the National Park Service to the author, March 18, 2013.
5. W. Livingston to L. Clarkson, April 10, 1778, in Prince et al. (eds.), *Livingston Papers* 2:287.
6. T. Stirling to H. Clinton, Feb. 26, 1779, PRO C/O, 5/97, British National Archives.
7. Extract of a letter from a correspondent relative to the enemy's late attempt on Elizabethtown, dated Feb. 25, 1779, *New Jersey Journal*, with dateline of March 2, 1779, quoted in Rivington's *Royal Gazette*, March 10, 1779, and in Nelson (ed.), *Documents Relating to the Rev.*

History of N.J. 3:160–61. This letter is also the source of the "profound silence" quote.

8. Extract of a letter from a correspondent relative to the enemy's late attempt on Elizabethtown, dated Feb. 25, 1779, *New Jersey Journal*, with dateline of March 2, 1779, quoted in Rivington's *Royal Gazette*, March 10, 1779 and in Nelson (ed.), *Documents Relating to the Rev. History of N.J.* 3:160–61; Prince et al. (eds.), *Livingston Papers* 3:50, n. 5 (citing *U.S. Magazine*, March 1779; *New Jersey Gazette*, March 3, 1779); Rivington's *Royal Gazette* (New York), March 10, 1779; and J. Fell to W. Livingston, March 25, 1779, in Prince et al. (eds.), *Livingston Papers* 3:48.

9. Extract of a letter from a correspondent relative to the enemy's late attempt on Elizabethtown, dated Feb. 25, 1779, *New Jersey Journal*, with dateline of March 2, 1779, quoted in Rivington's *Royal Gazette*, March 10, 1779 and in Nelson (ed.), *Documents Relating to the Rev. History of N.J.* 3:160–61; Prince et al. (eds.), *Livingston Papers* 3:49–50, n. 5; Kwasny, *Washington's Partisan War*, 235 (Maxwell's Continentals and some militia later provided stiff resistance to the raiders, who lost at least forty soldiers, with the Americans losing about thirty men).

10. W. Livingston to H. Clinton, March 29, 1779, in Prince et al. (eds.), *Livingston Papers* 3:49.

11. W. Smith Diary Entry, April 10, 1778, in Sabine (ed.), *Historical Memoirs of William Smith*, 2:92.

12. H. Clinton to W. Livingston, April 10, 1779, in Prince et al. (eds.), *Livingston Papers* 3:54.

13. Smith wrote, "I think the writer may be Parson Odell of Burlington or perhaps Governor Franklin." W. Smith Diary Entry, April 14, 1778, in Sabine (ed.), *Historical Memoirs of William Smith*, 2:95; see also Willcox, *Portrait of a General*, 267; *New York Gazette*, April 19, 1779 (printing two letters, with dateline of April 14).

14. W. Livingston to H. Clinton, April 15, 1779, in Prince et al. (eds.), *Livingston Papers* 3:55–58 and *New York Gazette*, April 26, 1779.

15. W. Franklin to G. Germain, Feb. 5, 1779, in Davies (ed.), *Documents of the A.R.* 17:53.

16. W. Livingston to W. Livingston, Jr., June 24, 1779, in Prince et al. (eds.), *Livingston Papers* 3:123–24; see also W. Livingston to Susannah Livingston, June 17, 1779, in *ibid.*, 115–16 (alerting his daughter to the plot and requesting that she remove his papers from the house for safekeeping); *New Jersey Journal*, July 28, 1779, quoted in Nelson (ed.), *Documents Relating to the Rev. History of N.J.* 3:515–16 (alleging involvement of Mayor Mathews).

17. *New Jersey Journal*, July 28, 1779, quoted in Nelson (ed.), *Documents Relating to the Rev. History of N.J.* 4:258–59.

18. W. Livingston to G. Washington, Jan. 15, 1780, in Prince et al. (eds.), *Livingston Papers* 3:291; see also W. Livingston to G. Washington, Jan. 13, 1780, in *ibid.*, 290; G. Washington to W. Livingston, Jan. 15, 1780, in Fitzgerald (ed.), *Washington Writings* 17:398.

19. *Royal Military Calendar* 2:23–58; Reuter, "'Petty Spy' or Effective Diplomat: The Role of George Beckwith," *Journal of the Early Republic* 10:4, 472 (Winter, 1990).

20. Ward, *Between the Lines*, 87–88; Israel Abner Pension Application, New Jersey, National Archives Building; Moody, *Memoirs*, 8–9.

21. British Intelligence Memorandum Book, MMC-2248, 1778, Library of Congress. The British secret service officer was probably Major Duncan Drummond. For more on Duncan and his memorandum book, see McBurney, *Spies of Revolutionary Rhode Island*, 50–53. Drummond spelled Moody's residence as "Nolton," which the author took to be Knowlton, a township in Sussex (now Warren) County. Moody also addressed this kidnapping attempt in his autobiography. Moody, *Memoirs*, 10.

22. Benjamin Sutton Rev. War Pension Application, 1834, in National Archives Building; see also Shenstone, *So Obstinately Loyal*, 57. Shenstone wrote further that a year later, William Brittain publicly exclaimed, "I will give any man two hundred and fifty hard dollars to take Isaac Martin to [British-held] Staten Island & I will pledge my estate for the performance of my promise." Brittain was then indicted for a misdemeanor in the Sussex County court for his impertinence. *Ibid.*, 70, n. 19.

23. James Moody Recollections, in Moody, *Memoirs*, 46, n. and 51–53.

24. G. Beckwith Orders, May 10, 1780, quoted in *New Jersey Gazette*, Aug. 9, 1780 and Nelson (ed.), *Documents Relating to the Rev. History of N.J.* 4:552; see also *New Jersey Gazette*, June 14, 1780 and quoted in Nelson (ed.), *Documents Relating to the Rev. History of N.J.* 4:436 (captive revealed that he had "received instructions from General Knyphausen").

25. Ward, *Between the Lines*, 87–90 and 95.

26. See sources in note immediately before the above note.

184 Notes—Chapter IV

27. Certification of John L. Roome, Secretary to Major General James Pattison, New York, May 11, 1782, in Moody, *Memoirs*, Appendix, 67.

28. *Ibid.* ("Moody ... confidentially consulted me on the practicability of several excursions he intended to make in rebel country, and particularly with respect to his intention to make Governor Livingston a prisoner").

29. Shenstone, *So Obstinately Loyal*, 75 (quoting from Moody's Loyalist post-war claim).

30. James Moody Recollections, in *ibid.*, 21.

31. *New Jersey Gazette*, June 14, 1780 and quoted in Nelson (ed.), *Documents Relating to the Rev. History of N.J.* 4:435; see also James Moody Recollections, in Moody, *Memoirs*, 21.

32. *New Jersey Journal*, Aug. 2, 1780, quoted in Nelson (ed.), *Documents Relating to the Rev. History of N.J.* 4:552.

33. James Moody Recollections, in Moody, *Memoirs*, 21.

34. Id.; Shenstone, *So Obstinately Loyal*, 78–79.

35. Shenstone, *So Obstinately Loyal*, 77–80. Shenstone's biography of James Moody contains the most complete and accurate description of his wartime activities, including an attempt to steal Continental Congress's papers. For another good description of Moody's activities, see Ward, *Between the Lines*, chapter 6.

36. *New Jersey Journal*, Aug. 2, 1780, quoted in Nelson (ed.), *Documents Relating to the Rev. History of N.J.* 4:553; see also Rivington's *Royal Gazette*, Aug. 9, 1780, quoting the *Pennsylvania Packet*, July 25, 1780 ("Lieutenant Moody and six of his party were taken on their return from an excursion to Sussex").

37. James Moody Proclamation, Aug. 25, 1781, in Rivington's *Royal Gazette*, Aug. 25, 1781 and Prince et al. (eds.), *Livingston Papers* 4:123–24; see also James Moody Recollections, in Moody, *Memoirs*, 21–24. For Livingston's proclamation offering a reward for the capture of John Moody (mistakenly identifying James for his brother) and three other men, see *New Jersey Gazette*, Aug. 22 and Oct. 24, 1781. For Moody's incarceration and escape, see Shenstone, *So Obstinately Loyal*, 82–90.

38. Diary Entry, March 31, 1781, in Mackenzie, *Diary* 2:497–98.

39. Sutherland, "Moody, James," in *Dictionary of Canadian Biography* 5, University of Toronto, 2003, at www.biographi.ca/en/bio/moody_james_5E.

40. John Moody to James Moody, Nov. 12, 1781, in Moody, *Memoirs*, 51–52.

41. W. Livingston to G. Washington, Jan. 1, 1782, in Prince et al. (eds.), *Livingston Papers* 4:357; see also G. Washington to W. Livingston, Jan. 12, 1782, in Fitzgerald (ed.), *Washington Writings* 23:445.

42. Ward, *Between the Lines*, 98–100.

43. Sutherland, "Moody, James," in *Dictionary of Canadian Biography* 5, University of Toronto, 2003, at www.biographi.ca/en/bio/moody_james_5E.

44. Quotations from Henry Clinton Memorandum, Aug. 1780, Henry Clinton Papers, William L. Clements Library, and quoted in Prince et al. (eds.), *Livingston Papers* 3:50, n. 6; see also Willcox, *Portrait of a General*, 331; Henry Clinton Recollections, in Willcox (ed.), *Clinton's Narrative*, 117 (describing raid against Elizabethtown but not attempt to kidnap Governor Livingston) and 203, n. 11 (describing purported poisoning attempt).

45. Willcox, *Portrait of a General*, 331–32. It is likely the case that the wine Clinton and his two aides drank had gone bad and had caused their mild nausea.

46. G. Washington to W. Livingston, Jan. 15, 1780, in Fitzgerald (ed.), *Washington Writings* 21:436; see also W. Livingston to G. Washington, Jan. 15, 1780, in Prince et al. (eds.), *Livingston Papers* 4:180.

47. W. Livingston to H. B. Livingston, Oct. 24, 1781, in Prince et al. (eds.), *Livingston Papers* 4:319; see also D. Romeyn to W. Livingston, Oct. 27, 1781, in *ibid.*, 322 ("a gentleman of credit assured him that there were near 30 of the enemy out in the country in different parties for the express purpose of capturing and carrying off your Excellency").

48. Ward, *Between the Lines*, 43; Rose, *Washington's Spies*, 227. Ward's book is an extensive study of the guerrilla war-type operations conducted during the Revolutionary War, including the whaleboat war of Long Island Sound.

49. It appears that the only source for Clinton approving the raid is the 1801 written recollections of Mary Silliman, wife of Gold Selleck Silliman, in which she recalled, "General Clinton the British commander of New York sent a whaleboat manned by the Tories to surprise and take him [Gold Selleck Silliman] prisoner." Mary Silliman Recollections, 1801, in Jones, *History of New York* 2:566. Mary probably obtained this information from her husband, who may or may not have obtained the correct information from British officers. Lieutenant Colonel John Graves Simcoe, the

Loyalist commander who apparently supervised the raid from Long Island, wrote in his memoirs that the raid to capture Silliman, as well as Continental general Samuel Holden Parsons, was authorized by headquarters in New York City. Simcoe, *Military Journal*, 99. The attempt on Parsons was not made.

Surviving accounts of the raid only refer to a Captain Glover, but a modern listing of Loyalists officers reveals that the man was Captain Isaac Glover of New York's King's Militia Volunteers, who was born in about 1736, lived in New Jersey prior to the war, and died in Nova Scotia in 1806. Dornfest, *Military Loyalists of the A.R.*, 40.

50. Mary Silliman Recollections, 1801, in Jones, *History of New York* 2:567.

51. Ibid. An unknown diarist, probably a civilian from Fairfield, Connecticut, reported that at "3 o'clock in the morning, an alarm turned out with the news that a party came from Long Island and took General Silliman and son off about 1 o'clock this morning and carried them to Long Island. This is the news of the night. This forenoon went to meeting. The parson prayed hearty for General and son and for Mrs. Silliman under her troubles and difficulties she labors under." Quoted in Brown, *Benjamin Silliman*, 15, n.

52. Mary Silliman Recollections, 1801, in Jones, *History of New York* 2:566.

53. Ibid., 567. For more on this raid, see G. S. Silliman to J. Fish, May 12, 1779, in *ibid.*, 564; Rivington's *Royal Gazette*, May 5, 1779; Buel and Buel, *The Way of Duty*, 162–71; Ward, *Between the Lines*, 43; Rose, *Washington's Spies*, 230–31; Brown, *Benjamin Silliman*, 15–17.

54. Quoted in Simcoe, *Military Journal*, 100; see also Rose, *Washington's Spies*, 229.

55. Mary Silliman Recollections, 1801, in Jones, *History of New York* 2:568.

56. Ibid.

57. Ibid., 568–71 and Buel and Buel, *The Way of Duty*, 162–71; see also Ward, *Between the Lines*, 43–44 and Rose, *Washington's Spies*, 230–31. A son and grandson of Mary and Gold Selleck Silliman became distinguished professors at Yale College. Brown, *Benjamin Silliman*, passim.

58. Excerpt from letter by Gold Selleck Silliman, in Onderdonk, *Revolutionary Incidents of Suffolk and Kings Counties*, 259–60.

59. Quoted in Buel and Buel, *The Way of Duty*, 171.

60. John Graves Simcoe Recollections, in Simcoe, *Military Journal*, 130.

61. *Ibid.*, 131.

62. "Morristown" Pamphlet, Morristown National Historical Park, National Park Service, 2013 ("December introduced the worst winter of the century to Morristown").

63. John Graves Simcoe Recollections, in Simcoe, *Military Journal*, 131.

64. "Morristown" Pamphlet, Morristown National Historical Park, National Park Service, 2013; G. Washington to N. Greene, Jan. 22, 1780, in Fitzpatrick (ed.), *Washington Writings* 17:423 (Washington began using the Ford house as his headquarters on December 1, 1779); R. K. Meade to T. Ford, July 26, 1780, in *ibid.*, 19:262 (same). Virtually all of Washington's correspondence he sent out during the winter of 1779 and 1780 was from Morristown. See Fitzpatrick (ed.), *Washington Writings* 17:334–507 and 18:1–7.

65. Baker, *Washington's Itinerary*, 169. The Ford house, now called the Ford Mansion, is currently part of the Morristown National Historical Park and is nicely furnished, as it would have been at the time it served as Washington's headquarters in the winter of 1779–1780. The main Continental encampment at Jockey Hollow to the west is also part of the Morristown National Historical Park. See "Morristown" Pamphlet, Morristown National Historical Park, National Park Service, 2013. For Jacob Ford, Jr.'s death, see Thayer, *Colonial and Revolutionary Morris County*, 164.

66. "Morristown" Pamphlet, Morristown National Historical Park, National Park Service, 2013.

67. For more on Washington's Life Guard, see Ward, *George Washington's Enforcers*, chapter 5.

68. Muster Rolls of The Commander-in-Chief's Guard, 1777–1783, m246–129, i182, National Archives Building. The total men in the unit dropped from 122 on November 1, 1779, to 118 on January 14, 1780 and to 97 on April 15, 1780. From those totals, the soldiers permitted to be absent on leave were 19 on November 1, 1779, 26 on January 14, 1780, and 39 on April 15, 1780. *Ibid.* Accordingly, in early February of 1780, I estimate that the unit had a total of about 115 men, with about 28 of them absent on permitted leave, leaving at their Morristown camp about 87 soldiers available for action.

69. *Ibid.*; Cunningham, *The Uncertain Revolution*, 124.

70. This estimate is based on an estimate by Eric Olsen of the National Park Service, sta-

tioned at Morristown National Historical Park, in an email to the author, August 20, 2015.

71. See Smith, *Winter at Morristown, 1779–1789*, 12 and 13 (showing map of Morristown, New Jersey, Dec. 12, 1779, New York Historical Society); see also "Washington at Morristown," *Harper's New Monthly Magazine*, vol. 18 (Feb. 1859), 297 ("In the meadow, southeast of the house, were cabins for the Life-Guard ….").

72. Diary Entries, Dec. 4, 6 and 9, 1779, "Elisha Fisher's Journal," *Magazine of History* 2:155 (1909) (members of the Life Guard arrived at Morristown on December 4 and pitched their tents; two days later they began to gather timber and work on their huts; and they finished their huts and moved into them on December 9).

73. Barber and Howe, *Historical Collections of the State of New Jersey*, 385–86.

74. Lossing, *Pictorial History of the Revolution* 1:310.

75. Diary Entry, Dec. 31, 1779, "Elisha Fisher's Journal," *Magazine of History* 2:156 (1909).

76. Lossing, *Pictorial History of the Revolution* 1:314.

77. Richard Kidder Meade Certification to Theodosia Ford, July 26, 1780, in Fitzpatrick (ed.), *Washington Writings* 19:262.

78. G. Washington to N. Greene, Jan. 22, 1780, in *ibid.*, 17:423; Richard Kidder Meade Certification to Theodosia Ford, July 26, 1780, in *ibid.*, 19:262 ("I certify that the commander-in-chief took up his quarters at Mrs. Ford's at Morristown the first day of December 1779 and that he left on the 23rd of June 1780 ….").

79. T. Stirling to J. G. Simcoe, Jan. 31, 1780, in Simcoe, *Military Journal*, Appendix, 288. For Stirling's service as brigadier general and no longer as a colonel, see *ibid.*; T. Stirling to W. Knyphausen, Jan. 15, 1780, in Davies (ed.), *Documents of the A.R.* 18:34; *New York Gazette*, July 3, 1780.

80. S. Condict to G. Washington, Jan. 31, 1780, George Washington Papers, microfilm reel 83, Manuscript Division, Library of Congress.

81. G. Washington to S. Condict, Feb. 1, 1780, *ibid.*

82. John Graves Simcoe Recollections, in Simcoe, *Military Journal*, 131.

83. Diary Entry, Feb. 7, 1780, General von Knyphausen's Journal, Henry Clinton Papers 83:2, William L. Clements Library. Knyphausen's Journal was probably used as his report to General Clinton.

84. *Ibid.*

85. Diary Entries, Feb. 7 and 9, 1780, in *ibid.*

86. Diary Entry, Feb. 8, 1780, General von Knyphausen's Journal, Henry Clinton Papers 83:2, William L. Clements Library. The information on the infantry regiment joining the dragoons is based on Diary Entry, Feb. 11, 1780, in Ford (ed.), *Journals of Hugh Gaine* 2:80 ("The Light Horse and Regiment of Foot went out last night, with a design as was said, to surprise G. Washington at Morristown"). The author has not discovered what regiment accompanied the cavalry. It is also possible that after raiding Elizabethtown, Stirling's and Skinner's troops were to fall back to the vicinity of Newark and wait for the return of the dragoons from Morristown.

87. Intelligence by John Jones, of Merionetshire in Wales, Taken 15th Febry, 1780, Tuesday, enclosed in a letter from William Tryon to Lord George Germain, Feb. 26, 1780, New York, in O'Callaghan (ed.), *Documents Relative to the History of the State of New York* 8:114.

88. New Jersey historian Todd Braisted informed the author that he reviewed a provisions return for the 17th Regiment of Light Dragoons that was taken between January 31 and February 6, 1780 showing that the regiment had a total of 315 soldiers based at Jamaica, Long Island. According to Braisted, the subsequent returns show the same number of men for the next two weeks, until it drops from 307 men to 246 men, or about sixty men. This may be the sixty dragoons sent on the raid across the ice towards Morristown. Email from T. Braisted to C. McBurney, Aug. 16. 2015. (Note that about one half of the regiment was not mounted.).

89. W. Smith Diary Entry, Feb. 11, 1780, in Sabine (ed.), *Historical Memoirs of William Smith*, 2:227.

90. A. St. Clair to G. Washington, Feb. 11, 1780, in Smith (ed.), *Life of St. Clair*, 500.

91. J. Abeel to Unidentified Aide-de-Camp to General Washington, Feb. 13, 1780, quoted in Vanderpool, *History of Chatham, New Jersey*, 307–08.

92. Diary Entry, Feb. 4, 1780, in Uhlendorf (ed.), *Major Baurmeister Journal*, 342. For the number of Diemar's Hussars, see Dornfest, *Military Loyalists of the A.R.*, 102 and 375 (Diemar's Hussars had about 80 rank and file effectives and 70 rank and file present and fit for duty as of Nov. 15, 1779 and April 1, 1780; commanded by Augustus Diemar, they consisted mostly of escaped Saratoga prisoners of

war from German regiments); email from Todd Braisted to the author, Jan. 8, 2014 (muster roll, dated March 19, 1780, for Diemar's Hussars listed one captain, one lieutenant, one cornet, one surgeon's mate, three sergeants, one trumpeter, three corporals, one volunteer, and sixty-two privates, for a total of seventy-four men).

93. John Graves Simcoe Recollections, in Simcoe, *Military Journal*, 109; Carrado, *The Black Hussars*, 12.

94. For the number of cavalry in Simcoe's Queen's Rangers, see muster roll of Wickham's Company, Queen's American Rangers, Dec. 25, 1779-Feb. 23, 1780, in On-Line Institute for Advanced Loyalist Studies, www.royalprovincial.com (sixty-five officers and other soldiers listed, with six of them sick in hospital, discharged, deserted or dead; this was the only mounted company in the Queen's Rangers at this time). For the number of dragoons in the 17th Light Dragoons, see muster rolls for the 17th Light Dragoons, Dec. 25, 1779-June 24, 1780, WO 12/1306, British National Archives (supplied to the author by Don N. Hagist) (listing about 350 men in six companies, with about 215 horses available for riding; some dragoons were dismounted). At the time of the attempt on Washington, one company of the 17th Light Dragoons was serving in South Carolina with General Clinton. Atkinson, "British Forces in North America, 1774–1781," *Journal of the Society for Army Historical Research* 16:18 (1937).

95. For information on the 17th Light Dragoons during the Revolutionary War, see Cannon, *Historical Record of the 17th Regiment of Light Dragoons*, 12–28. By doing a computer search of "British 17th Light Dragoons" and "Revolutionary War," some helpful websites appear, including the website for the reenactment regiment.

96. Carrado, *The Black Hussars*, 7.

97. Ibid. (summarizing painting by Queens Ranger Captain James Murray of a Hussar private of the Rangers).

98. See Jones, *History of New York* 1:324–325 and 341, and 2:67–75 and 87. From late 1780 through 1782, after being promoted to brigadier general, Birch served as Commandant of the City of New York, issuing various proclamations and orders to New Yorkers. See, e.g., *New York Gazette*, Nov. 6, 1780; *New York Gazette*, Jan. 15, 1781; Rivington's *Royal Gazette*, Dec. 25, 1782.

99. A. St. Clair to G. Washington, Feb. 11, 1780, in Smith (ed.), *Life of St. Clair*, 500 ("Their numbers are said to have been two thousand, which is improbable; but from General Stirling and General Skinner both being in command, they must have been considerable"); J. Abeel to Unidentified Aide-de-Camp to General Washington, Feb. 13, 1780, quoted in Vanderpool, *History of Chatham, New Jersey*, 308 (informer estimated that Stirling and Skinner's force numbered about 2,000). One of the reports by a resident of Elizabethtown had 3,000 infantry also crossing over to support the dragoons, with British Major General Charles Grey at their head. J. Abeel to Unidentified Aide-de-Camp to General Washington, Feb. 13, 1780, quoted in ibid., 308. However, this is the only evidence of this movement of this number of troops and Grey's participation. While it is possible this movement of troops occurred, the author does not believe enough proof exists to include it in the main text. The intelligence that Major General Charles Grey commanded the cavalry intended to ride to Morristown was not accurate—at the time Grey was in England. Nelson, *Sir Charles Grey*, 90–93.

100. Dornfest, *Military Loyalists of the A.R.*, 386–88 (at this time the 1st and 4th Battalions of the New Jersey Volunteers were on Staten Island, each with about 200 rank and files present and fit for duty).

101. W. Smith Diary Entry, Feb. 6, 1780, in Sabine (ed.), *Historical Memoirs of William Smith*, 2:223; Diary Entry, Feb. 11, 1780, in Ford (ed.), *Journals of Hugh Gaine* 2:79; A. St. Clair to G. Washington, Feb. 7, 1780, in Smith (ed.), *Life of St. Clair*, 408; see also G. Washington to N. Greene, Jan. 30, 1780, in Fitzpatrick (ed.), *Washington Writings* 17:469 (mentioning British impressment of sleds).

102. Quoted in W. Smith Diary Entry, Feb. 13, 1780, in Sabine (ed.), *Historical Memoirs of William Smith*, 229 ("made no impression") and J. Pattison to G. Germain, Feb. 22, 1780, in Davies (ed.), *Documents of the A.R.* 18:50 ("memory of man"); see also Diary Entry, Feb. 8, 1780, in Sabine (ed.), *Historical Memoirs of William Smith*, 2:223; Diary Entry, Feb. 4, 1780, in Schaukirk, *Occupation of New York City*, 12 ("This week sleighs have crossed over the ice from Staten Island to this city, which has hardly been known before").

103. Diary Entry, Feb. 7, 1780, General von Knyphausen's Journal, Henry Clinton Papers 83:2, William L. Clements Library; Diary Entry, Feb. 7, 1780, in Ford (ed.), *Journals of Hugh Gaine* 2:79. Knyphausen did not mention Diemar's Hussars, but the movement of this

188 Notes—Chapter IV

unit is inferred from the fact that it had ridden from Long Island to Staten Island on February 4. Diary Entry, Feb. 4, 1780, in Uhlendorf (ed.), *Major Baurmeister Journal*, 342. Diemar's Hussars often rode with the Queen's Rangers.

104. W. Smith Diary Entries, Feb. 7–8, 1781, in Sabine (ed.), *Historical Memoirs of William Smith*, 2:223.

105. See T. Stirling to G. Germain, Feb. 22, 1780, in Davies (ed.), *Documents of the A.R.* 18:50–51; Rivington's *Royal Gazette*, Jan. 29, 1780; J. Abeel to Unidentified Aide-de-Camp to General Washington, Feb. 13, 1780, quoted in Vanderpool, *History of Chatham, New Jersey*, 307–08; Diary Entry, Feb. 5, 1780, General von Knyphausen's Journal, Henry Clinton Papers 83:2, William L. Clements Library (forty new companies raised).

106. G. Washington to N. Greene, Jan. 30, 1780, in Fitzpatrick (ed.), *Washington Writings* 17:469; G. Washington to A. St. Clair, Jan. 30, 1780, in *ibid.*, 470; A. St. Clair to G. Washington, Feb. 7, 1780, in Smith (ed.), *Life of St. Clair*, 408.

107. G. Washington to A. St. Clair, Jan. 30, 1780, in Fitzpatrick (ed.), *Washington Writings* 17:470.

108. Huggins, "Raid Across the Ice," Dec. 17, 2013, in the online Journal of the American Revolution, at www.allthingsliberty.com (see text accompanying notes 23 and 24). For the New Jersey Privy Council orders authorizing the raising of forty-five horsemen to patrol between Newark and Perth Amboy for one month, see Minutes of the Council Meeting held at Elizabeth Town, Feb. 3, 1780, in Bernstein (ed.), *Minutes of the Privy Council* 1:144–46.

109. Diary Entry, Feb. 8, 1780, General von Knyphausen's Journal, Henry Clinton Papers 83:2, William L. Clements Library.

110. See Diary Entry, Feb. 7 and 8, 1780, in "John Barr's Diary," in Lauber (ed.), *Orderly Books*, 819 ("Snowed all last night and chief of this day"); see also Diary Entry, Feb. 7, 1780, in Ford (ed.), *Journals of Hugh Gaine* 2:79 ("The weather still very severe, and not the least probability of a change.... Snow this day.").

111. W. Smith Diary Entries, Feb. 11 and 14, 1780, in Sabine (ed.), *Historical Memoirs of William Smith*, 2:227 and 230; Diary Entry, Feb. 11, 1780, in Ford (ed.), *Journals of Hugh Gaine* 2:80.

112. John Graves Simcoe Recollections, in Simcoe, *Military Journal*, 132.

113. Huggins, "Raid Across the Ice," Dec. 17, 2013, in the online Journal of the American Revolution, at www.allthingsliberty.com.

114. John Graves Simcoe Recollections, in Simcoe, *Military Journal*, 133.

115. *Ibid.*, 133–34.

116. John Graves Simcoe Recollections, in Simcoe, *Military Journal*, 134.

117. A. St. Clair to G. Washington, Feb. 11, 1780, in Smith (ed.), *Life of St. Clair*, 500.

118. *Ibid.*

119. *Pennsylvania Packet*, Feb. 22, 1780 and quoted in Nelson (ed.), *Documents Relating to the Rev. History of N.J.* 4:182.

120. W. Smith Diary Entry, Feb. 11, 1780, in Sabine (ed.), *Historical Memoirs of William Smith*, 2:227.

121. A. St. Clair to G. Washington, Feb. 11, 1780, in Smith (ed.), *Life of St. Clair*, 500.

122. Diary Entry, Feb. 10, 1780, in General von Knyphausen's Journal, Henry Clinton Papers 83:2, William L. Clements Library.

123. John Graves Simcoe Recollections, in Simcoe, *Military Journal*, 134. For support for Simcoe's comment on the rain, see Diary Entry, Feb. 11, 1780, in "John Barr's Diary," in Lauber (ed.), *Orderly Books*, 819 ("rained a little today") and A. St. Clair to G. Washington, Feb. 11, 1780, in Smith (ed.), *Life of St. Clair*, 499–500 (same).

124. Jones wrote of the affair,"In the winter of this year, information was received at New York that Washington's quarters were in a house at Morristown, some distance from the huts occupied by the rebel army." Incorrectly stating that it was Clinton's plan to capture Washington, Jones continued, "Four hundred horse were dispatched for this purpose. This alert turned out as all others did—it failed. The guides got frightened, the party bewildered, they lost the road, and after a cold, tedious and fatiguing excursion of twenty-four hours, without ever seeing a rebel, returned to New York, all frost-bitten." According to Jones, "This maneuver was laughed at by the rebel army, derided by their militia, and cursed by the Loyalists." Jones, *History of New York* 1:318.

125. J. Abeel to Unidentified Aide-de-Camp to General Washington, Feb. 13, 1780, quoted in Vanderpool, *History of Chatham, New Jersey*, 308. The author of this letter, Colonel James Abeel, Deputy Quartermaster General, summarized his conversation with a resident of Elizabethtown, who had some accurate information, but probably exaggerated the number of infantry involved. See excerpt of the letter in Appendix A to this book.

126. Diary Entry, Feb. 11, 1780, in Ford (ed.), *Journals of Hugh Gaine* 2:80; see also

Diary Entry, Feb. 11, 1780, in *ibid*. ("The Light Horse and Regiment of Foot went out last night, with a design as was said, to surprise G. Washington at Morristown, but they all returned in half an hour after they set off, the weather proving unfavorable").
127. W. Smith Diary Entry, Feb. 11, 1780, in Sabine (ed.), *Historical Memoirs of William Smith*, 2:227.
128. Diary Entry, Feb. 8, 1780, in Jackson (ed.), *Diaries of George Washington* 3:344.
129. A. St. Clair to G. Washington, Feb. 11, 1780, in Smith (ed.), *Life of St. Clair*, 500.
130. *Ibid.*, 499–500.
131. J. Greenman Diary Entry, Feb. 20–22, 1780, in Bray and Bushnell (eds.), *Diary of a Common Soldier*, 168.
132. G. Washington to A. St. Clair, Feb. 12, 1780, in Fitzpatrick (ed.), *Washington Writings* 18:7.
133. *Ibid*.
134. G. Beckwith Reports, Intelligence No. 1, March 3, 1780 and Intelligence No. 2, March 9, 1780, Henry Clinton Papers 87:42, William L. Clements Library.
135. Diary Entry, March 19, 1780, in Jackson (ed.), *Diaries of George Washington* 3:348. It snowed another nine to ten inches at Morristown during the night of March 31 and early morning of April 1. *Ibid.*, 349.
136. Samuel Tallmadge Orderly Book, Fourth New York Regiment, Mar. 19, 1780, in Lauber (ed.), *Orderly Books*, 289; Ensign Griffin Diary Entry, March 20, 1780, quoted in West, *Stephen Griffing, His Ancestry and Descendants*, 10 ("This day Sergeant Vanaton and two privates were ordered to go and join His Excellency's Life Guard from our Regiment") (Ensign Griffin was in the Fourth New York Regiment). See also Huggins, "Raid Across the Ice," Dec. 17, 2013, in the online Journal of the American Revolution, at www.allthingsliberty.com (text accompanying notes 46 and 47).
137. Greenman Diary Entry, May 16, 1780, in Bray and Bushnell (eds.), *Diary of a Common Soldier*, 171.
138. See Baker, *Washington's Itinerary*, 226; Fitzpatrick (ed.), *Washington Writings* 22:331, n. 36.
139. C. Marquard to George Beckwith, July 28, 1781, Henry Clinton Papers 167:10, William L. Clements Library. Captain Ludwig August, an aide to General Knyphausen, in his letter indicated that Beckwith was working out of the Morris House in New York City.
140. G. Beckwith Intelligence Report, Aug. 11, 1781, Henry Clinton Papers 170:9, William L. Clements Library.
141. Quoted in Jacob and Case, *Treacherous Beauty*, 161–62.
142. G. Washington to H. Lee, Oct. 13, 1780, in Fitzpatrick (ed.), *Washington Writings* 20:178.
143. Henry Lee Recollections, in Lee, *Memoirs of the War*, 395. Lee's memoir is the main original source for information on Champe's activities. See also the recollections of John Champe and Captain Cameron, in Hall, "Sergeant Champe's Adventure," *William and Mary Quarterly*, 2nd Series, 18:3, 322–42 (July 1938); G. Washington to H. Lee, Oct. 13 and 20, 1780, in Fitzpatrick (ed.), *Washington Writings* 20:178 and 223 and Lee, *Memoirs of the War*, 407–08; H. Lee to G. Washington, undated (probably about October 19, 1780), excerpted in Fitzpatrick (ed.), *Washington Writings* 20:223, n. 34; H. Lee to G. Washington, Oct. 21 and 25, 1780, George Washington Papers, microfilm reels 71 and 72. The undated letter by Henry Lee is filed in the George Washington Papers at the end of September, but the author believes it was sent to Washington on October 19, based on his response the next day that he had "this moment" received Lee's letter "without a date." G. Washington to H. Lee, Oct. 20, 1780, in Fitzpatrick (ed.), *Washington Writings* 20:223.

The account of Champe's activities in Wilbur C. Hall's article is from a British officer named Captain Cameron, who had been Champe's superior officer during the time Champe was on board a transport vessel in the fleet carrying Arnold's force to Virginia. After the war, Cameron had accidentally met Champe while traveling on business through Virginia. After meeting with Champe and discussing his activities with Arnold's American Legion, Cameron wrote about the encounter, but his manuscript was not published until it was found years later. Cameron's account, as faithfully set forth in Hall's article, was originally published in London in *The United Service Journal and Naval and Military Magazine* in the December 1834 edition, at pages 438–52. The author of a 1939 article on Cameron's account, William Buckner McGroarty, wrote that he thought Cameron met Champe in Loudoun County in about 1782, but that seems unlikely, as the war had not yet officially ended and therefore Cameron could not freely travel in Virginia. Because Cameron was traveling in Virginia on personal business, it seems likely the meeting occurred shortly after war's end in 1783

190 Notes—Chapter IV

and before Champe's death in about 1798, perhaps some time in the mid to late 1780s. McGroarty also guessed that Cameron could have been Ensign Angus Cameron, but the three British officers with that name who fought in the war had each died by 1781. See Baule and Gilbert, *British Army Officers*, 27. It is also possible that Captain Cameron could have been one of the many Camerons who served as Loyalist officers during the war. See Dornfest, *Military Loyalists of the A.R.*, 55–57.

Some of the language used in Cameron's account is nearly identical to the language used in Lee's *Memoirs* and Cameron repeats some errors made by Lee due to Lee's lapse in memory. It is not clear who influenced whose writings on the subject. Henry Lee had his memoirs published in 1812. A petition submitted by Champe's wife to Congress in 1818 states that "she sent the papers belonging to her husband to General [Henry] Lee, who wished to consult them in preparing his memoirs; these included letters from General Washington." Quoted in McGroarty, "Sergeant John Champe and Certain of His Contemporaries," *William and Mary Quarterly*, 2nd Series, 17:2, 165 (April 1937). Thus, it is possible that Cameron, who likely met with Champe in the mid to late 1780s, wrote down some of Champe's own notes. It seems more likely that the man who found Cameron's recollections and had them published must have supplemented the account of Cameron's meeting with Champe by filling in gaps with information from Lee's *Memoirs*. William Buckner McGroarty agrees that this is the most likely scenario. McGroarty, "Captain Cameron and Sergeant Champe," *William and Mary Quarterly*, 2nd Series, 19:1, 51–52 (Jan. 1939).

The most glaring error in Lee's *Memoirs* is the frequently-stated purpose of Champe's kidnapping Arnold for Washington to spare John André's life by exchanging him for the newly-captured Arnold. Cameron's account repeats this version. André was hanged, however, on October 2, and all of the contemporary documents regarding Champe's activities are dated starting from October 13.

144. G. Washington to C. Lee, Oct. 20, 1780, in Fitzpatrick (ed.), *Washington Writings* 20:223; see also Henry Lee Recollections, in Lee, *Memoirs of the War*, 408.

145. Henry Lee Recollections, in Lee, *Memoirs of the War*, 395.

146. *Ibid.*, 397 ("bone and muscle"); H. Lee to G. Washington, undated (probably about October 19, 1780), in *ibid.*, 55 and excerpted in Fitzpatrick (ed.), *Washington Writings* 20;223, n. 34.

147. Henry Lee Recollections, in Lee, *Memoirs of the War*, 397–99; H. Lee to G. Washington, undated (probably about October 19, 1780), excerpted in Fitzpatrick (ed.), *Washington Writings* 20:223, n. 34 (offer of promotion and emphasizing glory to be gained); John Champe Recollections, in Hall, "Sergeant Champe's Adventure," *William and Mary Quarterly*, 2nd Series, 18:3, 334 (July 1938) ("immortal honor" quote).

148. H. Lee to G. Washington, undated (probably about October 19, 1780), excerpted in Fitzpatrick (ed.), *Washington Writings* 20:223, n. 34.

149. *Ibid.* Arnold issued a proclamation to fill his new American Legion on October 20, 1780, which appeared in editions of Rivington's *Royal Gazette* from November 8 through December 6, 1780.

150. H. Lee to G. Washington, undated (probably about October 19, 1780), in Lee, *Memoirs of the War*, excerpted in Fitzpatrick (ed.), *Washington Writings* 20;223, n. 34.

151. John Champe Recollections, in Hall, "Sergeant Champe's Adventure," *William and Mary Quarterly*, 2nd Series, 18:3, 341 (July 1938). Lee, in his memoirs, wrote: "Champe and his friend intended to have placed themselves each under Arnold's shoulder, and to have thus borne him through the most unfrequented alleys and streets to the boat; representing Arnold, in case of being questioned, as a drunken soldier, whom they were carrying to the guard-house." Henry Lee Recollections, in Lee, *Memoirs of the War*, 409.

152. John Champe Recollections, in Hall, "Sergeant Champe's Adventure," *William and Mary Quarterly*, 2nd Series, 18:3, 335 (July 1938).

153. G. Washington to C. Lee, Oct. 20, 1780, in Fitzpatrick (ed.), *Washington Writings* 20:223.

154. Henry Lee Recollections, in Lee, *Memoirs of the War*, 401.

155. Kranish, *Flight from Monticello*, 152.

156. *Ibid.*

157. *Ibid.*, 151–52.

158. Henry Lee Recollections, in Lee, *Memoirs of the War*, 400–03; John Champe Recollections, in Hall, "Sergeant Champe's Adventure," *William and Mary Quarterly*, 2nd Series, 18:3, 324–25 (July 1938).

159. Randall, *Benedict Arnold*, 579. Other good (and more detailed) descriptions of

Champe's adventures are in Kranish, *Flight from Monticello*, 149–55 and Scheer, "The Sergeant Major's Strange Mission," *American Heritage* 8:6, 26–29 and 98 (Oct. 1957).

160. H. Lee to G. Washington, Oct. 25, 1780, in George Washington Papers, microfilm reel 71 and excerpted in Fitzpatrick (ed.), *Washington Writings* 20:223, n. 34.

161. Kranish, *Flight from Monticello*, 153.

162. Clinton Recollections, in Clinton, *Narrative*, 235–36.

163. John Champe Recollections, in Hall, "Sergeant Champe's Adventure," *William and Mary Quarterly*, 2nd Series, 18:3, 341 (July 1938). Arnold's squadron of ships, due to wind and tide, did not depart New York harbor until December 21. *New York Gazette*, Jan. 15, 1781.

164. Henry Lee Recollections, in Lee, *Memoirs of the War*, 410; Kranish, *Flight from Monticello*, 155.

165. John Champe Recollections, in Hall, "Sergeant Champe's Adventure," *William and Mary Quarterly*, 2nd Series, 18:3, 341–42 (July 1938).

166. McGroarty, "Captain Cameron and Sergeant Champe," *William and Mary Quarterly*, 2nd Series, 19:1, 50 (Jan. 1939); McGroarty, "Sergeant John Champe and Certain of His Contemporaries," in *ibid.*, 17:2, 164 (April 1937).

167. Henry Lee Recollections, in Lee, *Memoirs of the War*, 410, n. Lee wrote: "When General Washington was called by President Adams to the command of the army, prepared to defend the country from French hostility, he sent to Lieutenant Colonel Lee to inquire for Champe, being determined to bring him into the field at the head of a company of infantry. Lee went to Loudoun County, where Champe settled after his discharge from the army, and learned that the gallant soldier had removed to Kentucky, and had soon after died." President Adams appointed Washington commander-in-chief of the army to be raised for a possible war against France in 1798 and the elderly Virginian concluded this service in December of 1799. Chernow, *Washington: A Life*, 785. Lee's information was not entirely accurate—Champe, after moving to Hampshire County, Virginia, in 1798 died on a trip visiting the frontier lands around what is now Morgantown, West Virginia. McGroarty, "Sergeant John Champe and Certain of His Contemporaries," *William and Mary Quarterly*, 2nd Series, 17:2, 164 (April 1937).

168. Kranish, *Flight from Monticello*, 262–63.

169. McGroarty, "Sergeant John Champe and Certain of His Contemporaries," *William and Mary Quarterly*, 2nd Series, 17:2, 166–67 (April 1937).

170. A. McDougall to G. Clinton, March 10, 1779, in Hastings (ed.), *George Clinton Papers* 4:626.

171. Resolution, Feb. 22, 1779, in Ford (ed.), *Journals of the Continental Congress* 13:218.

172. J. Jay to G. Washington, Feb. 23, 1779, in Twohig et al. (eds.), *Washington Papers* 19:248; G. Washington to A. McDougall, March 3, 1779, in *ibid.*, 344; G. Washington Ledger, Feb. 15, 1779, in *ibid.*, 344, n. 2.

173. G. Washington to A. McDougall, March 3, 1779, in *ibid.*, 344.

174. A. McDougall to G. Clinton, March 10, 1779, in Hastings (ed.), *George Clinton Papers* 4:626.

175. G. Clinton to A. McDougall, March 18, 1779, in *ibid.*, 645.

176. G. Washington's Instructions for Spies, undated (probably around Sept. 10, 1780), in Fitzpatrick (ed.), *Washington Writings* 20:26.

177. Humphreys, *Life and Times of David Humphreys* 1:96–99 and 116. Humphreys had previously served on the staffs of Generals Israel Putnam (starting December 1778) and Nathanael Greene (starting June 1780). *Ibid.*, 120–21 and 156–57.

178. William Heath Recollections, in Heath, *Memoirs*, 247–48. Heath identified Lieutenant John Hart of Webb's Regiment as signing on, but Hart had resigned in April of 1780. Heitman, *Historical Register of Officers*, 212. Heath also named the three ensigns as M'Calpin, Buchanan, and M'Guyer. *Ibid.*, 248. However, these men are not listed in either Heitman (ed.), *Historical Register of Officers* or in Johnston (ed.), *Record of Connecticut Men in the Military and Naval Service During War of the Revolution*. Humphreys's biographer states that the idea for the raid was Humphreys's. Humphreys, *Life and Times of David Humphreys* 1:194. This may be true; but because Washington wrote his letter first broaching the idea in March 1780 and had issued orders in September 1780 to determine the locations of the headquarters of Clinton and Knyphausen, the author credits him with the idea.

179. G. Washington to T. Pickering, Dec. 16, 1780, in Fitzpatrick (ed.), *Washington Writings* 20:486.

180. G. Washington to D. Humphreys, Dec. 23, 1780, in *ibid.*, 21:6–7.

181. See DeLancey (ed.), "Original Docu-

ments," *Magazine of American History* 10:414, n. (1883). The editor, Edward DeLancey, adds that Knyphausen "may have been, at this time, however, at Richmond Hill, not far from Greenwich village." *Ibid*.

182. William Heath Recollections, in Heath, *Memoirs*, 247–48.

183. Baurmeister Journal Entry, Dec. 24–25, 1780, in Uhlendorf (ed.), *Baurmeister Journals*, 406.

184. Diary Entry, Dec. 26, 1780, in Benians (ed.), *Hughes Journal*, 104.

185. Diary Entry, Jan. 2, 1781, in Krafft, "Journal," *N. Y. Hist. Soc. Coll.* 129 (1882).

186. Copy of a letter in cipher from Connecticut received February 4, 1781, in DeLancey (ed.), "Original Documents," *Magazine of American History* 10:410–14 (1883).

187. Hubert, *Major Philip M. Ulmer*, 402–03.

188. Charles Witham Stockton was officially an ensign in the King's American Rangers. See List of Officers Belonging to His Majesty's British American Forces in North America, New York City, November 25, 1783, British National Archives, Audit Office, CO/5/111, 234. He may have been temporarily promoted to lieutenant for service in Maine. Charles Witham Stockton had originally enlisted with the New Jersey Volunteers, as did his father. Charles Witham Stockton enlisted as an ensign with the first battalion of the New Jersey Volunteers on June 24, 1777. New Jersey Volunteers List of Officers, 1776–1783, in Braisted, The On-Line Institute for Advanced Loyalist Studies, at www.royalprovincial.com (search for the terms Charles, Witham and Stockton).

189. The information in the Peleg Wadsworth story is based on: *Royal Gazette* (New York), March 21, 1781, which is set forth in Braisted, The On-Line Institute for Advanced Loyalist Studies, at www.royalprovincial.com (search for the terms Stockton and Wadsworth); Dwight, Timothy, "The Story of General Wadsworth," *Maine Historical Society Quarterly* 15: 226–256 (1776); J. Campbell to H. Clinton, June 22, 1781, Maine Historical Society, Collection 112, Box 1/11; Higgins, *Hidden History of Midcoast Maine*, chapter 2. The author thanks Chris Hay, ancestor of the Stocktons, for bringing the capture of Wadsworth to his attention.

190. "The Sullivan Family," *The Bangor Historical Magazine* 6:277–79 (1890–91); Whittemore, *A General of the Revolution*, 169–73. See the prior two sources and the sources cited in them for the controversy as to whether Daniel Fletcher was trying to dupe the British Secret Service. Most Maine local histories do not mention Daniel[1]'s trip to Philadelphia.

Chapter V

1. Randall, *Benedict Arnold*, 583–84.
2. T. Jefferson to J. P. G. Muhlenberg, Jan. 31, 1781, in Boyd (ed.), *Jefferson Papers* 4:487.
3. *Ibid*.
4. *Ibid*., 488.
5. Bowen, "Life of Baron Steuben," in Sparks (ed.), *The Library of American Biography* 9:59.
6. Wallace, *The Muhlenbergs of Pennsylvania*, 210–12.
7. J. P. G. Muhlenberg to B. Steuben, Feb. 18, 1781, Baron von Steuben Papers, microfilm reel 4, Manuscript Division, Library of Congress; see also J. P. G. Muhlenberg to B. Steuben, Feb. 19, 1781, in *ibid*.; J. P. G. Muhlenberg to B. Steuben, Feb. 24, 1781, in Muhlenberg, *Life of Major General Muhlenberg*, 389 (slightly different version of Muhlenberg's February 18 letter).
8. Quoted in Muhlenberg, *Life of Major General Muhlenberg*, 212.
9. McBurney, *Spies in Revolutionary Rhode Island*, 102.
10. Lassiter, "Arnold's Invasion of Virginia," *Sewanee Review* 9:2, 190 (April 1901); see also Diary Entry, Feb. 18, 1781, in Mackenzie, *Diary* 2:474.
11. Quoted in Muhlenberg, *Life of Major General Muhlenberg*, 212.
12. Lassiter, "Arnold's Invasion of Virginia," *Sewanee Review* 9:2, 192 (April 1901).
13. G. Washington Instructions to Marquis de Lafayette, Feb. 20, 1781, in Fitzpatrick, *Washington Writings* 21:255.
14. Quoted in McBurney, *Spies in Revolutionary Rhode Island*, 105.
15. *Ibid*., 105–06; Randall, *Benedict Arnold*, 584.
16. Quoted in Muhlenberg, *Life of Major General Muhlenberg*, 215.
17. Diary Entry, March 26, 1781, in Mackenzie, *Diary* 2:495.
18. *Ibid*.
19. Quoted in Kranish, *Flight from Monticello*, 215.
20. Diary Entry, March 31, 1781, in Tustin (ed.), *Ewald Diary of the American War*, 295.
21. *Ibid*.
22. Diary Entry, March 19, 1781, in *ibid*., 291.

23. Quoted in Lassiter, "Arnold's Invasion of Virginia," *Sewanee Review* 9:2, 202, n. 126 (April 1901).
24. G. Washington to E. Dayton, April 11, 1781, in Fitzpatrick (ed.), *Washington Writings* 21:446–47.
25. See Kranish, *Flight from Monticello*, 265–66; Maas, *The Road to Yorktown*, 83–84 and 93–97; Maas, "The Greatest Terror Imaginable," *Goochland County Historical Society Magazine* 41:39 and 41–47 (2009).
26. E. Cornwallis to H. Clinton, June 30, 1781, in Maas, "The Greatest Terror Imaginable," *Goochland County Historical Society Magazine* 41:39 (2009).
27. Maas, *The Road to Yorktown*, 84–85.
28. Kranish, *Flight from Monticello*, 275–76. See also Mass, "The Greatest Terror Imaginable," *Goochland County Historical Society Magazine* 41:39 (2009). Historian John Maas writes, "Cuckoo is located at the intersection of U.S. highways 522 and 33. While many modern accounts of Jouett's ride claim that Jouett used the Three Notch'd Road to race toward Charlottesville, there is no contemporary evidence of this, and it is more likely that he took a parallel route north of Three Notch'd Road." *Ibid.*, 94, n. 52. Maas added that Cuckoo's Tavern was located on the Mountain Road, which is now U.S. Route 33. *Ibid.* For more on Jouett's likely route, see Maas, *Road to Yorktown*, 85 and 164.
29. Quoted in Maas, *Road to Yorktown*, 89–90.
30. Quoted in *ibid.*, 85.
31. Quoted in *ibid.*, 86; see also *ibid.*, 86–89; Kranish, *Flight from Monticello*, 275–80.
32. Kranish, *Flight from Monticello*, 281-82.
33. Quoted in Maas, *Road to Yorktown*, 92.
34. Kranish, *Flight from Monticello*, 284. Kranish surmises that McLeod and his men may not have ruined Monticello, "returning the courtesy with which Jefferson had treated British prisoners who until recently had been quartered at Charlottesville." *Ibid.* For another excellent description of the raid on Monticello, see Mass, *Road to Yorktown*, 89-93.
35. Quoted in Maas, *Road to Yorktown*, 92.
36. Boatner, *Encyclopedia of the American Revolution*, 600; Blanco (ed.), *The American Revolution* 1:906; Journal and Narrative of Capture and Confinement in the Tower of London, Aug. 13, 1780-April 4, 1782, in Chestnutt and Taylor (eds.), *Papers of Henry Laurens* 15:330–435 (see, e.g., pages 380 to 381 and n. 101); Petition to the House of Commons, Dec. 1, 1781, in *ibid.*, 456.
37. Historian John Maas writes, "Castle Hill is along Virginia Rt. 231, several miles northeast of Shadwell," which is a village in Albemarle County that was the former location, before it burned down in 1770, of Shadwell Plantation, the birthplace of Thomas Jefferson. Maas, "The Greatest Terror Imaginable," *Goochland County Historical Society Magazine* 41:94, n. 53 (2009).
38. P. Lyons to N. Brockenbrough, Sept. 20, 1784, in Wyllie, "New Documentary Light on Tarleton's Raid," *Virginia Magazine of History and Biography* 74:4 (Oct. 1966), 460–61.
39. John Reid Recollection, quoted in Blanco (ed.), *The American Revolution* 1:144.
40. Quoted in Morgan, *Boone*, 302; see also Faragher, *Daniel Boone*, 213 (this story has Boone as a lieutenant colonel of the militia, but Morgan indicates (at page 317) that that appointment did not come until 1782).
41. Quoted in Maas, *Road to Yorktown*, 90.
42. Quoted in Morgan, *Boone*, 303.
43. Faragher, *Daniel Boone*, 213; see also Morgan, *Boone*, 303; Maas, *Road to Yorktown*, 90.
44. Draper, *King's Mountain*, 436; Boatner, *Encyclopedia of the A.R.*, 234–35.
45. Powell (ed.), *Dictionary of North Carolina Biography* 385:218 (citing, in part, Surry County court records and other records).
46. Draper, *King's Mountain*, 446–47.
47. *Ibid.*, 436–37; see also Diary Entry, Oct. 14, 1780, in Draper (ed.), *Allaire Diary*, 31–32 (nine captured Loyalists court-martialed and executed after the battle).
48. William Lenoir Revolutionary War Pension Application, 1833, National Archives Building.
49. Diary Entry, Oct. 14, 1780, in Draper (ed.), *Allaire Diary*, 31–32.
50. Diary Entries, Oct. 30 and November 1, 1780, in *ibid.*, 33.
51. Wheeler, *Historical Sketches of North Carolina*, 444.
52. See *ibid.*; see also Crouch, *Historical Sketches of Wilkes County*, 20–27; Draper, *King's Mountain*, 437–44; Elisha Reynolds Revolutionary War Pension Application, 1832, National Archives Building. (Reynolds affirmed that he volunteered for one week with a small party from Wilkes County that recaptured Colonel Cleveland who was a prisoner with the Tories; Captain Samuel Johnson, who filed an affidavit supporting Reynolds, confirmed that account

and stated that he accompanied the party too). John H. Wheeler, who published his book in 1851, and Theodore Draper, who published his in 1881, had slightly different accounts of Cleveland's rescue. Wheeler wrote that the rescuers were led by Cleveland's brother, Captain Robert Cleveland, but Draper does not mention the brother. Wheeler also stated that Riddle and his party all escaped the rescue attempt, but he, his son and one other of his party were captured shortly afterwards. Draper wrote that Riddle and the two others were captured during Cleveland's rescue. John Crouch, whose history of Wilkes County was published in 1902, follows Wheeler's version, and provides even more details than either Wheeler or Draper. The author believes Wheeler's earlier version is more reliable that Draper's later version. Wheeler further wrote that the hanging of Riddle, his son, and the man occurred "near the Mulberry Meeting House, now Wilkesboro." Wheeler, *Historical Sketches of North Carolina*, 444. Crouch confirmed that, adding, "The three Tories were accordingly hung on the notorious oak that is yet standing in the town of Wilkesboro." Crouch, *Historical Sketches of Wilkes County*, 27.

53. Buchanan, *Road to Guilford Court House*, 216; Draper, *King's Mountain*, 452.

54. The information on Williamson is from Toulmin, "Backcountry Warrior: Brig. Gen. Andrew Williamson, The 'Benedict Arnold of South Carolina' and America's First Major Double Agent," *Journal of Backcountry Studies* 7:1, 1–46 (Spring 2012), which is by far the most detailed and accurate account of Williamson's wartime career. Toulmin believes that Williamson took the protection of the British Crown. Ibid., 38–42. See also *Scots Magazine* 43:704 (1781) (Williamson had "taken the opportunity of submitting himself [to the protection of the Crown] upon the first proclamation that was issued in South Carolina)."

55. Toulmin, "Backcountry Warrior: Brig. Gen. Andrew Williamson," *Journal of Backcountry Studies* 7:1, 42–43 and 45, n. 229 (Spring 2012).

56. McCrady, *History of S.C. in the Revolution*, 130–31.

57. *Scots Magazine* 43:704 (1781).

58. J. Rutledge to J. Dickinson, undated [probably July 1782], in Smith (ed.), *Letters to Delegates* 18:697.

59. Lee, *Memoirs of the War*, 450–51.

60. W. Harden to F. Marion, April 7, 1781, quoted in McCrady, *History of S.C. in the Revolution*, 134.

61. Lee, *Memoirs of the War*, 451–52.

62. *Scots Magazine* 43:704 (1781).

63. Bowden, *The Execution of Isaac Hayne*, 29; Parker, *Parker's Guide to the Revolutionary War in South Carolina*, 84–85, 184; Earl of Moira (formerly F. Rawdon) to H. Lee, June 24, 1813, in Lee, *Memoirs of the War*, 618 (Williamson was captured at his home); *Scots Magazine* 43:704 (1781) (Hayne, within a few miles of Charleston heading a party of horse, took several Loyalists as well as General Williamson; Williamson was captured at his home).

64. *Royal South Carolina Gazette*, July 11, 1781.

65. Earl of Moira (formerly F. Rawdon) to H. Lee, June 24, 1813, in Lee, *Memoirs of the War*, 618.

66. Toulmin, "Backcountry Warrior: Brig. Gen. Andrew Williamson," *Journal of Backcountry Studies* 7:1, 45 (Spring 2012).

67. Quoted in Bowden, *The Execution of Isaac Hayne*, 29; see also, Parker, *Parker's Guide to the Revolutionary War in South Carolina*, 84–85, 184 and 253.

68. Quoted in Lee, *Memoirs of the War*, 453; another similar, but perhaps more credible, description of Hayne's capture, is in McCrady, *History of S.C. in the Revolution*, 319–20.

69. Quoted in Toulmin, "Backcountry Warrior: Brig. Gen. Andrew Williamson," *Journal of Backcountry Studies* 7:1, 43, n. 220 (Spring 2012).

70. N. Balfour to L. Cornwallis, April 26, 1781, quoted in Quoted in Toulmin, "Backcountry Warrior: Brig. Gen. Andrew Williamson," *Journal of Backcountry Studies* 7:1, 44 (Spring 2012).

71. *Royal South Carolina Gazette*, May 7, 1781.

72. Bowden, *The Execution of Isaac Hayne*, 31 and 34–35. In a subsequent letter to Major General Nathanael Greene, Lieutenant Colonel Balfour argued that "on the subjection of any territory, the inhabitants of it owe allegiance to the conquering power (in the present case a voluntary acknowledgement was given, and consequent protection received); and that, on any account to recede from it, is punishable by death, by whatever law, either civil or military, is then present." N. Balfour to N. Greene, Sept. 3, 1781, in Conrad et al. (eds.), *Greene Papers* 11:283. Hayne, in contrast, argued that "allegiance due to a conqueror ceased with his

expulsion from the subdued territory." Quoted in Lee, *Memoirs of the War*, 452; see also J. Rutledge to J. Dickinson, undated [probably July 1782], in Smith (ed.), *Letters to Delegates* 18:697 ("the Americans had so far reconquered the country and that all his neighbors thought themselves obliged to declare for them [the Americans] and insisted on his doing so"). It was also argued that Hayne, as a subject under British protection, merited a proper trial and not the rump military tribunal he received. Lee, *Memoirs of the War*, 461. In a defense of his actions published in 1813, Lord Rawdon, then Earl of Moira, also argued that Hayne was as much a spy as Major John André, which was not a compelling argument. Earl of Moira (formerly F. Rawdon) to H. Lee, June 24, 1813, in Lee, *Memoirs of the War*, 617.

73. Earl of Moira (formerly F. Rawdon) to H. Lee, June 24, 1813, in Lee, *Memoirs of the War*, 618.

74. Bowden, *The Execution of Isaac Hayne*, 32–34; Parker, *Parker's Guide to the Revolutionary War in South Carolina*, 84.

75. Toulmin, "Backcountry Warrior: Brig. Gen. Andrew Williamson," *Journal of Backcountry Studies* 7:1, 46 (Spring 2012).

76. Lee, *Memoirs of the War*, 449 and 455.

77. N. Greene to W. Henderson, Aug. 16, 1781, in Conrad et al. (eds.), *Greene Papers* 9:169–71 and 177.

78. Petition from the Officers of the Southern Army to N. Greene, Aug. 20, 1781, in ibid., 217.

79. N. Greene to N. Balfour, Aug. 26, 1781, in ibid., 249–51.

80. N. Balfour to N. Greene, Sept. 19, 1781, in ibid., 283.

81. J. Varnum to N. Greene, Sept. 17, 1781, in Smith (ed.), *Letters to Delegates* 18:51–52.

82. N. Greene to G. Washington, Nov. 21, 1781, in ibid., 605 and N. Greene to T. McKean, Dec. 9, 1781, in ibid., 10:17.

83. Ibid., 11:15, n. 8.

84. G. Washington to N. Greene, Dec. 15, 1781, in Fitzpatrick (ed.), *Washington Writings* 23:391.

85. Lee, *Memoirs of the War*, 461.

86. Debates in the House of Lords, Jan. 31 and Feb. 4, 1782, in *Parliamentary History of England* 22:963–83.

87. Correspondence between Lord Rawdon and Duke of Richmond, Feb. 21–22, 1782, in ibid., 967–70.

88. Fletchall et al. to King George III, April 19, 1782, South Carolina Loyalists and Rebels, http://sc_tories.tripod.com/list_of_murdered_loyalists.htm (accessed July 11, 2002).

89. Piecuch, *Three Peoples, One King*, 274.

Chapter VI

1. Gerlach, *Proud Patriot*, 458.

2. R. Mathews to J. Sherwood, July 4, 1781, quoted in Maguire, "The British Secret Service and the Attempt to Kidnap General Jacob Bayley of Newbury, Vermont, 1782," *Vermont History* 44:146 (Summer 1976).

3. Fryer, *King's Men*, 284–85; *Loyalist Spy*, 124.

4. Quoted in Fryer, *Loyalist Spy*, 122.

5. "Meyers, John Walden," *Dictionary of Canadian Biography* 6:502. John Walden Meyers had numerous versions of his names. Baptized Johannes Waltermyer, he was sometimes known as Hans Waltermeyer. His last name was sometimes spelled Meyer, Myers, Mayers, Mires, or Myres, while his middle name was variously given as Walten or Walter. Ibid. The author uses the version adopted in the *Dictionary of Canadian Biography*.

6. A recent thorough study of Loyalist officers states that Meyers was appointed captain in the 2nd Battalion of the King's American Rangers (Robert Rogers's outfit) on November 24, 1780 and served as a captain of his own unit, Meyers's Independent Company, in June of 1781. Dornfest, *Military Loyalists of the A.R.*, 244. See also Loyalist Rev. War Claim, summarized in Coldham (ed.), *American Migrations*, 307 (Meyers of Albany County had a 200-acre farm, with house and cattle).

7. Dornfest, *Military Loyalists of the A.R.*, 437.

8. Fryer, *Loyalist Spy*, 124 and 128.

9. Ibid., 128–31; Commissioner Minutes, July 30–31, 1781, in Paltsits (ed.), *Minutes of the Commissioners for Detecting and Defeating Conspiracies* 2:754–55; Maguire, "The British Secret Service and the Attempt to Kidnap General Jacob Bayley of Newbury, Vermont, 1782," *Vermont History* 44:147 (Summer 1976); *Massachusetts Spy*, Sept. 6, 1781 (when he was captured and searched, "Howard … had his orders in writing from Col. St. Leger, commanding at St. John's").

10. P. Schuyler to G. Clinton, Aug. 9, 1781, in Hastings (ed.), *George Clinton Papers* 7:184.

11. Ibid., 184–86. Author Don Gerlach wrote that Schuyler's guard was from the Second New York Regiment, but based on the iden-

tities of the two captured soldiers, the author believes they might all have served in the First New York Regiment. See note 28 below.

12. Fryer, *Loyalist Spy*, 131 and 132 (floor plan of house).

13. Gerlach, *Proud Patriot*, 458–59.

14. *Connecticut Gazette*, Aug. 24, 1781; *Providence Gazette*, Aug. 25, 1781.

15. P. Schuyler to G. Washington, Aug. 8, 1781, quoted in Gerlach, *Proud Patriot*, 459–60; see also P. Schuyler to G. Clinton, Aug. 9, 1781, in Hastings (ed.), *George Clinton Papers* 7:185. Schuyler biographer Don Gerlach further wrote: "John Van Zandt (1767–1858), then a boy of about fourteen, later remembered hearing the signal gun from the Schuyler house when the raiders surprised the general. Joel Munsell, *The Annals of Albany*, 10 vols. (Albany, 1850–59) 10:413." Gerlach, *Proud Patriot*, 584, n 46. The Schuyler Mansion in Albany is located at 32 Catherine Street.

16. Fryer, *Loyalist Spy*, 133.

17. P. Schuyler to H. Glen, Aug. 7, 1781, quoted in Gerlach, *Proud Patriot*, 460.

18. *Ibid.*

19. Commissioner Minutes, Aug. 8 to 17, 1781, in Paltsits (ed.), *Minutes of the Commissioners for Detecting and Defeating Conspiracies* 2:758–60 and 765–66.

20. P. Schuyler to G. Clinton, Aug. 9, 1781, in Hastings (ed.), *George Clinton Papers* 7:185.

21. Quoted in Gerlach, *Proud Patriot*, 460; see also Fryer, *Loyalist Spy*, 132–33.

22. Fryer, *Loyalist Spy*, 133.

23. Quoted in Gerlach, *Proud Patriot*, 460.

24. Fryer, *Loyalist Spy*, 133. This is the only report of the death.

25. See sources in the next note.

26. *Connecticut Gazette*, Aug. 24, 1781; *Providence Gazette*, Aug. 25, 1781.

27. *Massachusetts Spy*, Sept. 6, 1781 (Poughkeepsie, August 20 dateline).

28. Fryer, *Loyalist Spy*, 156. For the names of the guards, their regiment, and their returning to Albany after the war, see Watt, *A Dirty, Trifling, Piece of Business*, 247 (Cockley, Tubbs and Ward of First New York); Richard-Morrow, "The Attempt to Abduct General Phillip Schuyler and the Great Kidnap Plot of 1781," *The Burning Issues* 14:1, 4 (March 2006) (Lockey (not Cockley) and Tubbs of the First New York; returned to Albany after the war); "Regimental History of the First New York Regiment," online at www.1stnewyorkmccrackensco.org (Cockley and Tubbs returned from Canada after the war). Stone, in his *Life of Joseph Brant*, published in 1838, mentioned in a footnote, "The names of the guard were, John Tubbs, John Corlies, and Hans (John) Ward. They were carried to Canada, and when exchanged, the General gave them each a farm in Saratoga County. Ward is still, or was very lately, living (Dec. 1837.)" *Ibid.*, 177. Stone apparently mixed up the name of Cockley, calling him Corlies, and mistakenly stated that there were three prisoners seized by Meyers. He obtained his information from Catherine Schuyler, a daughter of General Schuyler (see *ibid.*) who was just six months old at the time of the raid. Catherine's recollections seem to be a mix of fact and fiction. See note following the one immediately below and accompanying text. Schuyler's statement that one of the captives was a mere overseer on his estate is inconsistent with the above reports, although it is possible that the overseer was also enlisted in the First New York.

29. G. Smyth to R. Mathews, Oct. 30, 1782, excerpted in Marsh and Brown, *William Marsh*, 216.

30. For the earliest published version of the story, based on the recollections of Catherine Schuyler, see Stone, *Life of Joseph Brant*, 176–77, which was first published in 1838. It was repeated in Stone, *Border Wars of the American Revolution*, 162, which was first published in 1844. J. Benson Lossing mentions the story in his history of the Revolutionary War published in 1850, and otherwise relies on Stone's version, but does not say that the attacker who hurled the tomahawk was an Indian. Lossing, *Field Book of the Revolution* 2:222–23. For modern historians who doubt the veracity of the story, see Gerlach, *Proud Patriot*, 583; Fryer, *Loyalist Spy*, 134; and Watt, *A Dirty, Trifling, Piece of Business*, 445.

31. Fryer, *Loyalist Spy*, 134.

32. Maguire, "The British Secret Service and the Attempt to Kidnap General Jacob Bayley of Newbury, Vermont, 1782," *Vermont History* 44:147 (Summer 1976).

33. Sabine, *Biographical Sketches of Loyalists* 1:228.

34. *Ibid.*; Graydon, *Anecdotes of the American Revolution*, 167–70; payroll list of the gondola *Philadelphia*, Aug. 1-Oct. 16, 1776, Smithsonian Institution, Washington, D.C.

35. Sabine, *Biographical Sketches of Loyalists* 1:228; Fryer, *Loyalist Spy*, 128–30.

36. Fryer, *Loyalist Spy*, 136.

37. *Ibid.*

38. Quoted in Maguire, "The British Secret

Service and the Attempt to Kidnap General Jacob Bayley of Newbury, Vermont, 1782," *Vermont History* 44:147–48 (Summer 1976).
  39. *Connecticut Gazette*, Aug. 24, 1781; *Providence Gazette*, Aug. 25, 1781.
  40. *Massachusetts Spy*, Sept. 6, 1781 (when he was captured and searched, "Howard ... had his orders in writing from Col. St. Leger, commanding at St. John's"); Fryer, *Loyalist Spy*, 130–31.
  41. P. Schuyler to G. Clinton, Aug. 9, 1781, in Hastings (ed.), *George Clinton Papers* 7:186.
  42. Fryer, *Loyalist Spy*, 249.
  43. Ibid., 164.
  44. J. Sherwood to R. Mathews, Aug. 3, 1781, quoted in Maguire, "The British Secret Service and the Attempt to Kidnap General Jacob Bayley of Newbury, Vermont, 1782," *Vermont History* 44:147 (Summer 1976).
  45. *Massachusetts Spy*, Sept. 6, 1781 (with Poughkeepsie, August 20 dateline).
  46. Fryer, *Loyalist Spy*, 163–66.
  47. Quoted in Stone, *Border Wars*, 159–60.
  48. G. Washington to G. Clinton, Aug. 10, 1781, in Fitzpatrick (ed.), *Washington Writings* 20:491 (Washington provides detailed threat of kidnapping plot against Clinton); G. Clinton to P. Schuyler, Aug. 14, 1781, ibid., 193–99 (Clinton informed Schuyler that this was the third plot to kidnap him).
  49. Memorandum of Names of Persons Said to be in the Secret Service of the Enemy, undated [probably November 8, 1781], in Hastings (ed.), *George Clinton Papers* 7:185.
  50. "Pritchard, Aaron," *Dictionary of Canadian Biography* 6:616.
  51. Hemenway (ed.), *Vermont Historical Gazetteer* 2:928; Thomas Johnson Journal Entry, March 8, 1781, in ibid. According to Hemenway, the other prisoners were Jacob Page, and Jonathan and Joseph Elkins. "The fortune of Page and Jonathan Elkins was very different. Page was sent to Montreal, and never heard of afterwards—and Elkins was carried immediately to Quebec, where he was imprisoned till fall, and then sent in a prison ship to England, where he suffered many hardships in Mill prison till the great exchange of prisoners in June, 1780." Ibid., 928–29. Hemenway does not provide the details of the fate of Joseph Elkins.
  52. Thomas Johnson Journal Entry, March 8, 1781, in ibid., 928.
  53. Thomas Johnson Journal Entries, March 10–13, 1781, in ibid.
  54. J. Sherwood to R. Mathews, June 5, 1781, quoted in Marsh and Brown, "William Marsh," 195.
  55. Quoted in Marsh and Brown, *Marsh*, 195–96.
  56. Hemenway (ed.), *Vermont Historical Gazetteer* 2:929; Fryer, *King's Men*, 258.
  57. T. Johnson to G. Washington, May 30, 1782, in Hemenway (ed.), *Vermont Historical Gazetteer* 2:929–30.
  58. Colonel Thomas Johnson's Statement to the Committee of Newbury, in Maguire, in "The British Secret Service and the Attempt to Kidnap General Jacob Bayley of Newbury, Vermont, 1782," *Vermont History* 44:157 (Summer 1976).
  59. Joseph White Report, June 30, 1782, in ibid., 158.
  60. Maguire, "The British Secret Service and the Attempt to Kidnap General Jacob Bayley of Newbury, Vermont, 1782," *Vermont History* 44:158 (Summer 1976)
  61. Ibid., 162–63.
  62. Maguire, "The British Secret Service and the Attempt to Kidnap General Jacob Bayley of Newbury, Vermont, 1782," *Vermont History* 44:164 (Summer 1976) ("treachery"); Fryer, *King's Men*, 331.
  63. Hemenway (ed.), *Vermont Historical Gazetteer* 2:929.
  64. See T. Johnson to G. Washington, May 30, 1782, in ibid., 929–30; T. Johnson to G. Washington, July 20, 1782, in ibid., 930; M. Weare to G. Washington, Nov. 25, 1782, in ibid.; N. Peabody to G. Washington, Nov. 27, 1782, in ibid., 930–31; see also G. Washington to T. Johnson, June 14, 1782, in ibid., 930 and Fitzpatrick (ed.), *Washington Writings* 24:341–42; G. Washington to J. Bayley, June 13, 1782, in ibid., 337–39.
  65. See Johnson Family of Newbury, Vermont Papers, 1775–1886, on-line catalogue entry, www.vermonthistory.org (see bibliography under Unpublished Records and "Johnson Family" for directions on how to access this entry).
  66. Maguire, "The British Secret Service and the Attempt to Kidnap General Jacob Bayley of Newbury, Vermont, 1782," *Vermont History* 44:167 (Summer 1976).
  67. Watt, *A Dirty, Trifling, Piece of Business*, 312; Marsh and Brown, *William Marsh*, 198.

Chapter VII

  1. Massey, "The British Expedition to Wilmington," *North Carolina Historical Review* 66:4 (Oct. 1989), 388–92.
  2. "Civil War 1781–82—Colonel David

Fanning," *North Carolina University Magazine* (1853), 70.

3. Quoted in Russell, *North Carolina in the Revolutionary War*, 275–76.

4. H. Ramsey et al. to T. Burke, July 22, 1781, in Clark (ed.), *North Carolina State Records* 22:550–51. The first signature line is printed as that of General Herndon Ramsey, but the author does not believe any such general existed. It was probably Colonel Ambrose Ramsey, the ranking prisoner, and then George Herndon. See also Wheeler, *Historical Sketches of North Carolina*, 324–26.

5. "Civil War 1781–82—Colonel David Fanning," *North Carolina University Magazine* (1853), 71; J. Butler to T. Burke, Aug. 10, 1781, in *ibid.*, 83.

6. Quoted in Rankin, *North Carolina Continentals*, 363.

7. Watterson, "The Ordeal of Governor Burke," *North Carolina Historical Review* 44:2 (April 1971), 104–05. For the mid–August warning, see Massey, "The British Expedition to Wilmington," *North Carolina Historical Review* 66:4 (Oct. 1989), 407, n. 68.

8. Fanning, *Narrative*, 32.

9. Watterson, "The Ordeal of Governor Burke," *North Carolina Historical Review* 44:2 (April 1971), 105.

10. Quoted in Massey, "The British Expedition to Wilmington," *North Carolina Historical Review* 66:4 (Oct. 1989), 407.

11. Watterson, "The Ordeal of Governor Burke," *North Carolina Historical Review* 44:2 (April 1971), 105.

12. Fanning, *Narrative*, 33.

13. *Ibid.*, 33–34; Massey, "The British Expedition to Wilmington," *North Carolina Historical Review* 66:4 (Oct. 1989), 407.

14. Rankin, *North Carolina Continentals*, 365.

15. Massey, "The British Expedition to Wilmington," *North Carolina Historical Review* 66:4 (Oct. 1989), 407.

16. Rankin, *North Carolina Continentals*, 371–72; T. Burke to N. Greene, April 8, 1782, in Conrad et al. (eds.), *Greene Papers* 11:13 (Burke claimed he feared for his life).

17. Quoted in Conrad et al. (eds.), *Greene Papers* 11:15, n. 2.

18. *Ibid.*, 371–73 and 382. See also Thomas Burke's Speech to the Assembly, April 16, 1782, Clark (ed.), *North Carolina State Records* 26:202; Wheeler, *Historical Sketches of North Carolina*, 333.

19. Quoted in Massey, "The British Expedition to Wilmington," *North Carolina Historical Review* 66:4 (Oct. 1989), 411.

20. J. Williams to T. Burke, Jan. 27, 1782, in "Civil War 1781–82—Colonel David Fanning," *North Carolina University Magazine* (1853), 84.

21. D. Fanning to T. Burke, Feb. 26, 1782, in *ibid.*, 84.

22. Fanning, *Narrative*, 35–37.

23. These quotes and incidents are from Parker, "Fanning's Bloody Sabbath as Traced by Alexander Gray," May 4, 2015, in the online Journal of the American Revolution, at www.allthingsliberty.com. The article's author, Hershel Parker, rediscovered a letter written by Alexander Gray and dated March 30, 1847, which was published in Salisbury, North Carolina, in the June 4, 1847 edition of the *Carolina Watchman*. It is possible that Gray fabricated the stories or that the elder men he interviewed had imperfect memories, but I believe the recollections are credible and that it is unlikely such specific stories were made from whole cloth. Reports of some of Fanning's brutalities were set forth in John Wheeler's *Historical Sketches of North Carolina*, 84–85, published in 1851. E. W. Caruthers, in his book *Revolutionary Incidents, and Sketches of Character*, 139–344, published in 1854, has thirteen chapters on Fanning, including one chapter entitled, "Miscellaneous Deeds of Atrocity," which covered events that reportedly occurred in Cumberland County. Caruthers has an extensive chapter on the murder of Andrew Balfour, which includes excerpts from several letters written by contemporaries that referred to it. In one letter, one of Balfour's sisters who witnessed the scene wrote to another sister who was then visiting Newport, Rhode Island, where the Balfours often wintered, stated that Fanning shot her brother in the head after he had been wounded. *Ibid.*, 297–343. The June 22, 1782 edition of the *Boston Evening Post* reported an item it picked up from a Newport, Rhode Island, newspaper: "Col. Andrew Balfour, formerly of this town, was on the 12th of March killed in his own house in Randolph County, North Carolina, by a party of Tories, commanded by the infamous Fanning." See also Extract of a Letter from New Providence, April 16, 1782, in *Pennsylvania Packet*, May 23, 1782 (Fanning murdered Balfour).

Judge Murphey's narrative of Fanning's life, which he wrote in or around 1822, is also consistent with Gray's 1847 letter. Judge Murphey described the attack on Colonel Balfour's house and his being shot in the head at close range by Fanning. Murphey continued: "They [Fanning and his men] then went to Col. Collins's and not finding him at home, they burnt his house. From that place they proceeded to John Bryant's. He closed his doors; they called on him to come out and surrender. He refused. They then threatened to burn down his house. The agreed to surrender himself, if they would treat him as a prisoner of war, which they promised to do. Bryant came out and they instantly shot him down." Murphey then wrote that on the same day Fanning and his men took prisoner Daniel Clifton, who had been visiting relations and was returning to Virginia, Clifton was hanged on limb from a nearby tree. Judge Murphey's narrative of Fanning, 1822, in "Civil War 1781–82—Colonel David Fanning," *North Carolina University Magazine* (1853), 78. Clifton was apparently the traveler whom Captain Bell had seen dead lying naked in the road. Finally, putting Fanning's killings in the context of retaliation for the hanging of his own men in February 1782 makes Gray's letter (and Murphey's narrative) more credible.

24. Quoted in Caruthers, *Revolutionary Incidents, and Sketches of Character*, 324–25.

25. Quoted in *ibid.*, 319.

26. Fanning, *Narrative*, 59–60.

27. Judge Murphey's narrative of Fanning, 1822, in "Civil War 1781–82—Colonel David Fanning," *North Carolina University Magazine* (1853), 80.

28. See citation to letter by Alexander Gray in note 23 above. For more on Andrew Hunter's escape, see Caruthers, *Revolutionary Incidents, and Sketches of Character*, 273–78.

29. The *Virginia Gazette* article is quoted in Conrad et al. (eds.), *Greene Correspondence* 11:260, n. 2. See also Henry Lee Recollection; in Lee, *Memoirs of the War*, 547. For a good discussion of this plot see Nagy, *Rebellion in the Ranks*, 190–97.

30. T. Farr to N. Greene, Sept. 9, 1783, in *ibid.*, 639.

31. Fanning, *Narrative*, 62–63; see also Conrad et al. (eds.), *Greene Correspondence* 11:640, n. 7.

32. *Royal Georgia Gazette*, Sept. 20, 1781 and March 14, 1782.

33. McCall, *History of Georgia*, 535.

34. N. Brownson to N. Greene, Dec. 15, 1781, summarized in Conrad et al. (eds.), *Greene Papers* 10:58–59 and n. 4.

35. *Pennsylvania Packet*, Oct. 4, 1781.

36. Allen, *King William IV*, 28.

37. Ziegler, *King William IV*, 30–31.

38. Pocock, *Sailor King*, 8.

39. Quoted in *ibid.*, 12–13.

40. Quoted in Ziegler, *King William IV*, 26–27.

41. *Ibid.*, 28.

42. W. Smith Diary Entry, Sept. 26, 1781, in Sabine (ed.), *Historical Memoirs of William Smith* 2:447. Prince William had arrived on September 24 at Sandy Hook, New Jersey on board Digby's flagship, HMS *Prince George*, accompanied by two other warships. Diary Entry, Sept. 24, 1781, in *ibid.*, 446; see also Rivington's *Royal Gazette*, Sept. 26, 1781.

43. Quoted in Pocock, *Sailor King*, 34.

44. Quoted in Ziegler, *King William IV*, 36.

45. Quoted in Pocock, *Sailor King*, 35.

46. Quoted in Ziegler, *King William IV*, 36.

47. See Heath, *Heath's Memoirs*, 418; Lossing, *Pictorial History of the Revolution* 2:629, n. 1; Booth, *City of New York*, 511.

48. Diary Entry, Sept. 26, 1781, in Schaukirk, *Occupation of New York City*, 21.

49. Quoted in Pocock, *Sailor King*, 35.

50. *The Athenaeum* 186:321 (May 21, 1831).

51. Quoted in Pocock, *Sailor King*, 34.

52. M. Ogden to G. Washington, March (probably on or around 26), 1782, George Washington Papers, microfilm reel 83, Manuscript Division, Library of Congress.

53. G. Washington to M. Ogden, March 28, 1782, in Fitzpatrick (ed.), *Washington Writings* 24:91.

54. *Ibid.*

55. M. Ogden to G. Washington, March (probably on or around 26), 1782, George Washington Papers, microfilm reel 83, Manuscript Division, Library of Congress. Parts of this letter were quoted (and slightly altered from the original) in *The Athenaeum* 186:321–22 (May 21, 1831), but the editors did not realize that the quotes were from Ogden's initial March 1782 letter to Washington. The author is not aware that the entire letter has ever been previously published. The entire original letter is set forth in Appendix B to this book.

It appears Ogden mistakenly reported that Prince William Henry was then residing at Bateman's house, which the author has not identified. The Prince and Admiral Digby stayed at the Beekman house on Hanover Square, which had been taken over by British naval officers. See Heath, *Heath's Memoirs*, 418; Lossing, *Pictorial History of the Revolution* 2:629, n. 1; Booth, *City of New York*, 511. Lossing writes that the Beekman house was located "on the northwest corner of Sloat Lane and Hanover Square." Lossing, *Pictorial History of the Revolution* 2:629, n. 1. William Beekman had a "country seat" at what is now 51st Street and First Avenue, which was also used by British and German generals during the Revolutionary War. His downtown house on Hanover Square was located at the site of what became the Journal of Commerce building. Stone, *History of New York City*, 272. The current India House, one of the few pre–Civil War buildings left in New York City, is at One Hanover Square. The reference to Lord Stirling is to Major General William Alexander Stirling of the Continental army—he stayed at a house on Broad Street when the main Continental army occupied Manhattan Island in 1776. Coenties Market, also called the Great Fish Market, was at Coenties Slip at Pearl Street on the East River. The slip was filled to South Street about 1880. Only the apex, between Pearl and Water Streets, retains its historic name. Old Slip, the city's first slip, was known as Old Slip by 1730. It was filled to South Street in 1834 but the filled-in area currently retains the name. See the website "Old Streets of New York," at www.oldstreets.com.

56. The Estimate of the Enemy's Force in New York and Its Dependencies with the Disposition of It, February 1782, in George Washington Papers, microfilm reel 83, Manuscript Division, Library of Congress, with Colonel Ogden's name on it, indicated that the following units were stationed at the "Garrison of the City" of New York: British 40th Regiment, 200 soldiers; one battalion of Hessians, 200 soldiers; and 2 battalions of Hessian grenadiers, 1,100 soldiers. See also A List of the Enemy's Corps in New York and Its Dependencies with the Distribution of Them, February 1782, in *ibid*. ("City of New York": British 40th Regiment; four battalions of Hessian grenadiers; Hessian Landgrave Regiment; and the Hessian Knyphausen Regiment).

57. Col. Ogden's Plan for Surprising Characters in New York, undated (probably March 26, 1782), George Washington Papers, Manuscript Division, Library of Congress (microfilm reel 83; filed with other undated documents at the end of March 1782).

58. Intelligence Report sent to G. Washington, March 23, 1782, quoted in *The Athenaeum* 186:322 (May 21, 1831). The *Athenaeum* indicates that the handwritten report was taken from a fragment of a letter written by Washington to Ogden, but it appears from its language that it was written by the secret agent in New York for Washington's eyes. The *Athenaeum* likely received handwritten copies of the original correspondence, not the originals themselves. The *Athenaeum's* report was republished in *The Mirror of Literature, Amusement, and Instruction* (London) 17:492, 380–81 (June 4, 1831).

59. G. Washington to M. Ogden, April 2, 1782, in Fitzpatrick (ed.), *Washington Writings* 24:99–100.

60. Quoted in Pocock, *Sailor King*, 49.

61. Quoted in Fitzpatrick (ed.), *Washington Writings* 24:91, n. 45. John C. Fitzpatrick, editor of *Washington Writings*, wrote in note 45, accompanying Washington's March 28 letter: "On the letter sent, which was sold at auction in 1920, is an endorsement by Robert Gilmore that he secured this letter from Louis McLane, then United States Minister to Great Britain, who at one time showed it to the King (formerly Prince William Henry and then William IV, of Great Britain), who had remarked: 'I am obliged to General Washington for his humanity, but I'm damn'd glad I did not give him an opportunity of exercising it towards me.'"

62. Huish, *History of the Life and Reign of William the Fourth*, 108. Huish continued, "That the capture of Prince William would have been advantageous to the Americans there is no doubt, but on the other hand, the hazard with which the undertaking was attended, was perhaps greater than the advantage which would have been derived from the possession of his person." *Ibid*.

63. G. Washington to R. Digby, June 15, 1782, in Fitzpatrick (ed.), *Washington Writings* 24:315–16.

64. G. Washington to N. Greene, Aug. 6, 1786, in *ibid*., 471 (quoting from Aug. 2 letter); see also G. Washington to President of Congress, Aug. 5, 1782, in *ibid*. (forwarding letter to Congress), 466–67 and G. Washington to G. Carleton and R. Digby, Aug. 5, 1782, in *ibid*., 468–69 (confirming receipt of letter).

65. Allen, *King William IV*, 32.

66. Pocock, *Sailor King*, 226–27.

67. Frederika Riedesel Journal Entry, undated, in Riedesel, *Letters and Journals*, 183–84.

68. W. Livingston to R. Macnair, Aug. 21, 1782, in Prince et al. (eds.), *Livingston Papers* 4:459.

69. G. Washington to W. Livingston, Feb. 2, 1778, in Twohig et al. (eds.), *Washington Papers* 13:442.

Appendix A

1. Conrad et al. (eds.), *Greene Papers* 2:314, n. 1.

2. J. Abeel to Unidentified Aide-de-Camp to General Washington, Feb. 13, 1780, quoted in Vanderpool, *History of Chatham, New Jersey*, 307–08.

Appendix B

1. Col. Ogden's Plan for Surprising Characters in New York, undated (probably March 26, 1782), George Washington Papers, Manuscript Division, Library of Congress (microfilm reel 83; filed with other undated documents at the end of March 1782).

Bibliography

Published Primary Sources—Diaries, Letters and Others

Acomb, Evelyn M., ed. *The Revolutionary Journal of Baron Ludwig von Closen, 1780–1783.* Chapel Hill: University of North Carolina Press, 1958.

Atkinson, C. T. "British Forces in North America, 1774–1781: Their Distribution and Strength." *Journal of the Society for Army Historical Research* 16 (1937), 2–23.

Baker, William S. *Itinerary of General Washington from June 15, 1775, to December 23, 1783.* Philadelphia: J. B. Lippincott, 1892.

Baule, Steven M., and Stephen Gilbert, eds. *British Army Officers Who Served in the American Revolution, 1775–1783.* Westminster, MD: Heritage Books, 2004.

Benians, E. A., ed. *A Journal by Thos. Hughes for his Amusement, & Designed for his Perusal by the Time He Attains Age 50 if He Lives So Long (1778–1779).* Cambridge: Cambridge University Press, 1947.

Bernstein, David A., ed. *Minutes of the Governor's Privy Council, 1777–1789.* New Jersey Archives. 3rd Series, Vol. 1. Trenton: New Jersey State Library, 1974.

Boyd, Julian, ed. *Papers of Thomas Jefferson.* Vols. 1–5 and 16. Princeton: University of Princeton Press, 1950–52 and 1961.

Bray, Robert, and Paul Bushnell, eds. *Diary of a Common Soldier in the American Revolution, 1775–1783: An Annotated Edition of the Military Journal of Jeremiah Greenman.* DeKalb: Northern Illinois University Press, 1978.

Bushnell, Charles I., ed. *Journal of Solomon Nash, a Soldier of the Revolution, 1776–1777.* New York: Privately printed, 1861.

Butterfield, L. H., ed. *Letters of Benjamin Rush.* 2 vols. Princeton: Princeton University Press, 1951.

Chestnutt, David R., and C. James Taylor. *The Papers of Henry Laurens.* Vol. 15. Columbia: University of South Carolina Press, 2000.

Clark, Walter, ed. *The State Records of North Carolina.* Vols. 22 and 26. Winston and Goldsboro, NC: M. I. and J. C. Stewart, and Nash Brothers, 1895 and 1899.

Clark, William B., William J. Morgan, and Michael J. Crawford, eds. *Naval Documents of the American Revolution.* Vols. 1–12. Washington, D.C.: U.S. Naval Department, 1964–2013.

Coldham, Peter W. *American Migrations, 1765–1799, The Lives, Times and Families of Colonial Americans Who Remained Loyal to the British Crown before, during and after the Revolutionary War, as Related in their own Words and Through Their Correspondence.* Baltimore: Genealogical Publishing Co., 2000.

Connolly, John. *A Narrative of the Transactions, Imprisonment, and Sufferings of John Connolly, an American Loyalist and Lieutenant Colonel in His Majesty's Service.* London: Privately printed, 1783. Reprinted in part in *Pennsylvania Magazine of History and Biography* 13:61–70 (1889).

Conrad, Dennis, Richard K. Showman, and Roger Parker, eds. *The Papers of General Nathanael Greene.* Vols. 1–13. Chapel Hill: University of North Carolina Press, 1976–2005.

Davies, K.G., ed. *Documents of the American Revolution, 1770–1783.* Colonial Office Series 12. 21 vols. Dublin: Irish University Press, 1972–81.

DeLancey, Edward F. "Original Documents. Sir Henry Clinton's Original Secret Record of Private Daily Intelligence." *Magazine of American History* 10:327–42, 409–19 and 497-507 (July-Dec. 1883).

204 Bibliography

Delaware Archives. Revolutionary War. Published by the Public Archives Commission of Delaware. Wilmington: Chas. L. Story Company Press, 1919.

Dexter, Franklin B., ed. *Literary Diary of Ezra Stiles*. Vol. 2. New York: Charles Slocum Co., 1901.

Dornfest, Walter T. *Military Loyalists of the American Revolution. Officers and Regiments, 1775–1783*. Jefferson, NC: McFarland, 2011.

Draper, Lyman C., ed. *Diary of Lieutenant Anthony Allaire*. New York: New York Times and Arno Press, 1968. Originally published in 1881.

Egerton, Edward H., ed. *The Royal Commission on the Losses and Services of American Loyalists, 1783 to 1785*. Oxford: The Roxburghe Club, 1915.

"Elisha Fisher's Journal While in the War for Independence." *Magazine of History* 2:125–202 (1909).

Evans, Mary T., ed. "Letters of Dr. John McKinly to His Wife, While a Prisoner of War, 1777–1778." *Pennsylvania Magazine of History and Biography* 34:1–20 (1910).

Fanning, David. *The Narrative of Colonel David Fanning (A Tory in the Revolutionary War with Great Britain) Giving an Account of his Adventures in North Carolina from 1775 to 1783*. Richmond: Privately printed, 1861.

Fanning, Nathaniel. *Fanning's Narrative: The Memoirs of Nathaniel Fanning, an Officer of the American Navy, 1778–1783*. Republished by Heritage Books, 2003.

Fitzpatrick, John C., ed. *The Writings of George Washington from the Original Manuscript Sources, 1745–1799*. Vols. 11–24. Washington, D.C.: Library of Congress, 1934–38.

Force, Peter, ed. *American Archives*. 4th Series, Vol. 6 and 5th Series, Vol. 5. Washington, D.C.: M. St. Clair Clarke and Peter Force, 1853.

Ford, Paul L., ed. *The Journals of Hugh Gaine, Printer*. 2 vols. New York: Dodd, Mead, 1902.

Ford, Worthington C., ed. *British Officers Serving in the American Revolution, 1775–1783*. Brooklyn: Historical Printing Club, 1897.

_____. *Correspondence and Journals of Samuel B. Webb*. Vol. 2. New York: Wickersham, Press, 1893.

_____. *The Journals of the Continental Congress*. 34 vols. Washington, D.C.: Library of Congress, 1905–37.

Gerlach, Larry, ed. *New Jersey in the American Revolution, 1763–1783, A Documentary History*. Trenton: New Jersey Historical Commission, 1975.

Green, William, ed. *Diary of Ezra Green, M.D., Surgeon on Board the Continental Ship-of-War "Ranger," Under John Paul Jones, from November 1, 1777, to September 27, 1778*. Boston: David Clapp and Sons, 1875. Reprinted by Arno Press, 1971.

Hall, Wilbur C. "Sergeant Champe's Adventure." *William and Mary College Quarterly Historical Magazine*, 2nd Series, 18:322–42 (July 1938). (Captain Cameron's account of Sergeant John Champe's activities.)

Hammond, Otis. G., ed. *Letters and Papers of Major-General John Sullivan, Continental Army*. Vol. 2. Concord: New Hampshire Historical Society, 1931.

Hastings, Hugh, ed. *Public Papers of George Clinton, First Governor of New York, 1777–1795—1801–1804*. Vols. IV and VII. Albany: Oliver A. Quayle, 1901 and 1904.

Hazard, Samuel, ed. *Pennsylvania Archives*. Series 1, Vol. VI. Philadelphia: Joseph Severn & Co., 1853.

Heath, William. *Heath's Memoirs of the American War*. Boston: Thomas and E.T. Co., 1798. Reprinted by Books for Libraries Press, 1970.

Heitman, Francis B. *Historical Register of Officers of the Continental Army During the War of the Revolution*. Baltimore: Genealogical Publishing Society, 1969. Originally published in 1893.

Hutchinson, Richard S., ed. *Abstracts of the Council of Safety Minutes, State of New Jersey, 1777–1778*. Westminster, MD: Heritage Books, 2005.

"Huntington Papers: Correspondence of the Brothers Joshua and Jedediah Huntington During the Period of the American Revolution, 1771–1783." *Collections of the Connecticut Historical Society* 20 (1923).

Jackson, Donald. *The Diaries of George Washington*. Vol. III. Charlottesville: University Press of Virginia, 1978.

"John Barr's Diary, June 17, 1779, to October 20, 1782." *Orderly Books of the Fourth New York Regiment, 1778–1780 and the Second New York Regiment, 1780–1783*. Edited by Almon W. Lauber. Albany: University of the State of New York, 1932.

Johnston, Henry P., ed. *Record of Connecticut Men in the Military and Naval Service During the War of the Revolution, 1775–1783*. Hartford: Adjutant General's Office, 1889.

Kemble Papers. Vol. 1. "Journals of Lieut.-Col.

Stephen Kemble, 1773–1789." *New York Historical Society Collections for the Year 1882* 16:1–287 (1883).

Krafft, John Charles Philip von. *Journal of Lieutenant John Charles Philip von Krafft.* New York: New York Times and Arno Press, 1968. Originally published in 1883.

Lee, Francis B., ed. *Documents Relating to the Revolutionary History of the State of New Jersey. Extracts from American Newspapers.* Vol. 2. Trenton: The John L. Murphy Publishing Co., 1903.

Lee, Henry. *Memoirs of the War in the Southern Department of the United States.* 2 vols. New York: University Publishing Company, 1869. Originally published in Philadelphia by Bradford and Inskeep, 1812.

Lee Papers. Vol. I. Charles Lee correspondence. *Collections of the New York Historical Society for the Year 1871* (1872).

Mackenzie, Frederick. *Diary of Frederick Mackenzie ... During the Years 1775–1781 in Massachusetts, Rhode Island and New York.* 2 vols. Cambridge: Harvard University Press, 1930. Reprinted by New York Times, 1969.

Minutes of the Council of Safety of the State of New Jersey. Jersey City: John H. Lyon, 1872.

Minutes of the Provincial Congress and the Council of Safety of the State of New Jersey. Trenton: Naar, Day & Naar, 1879.

Moody, James. *Narrative of the Exertions and Sufferings of Lieut. James Moody, in the Cause of the Government since the Year 1776. Written by Himself, with the Author's Last Corrections.* Introduction and notes by Charles I. Bushnell. New York: Privately published, 1865. Originally published in London, 1783.

Nelson, William, ed. *Documents Relating to the Revolutionary History of the State of New Jersey. Extracts from American Newspapers.* Vols. 3 and 4. Trenton: The John L. Murphy Publishing Co., 1906 and State Gazette Publishing Co., 1914.

O'Callaghan, E. B., ed. *Documents Relative to the History of the State of New York.* Albany: Weed, Parsons & Co., 1857).

Paltsits, Victor Hugo, ed. *Minutes of the Commissioners for Detecting and Defeating Conspiracies in the State of New York, Albany County Sessions, 1778–1781.* Vol. 2. Albany: State of New York, 1909.

The Parliamentary History of England from the Earliest Period to the Year 1803. ... The Parliamentary Debates. Vol. 22. London: T. C. Hansard, 1814.

Powell, William S., ed. *The Correspondence of William Tryon and Other Selected Papers.* Vol. 2. Raleigh: North Carolina Division of Archives and History, 1981.

Prince, Carl E., Dennis P. Ryan, Brenda Parnes, and Mary Lou Lustig, eds. *The Papers of William Livingston.* 4 vols. Trenton: New Jersey Historical Commission, 1979–97.

Read, William Thompson, ed. *Life and Correspondence of George Read, Signer of the Declaration of Independence.* Philadelphia: J. B. Lippincott, 1870.

Riedesel, Friederika Charlotte Louise. *Letters and Journals Relating to the War of the American Revolution, and the Capture of the German Troops at Saratoga, by Mrs. General Riedesel.* Transcribed by William L. Stone. Albany: Joel Munsell's Sons, 1867.

Rush, Benjamin. *The Autobiography of Benjamin Rush. His "Travels Through Life" Together with His "Commonplace Books" for 1789–1813.* Edited by George W. Corner. Princeton: Princeton University Press, 1948.

Ryden, George Herbert, ed. *Letters to and from Caesar Rodney, 1756–1784.* Philadelphia: University of Pennsylvania Press, 1933.

"Samuel Tallmadge Orderly Book, Fourth New York Regiment." *Orderly Books of the Fourth New York Regiment, 1778–1780 and the Second New York Regiment, 1780–1783.* Edited by Almon W. Lauber. Albany: University of the State of New York, 1932.

Sabine, William H. W., ed. *Historical Memoirs of William Smith.* New York: W. H. W. Sabine, 1956. Vol. 2. Reprinted by New York Times and Arno Press, 1969.

Simcoe, John Graves. *Simcoe's Military Journal. A History of the Operations and Partisan Corps, called The Queen's Rangers, Commanded by Lieut. Col. J. G. Simcoe, During the War of the American Revolution.* New York: Bartlett and Welford, 1844. Reprinted in New York Times and Arno Press, 1968.

Slafter, Edward F., ed. "Letter of Governor Eustis—With Notes." *New England Historical and Genealogical Register* 23:205–09 (1869).

Smith, Paul H., ed. *Letters of Delegates to Congress, 1774–1789.* Vols. 2–14. Washington, D.C.: 1977–1987.

Smith, William Henry, ed. *The Life and Public Services of Arthur St. Clair, Soldier of the Revolutionary War; President of the Continental Congress; and Governor of the North-Western Territory, with his Correspondence and Other Papers.* Vol. 1. Cincinnati: Robert Clarke and Co., 1882.

206 Bibliography

Stryker, William S., ed. *Documents Relating to the Revolutionary History of the State of New Jersey. Extracts from American Newspapers, 1776–1777.* Vol. 1. In *Archives of the State of New Jersey*. Second Series. Vol. 1. Trenton: John L. Murphy Publishing Co., 1901.

Tustin, Joseph P., ed. *Diary of the American War: A Hessian Journal.* New Haven: Yale University Press, 1979. Diary of Johann von Ewald.

Twohig, Dorothy, Philander D. Chase, Theodore J. Crackel, and W. W. Abbot, eds. *The Papers of George Washington. Revolutionary War Series.* Vols. 1–18. Charlottesville: University of Virginia Press, 1985–2010.

Uhlendorf, Bernhard A., ed. *Revolution in America: Confidential Letters and Journals, 1776–1784, of Adjutant General Major Baurmeister of the Hessian Forces.* New Brunswick: Rutgers University Press, 1957.

West, Edith Willoughby. *Stephen Griffing, His Ancestry and Descendants.* Warrensburgh, NY: Privately Printed, 1911. Contains the Revolutionary War Journal of Ensign Stephen Griffing of the Fourth New York Regiment.

Wilkinson, James. *Memoirs of My Own Times.* Vol. 1. Philadelphia: Abraham Small, 1816.

Willcox, William B., ed. *The American Rebellion, Sir Henry Clinton's Narrative of His Campaigns, 1775–1782.* New Haven: Yale University Press, 1954.

Published Secondary Sources—Books

Alden, John R. *General Charles Lee: Traitor or Patriot?* Baton Rouge, LA: Louisiana State Press, 1951.

Barber, John W., and Henry Howe. *Historical Collections of the State of New Jersey; Containing a General Collection of the Most Interesting Facts, Traditions, Biographical Sketches, Anecdotes, Etc. Relating to its History and Antiquities, with the Geographical Descriptions of Every Township in the State.* New York: S. Tuttle, 1845.

Bayles, Richard M. *History of Newport County, Rhode Island. From the Year 1638 to the Year 1887, Including the Settlement of the Towns, and Their Subsequent Progress.* New York: I. E. Preston and Co., 1888.

Berger, Carl. *Broadsides and Bayonets: The Propaganda War of the American Revolution.* Philadelphia: University of Pennsylvania Press, 1961.

Bill, Alfred Hoyt. *A House Called Morven: Its Role in American History.* Princeton: Princeton University Press, 1954.

Blanco, Richard L. *The American Revolution, 1775–1783: An Encyclopedia.* Vol. I. New York: Garland, 1993.

Boatner, Mark M. *Encyclopedia of the American Revolution.* New York: D. McKay Co., 1974.

Booth, Mary. *History of the City of New York, from Its Earliest Settlement to the Present Time.* New York: W. R. C. Clark and Meeker, 1859.

Bowden, David K. *The Execution of Isaac Hayne.* Lexington, SC: Sandlapper Publishing Co., Inc., 1977.

Bowen, Francis. "Life of Baron Steuben." In *The Library of American Biography.* Edited by Jared Sparks. Vol. 9. Boston: Hilliard, Gray and Co., 1838.

Bowman Larry, G. *Captive Americans: Prisoners During the American Revolution.* Athens, Ohio University Press, 1976.

Brooks, Victor. *The Boston Campaign, April 1775–March 1776.* Conshohocken, PA: Combined Publishing, 1999.

Brown, Chandos Michael. *Benjamin Silliman: A Life in the Young Republic.* Princeton: Princeton University Press, 1989.

Brown, Henry Collins, ed. *Valentine's Manual of Old New York 1925.* New York: Gracie Mansion, 1925.

Buchanan, John. *The Road to Guilford Courthouse: The American Revolution in the Carolinas.* New York: John Wiley & Sons, 1997.

Buel, Joy D., and Richard Buel. *The Way of Duty: A Woman and Her Family in Revolutionary America.* New York: W. W. Norton, 1984.

Burrows, Edwin G. *Forgotten Patriots: The Untold Story of American Prisoners During the Revolutionary War.* New York: Basic Books, 2008.

Cannon, Richard. *Historical Record of the Seventeenth Regiment of Light Dragoons-Lancers: Containing an Account of the Formation of the Regiment in 1759, and of its Subsequent Services to 1841.* London: John W. Parker, 1841.

Caruthers, E. W. *Revolutionary Incidents and Sketches of Character, Chiefly of the "Old North State."* Philadelphia: Hayes & Zell, 1854.

Corrado, Gary. *The Black Hussars: A Brief and Concise History of Frederick Diemar's Hussars.* Westminster, MD: Heritage Books, 1999.

Coleman, John M. *Thomas McKean: Forgotten Leader of the Revolution.* Rockaway, NJ: American Faculty Press, 1975.

Chernow, Ron. *Washington: A Life.* New York: Penguin Press, 2010.
Coggins, Jack. *Ships and Seamen of the American Revolution.* Mineola, NY: Dover, 2002.
Cunningham, John T. *The Uncertain Revolution: Washington & the Continental Army at Morristown.* West Creek, NJ: Cormorant Publishing, 2007.
Dictionary of Canadian Biography. Vol. 6, 1821–35. Toronto: University of Toronto Press, 1987.
Di Ionno, Mark. *A Guide to New Jersey's Revolutionary War Trail for Families and History Buffs.* New Brunswick: Rutgers University Press, 2000.
Draper, Lyman C. *King's Mountain and Its Heroes History of the Battle of King's Mountain, October 7, 1780, and the Events which Led to It.* Cincinnati: Peter G. Thomson, 1881.
Faragher, John Mack. *Daniel Boone: The Life and Legend of an American Pioneer.* New York: Henry Holt, 1992.
Ferris, Robert G., ed. *Signers of the Declaration. Historic Places Commemorating the Signing of the Declaration of Independence.* Washington, D.C.: United States Department of the Interior, National Park Service, 1973.
Fischer, David Hackett. *Paul Revere's Ride.* New York: Oxford University Press, 1994.
———. *Washington's Crossing.* New York: Oxford University Press, 2004.
Flavell, Julia. *When London was Capital of America.* New Haven: Yale University Press, 2010.
Fryer, Mary Beacock. *King's Men: The Soldier Founders of Ontario.* Toronto: Dundurn Press, 1980.
———. *Loyalist Spy: The Experiences of Captain John Walton Meyers during the American Revolution.* Brockville, Ontario: Besancourt Publishers, 1974.
Gerlach, Don R. *Proud Patriot: Philip Schuyler and the War of Independence.* Syracuse: Syracuse University Press, 1987.
Hallahan, William. *The Day the American Revolution Began, 19 April 1776.* New York: Perennial, 2000.
Hammond, Cleon E. *John Hart: The Biography of a Signer of the Declaration of Independence.* Newfane, VT: Pioneer Press, 1977.
Hemenway, Abby Maria, ed. *Vermont Historical Gazetteer: A Magazine Embracing a History of Each Town, Civil, Ecclesiastical, Biographical and Military.* Vols. 2–3. Claremont, NH: Claremont Manufacturing Company, 1877. Also privately published in Burlington, VT, 1971.

Higgins, Patricia M. *Hidden History of Midcoast Maine.* Charleston, SC: History Press, 2014.
Hubert, Patricia M. *Major Philip M. Ulmer: A Hero of the American Revolution.* Charleston, SC: History Press, 2014.
Hughes, Rupert. *George Washington: The Rebel and the Patriot, 1762–1777.* New York: William Morrow, 1927.
Huish, Robert. *The History of the Life and Reign of William the Fourth, the Reform Monarch of England.* London: William Emans, 1837.
Humphreys, Frank Landon. *Life and Times of David Humphreys: Soldier-Statesmen-Poet.* Vol. 1. New York: G. P. Putnam's Sons, 1917.
Jacob, Mark, and Stephen H. Case. *Treacherous Beauty: Peggy Shippen, the Woman Behind Benedict Arnold's Plot to Betray America.* Guilford, CT: Guilford Press, 2012.
Jones, Charles C. *The History of Georgia.* Vol. 2. Boston: Houghton, Mifflin, 1883.
Jones, E. Alfred. *The Loyalists of New Jersey: Their Memorials, Petitions, Claims, Etc. from English Records.* Newark: New Jersey Historical Society, 1927.
Jones, Thomas. *History of New York During the Revolutionary War.* 2 vols. New York: New York Historical Society, 1879. Reprinted by New York Times, 1968.
Kranish, Michael. *Flight from Monticello: Thomas Jefferson at War.* New York: Oxford University Press, 2010.
Kwasney, Mark V. *Washington's Partisan War, 1775–1783.* Kent, OH: Kent State University Press, 1998.
Lincoln, Anna T. *Wilmington, Delaware: Three Centuries under Four Flags, 1609–1937.* Rutland, VT: Tuttle, 1937.
Livingston, William F. *Israel Putnam: Pioneer, Ranger, and Major-General.* New York: The Knickerbocker Press, 1901.
Lossing, Benson. J. *The Pictorial Field-Book of the Revolution.* 2 vols. New Rochelle, NY: Caratzas Bros., 1976. Originally published in New York by Harper and Brothers in 1850.
Maring, Norman H. *Baptists in New Jersey.* Valley Forge, PA: The Judson Press, 1964.
Marsh, Jennifer S. H. and Wilson B. Brown. *Col. William March: Vermont Patriot & Loyalist.* Denver: Tiger Rock Press, 2013.
Mass, John R. *The Road to Yorktown: Jefferson, Lafayette and the British Invasion of Virginia.* Charleston, SC: History Press, 2015.
McBurney, Christian M. *Kidnapping the Enemy: The Special Operations to Capture Generals Charles Lee and Richard Prescott.* Yardley, PA: Westholme, 2014.

_____. *The Rhode Island Campaign: The First French and American Operation in the Revolutionary War.* Yardley, PA: Westholme, 2011.

_____. *Spies in Revolutionary Rhode Island.* Charleston, SC: History Press, 2014.

McCall, Hugh Capt. *The History of Georgia. Containing Brief Sketches of the Most Remarkable Events Up to the Present Day (1784).* Reprinted by A. B. Caldwell, Atlanta, 1909.

McCrady, Edward. *The History of South Carolina in the Revolution, 1780–1783.* London: Macmillan, 1902.

McCullough, David. *1776.* New York: Simon & Schuster, 2005.

Morgan, Robert. *Boone: A Biography.* Chapel Hill: Algonquin Books of Chapel Hill, 2007.

Muhlenberg, Henry A. *The Life of Major-General Peter Muhlenberg of the Revolutionary Army.* Philadelphia: Cary and Hart, 1849.

Nagy, John A. *Rebellion in the Ranks: Mutineer of the American Revolution.* Yardley, PA: Westholme, 2008.

Nelson, Paul David. *Sir Charles Grey, First Earl Grey: Royal Soldier, Family Patriarch.* Madison: Fairleigh Dickinson University Press, 1996.

O'Kelley, Patrick. "Nothing but Blood and Slaughter." *Military Operations and Order of Battle of the Revolutionary War in the Carolinas.* Vol. 1. Booklocker.com, Inc., 2004.

O'Shaughnessy, Andrew Jackson. *The Men Who Lost America. British Leadership, the American Revolution, and the Fate of the Empire.* New Haven: Yale University Press, 2013.

Papas, Phillip. *That Ever Loyal Island. Staten Island and the American Revolution.* New York: New York University Press, 2009.

Parker, John C., Jr. *Parker's Guide to the Revolutionary War in South Carolina. Battles, Skirmishes and Murders.* West Conshohocken, PA: Infinity Publishing, 2013.

Pasko, W. W., ed. *Old New York. A Journal Relating to the History and Antiquities of New York City.* New York: Privately printed, 1890.

Philbrick, Nathaniel. *Bunker Hill: A City, a Siege, a Revolution.* New York: Viking, 2013.

Piecuch, Jim. *Three Peoples, One King. Loyalists, Indians, and Slaves in the Revolutionary South, 1775–1782.* Columbia: University of South Carolina Press, 2008.

Pocock, Tom. *Sailor King. The Life of King William IV.* London: Sinclair-Stevenson, 1991.

Powell, William S. *Dictionary of North Carolina Biography.* Vols. 1 and 3. Chapel Hill: University of North Carolina Press, 1979 and 1988.

Randall, Willard Sterne. *Benedict Arnold: Patriot and Traitor.* New York: William Morrow, 1990.

Rankin, Hugh F. *The North Carolina Continentals.* Chapel Hill: University of North Carolina Press, 1971.

Rose, Alexander. *Washington's Spies: The Story of America's First Spy Ring.* New York, NY: Bantom, 2006.

The Royal Military Calendar, or Army Service and Commission Book. Vol. 2, 3d ed. London: A. J. Valpy, 1820.

Russell, Phillips. *North Carolina in the Revolutionary War.* Charlotte: Heritage Printers, 1965.

Schama, Simon. *Rough Crossings: Britain, the Slaves and the American Revolution.* New York: HarperCollins, 2006.

Scharf, J. Thomas. *History of Delaware, 1609–1888.* Volume 1. Philadelphia: L. J. Richards & Co., 1888.

Schaukirk, Ewald Gustav. *Occupation of New York City by the British.* New York: New York Times and Arno Press, 1969. Reprinted from a copy in the collections of The New York Public Library.

Scoville, Joseph Alfred. *The Old Merchants of New York City.* Vol. 1. New York: Carleton, 1864.

Shenstone, Susan Burgess. *So Obstinately Loyal: James Moody, 1744–1809.* Montreal: McGill-Queens University Press, 2000.

Sherman, Frederic Fairchild. *Early American Painting.* New York, NY: The Century Co., 1932.

Smith, Howard W. *Benjamin Harrison and the American Revolution.* Williamsburg, Va.: Virginia Independence Bicentennial Commission, 1978.

Smith, Samuel Stelle. *Winter at Morristown 1779–1780. The Darkest Hour.* Monmouth Beach, NJ: Philip Freneau Press, 1979.

Stokes, I.N. Phelps. *The Iconography of Manhattan Island, 1498–1909.* 3 vols. New York: Robert H. Dodd, 1915–28.

Stone, William Leete, Jr. *History of New York City, from the Discovery to the Present Day.* New York: Virtue and Yorston, 1872.

Stone, William Leete, Sr. *Life of Joseph Brant, Thayen Danegea…Including the Border Wars of the American Revolution.* 2 vols. New York: A. V. Blake, 1838.

_____. *Border Wars of the American Revolution.* 2 vols. New York, 1844.

Thayer, Theodore. *Colonial and Revolutionary Morris County.* Morris County, NJ: Morris County Heritage Commission, 1975.

Thomas, Evan. *John Paul Jones: Soldier, Hero, Father of the American Navy*. New York: Simon & Schuster, 2003.
Tonsetic, Robert L. *Special Operations During the American Revolution*. Philadelphia: Casemate, 2013.
Trask, Spencer. *Bowling Green*. New York: G. P. Putnam's Sons, 1898.
Valentine's *Manual of Old New York*. New York: Valentine's Manual Inc., 1921.
Vanderpool, Ambrose E. *History of Chatham, New Jersey*. New York: Charles Francis Press, 1921.
Wade, Hebert T., and Lively, Robert A. *This Glorious Cause. The Adventures of Two Company Officers in Washington's Army*. Princeton: Princeton University Press, 1958.
Wallace, Paul A. *The Muhlenbergs of Pennsylvania*. Philadelphia: University of Pennsylvania Press, 1950.
Ward, Harry M. *Between the Lines: Banditti of the American Revolution*. Westport, CT: Praeger, 2002.
———. *George Washington's Enforcers: Policing the Continental Army*. Carbondale: Southern Illinois University Press, 2006.
Watt, Gavin K. *A Dirty, Trifling, Piece of Business: The Revolutionary War as Waged from Canada in 1781*. Vol. 1. Toronto: Dundern, 2009.
Weintraub, Stanley. *Iron Tears: America's Battle for Freedom, Britain's Quagmire: 1775–1783*.
Wheeler, John H. *Historical Sketches of North Carolina from 1584 to 1851*. Philadelphia: Lippincott, Grambo and Co., 1851.
Whittemore, Charles P. *A General of the Revolution. John Sullivan of New Hampshire*. New York, NY: Columbia University Press, 1961.
Wickes, Stephen. *History of Medicine in New Jersey and of its Medical Men from the Settlement of the Province to A.D. 1800*. Newark: Martin R. Denis and Co., 1879.
Willcox, William B. *Portrait of a General: Sir Henry Clinton in the War of Independence*. New York: Alfred A. Knopf, 1964.
Winfield, Charles H. *History of the County of Hudson, New Jersey. From Its Earliest Settlement to the Present Time*. New York: Kennard & Hay, 1874.
Ziegler, Philip. *King William IV*. First U.S. edition. New York: Harper & Row, 1971.

Published Secondary Sources— Articles

"Civil War 1781–82—Colonel David Fanning." *North Carolina University Magazine* 70–86 (1853). Also contains Judge Murphey's narrative of the life of David Fanning, written about 1822.
Dwight, Timothy. "The Story of General Wadsworth," *Maine Historical Society Quarterly* 15: 226–256 (1776).
Fowler, David J. "'Loyalty is Now Bleeding in New Jersey.' Motivations and Mentalities of the Disaffected." In Joseph S. Tiedemann, Eugene R. Fingerhut, and Robert W. Venables, eds, *The Other Loyalists: Ordinary People, Royalism, and the Revolution in the Middle Colonies, 1763–1787*. New York: State University of New York Press, 2009.
Hall, Wilbur. "Sergeant Champe's Adventure." *William and Mary College Quarterly Historical Magazine*. 2nd Series, 18:322–42 (July 1938).
Lander, James. "A Tale of Two Hoaxes in Britain and France in 1775." *The Historical Journal* 49:4, 995–1024 (2006).
Lassiter, Frances Rives. "Arnold's Invasion of Virginia." *The Sewanee Review* 9, no. 2 (April 1901), 185–203.
Lee, Thomas Armory. "The Lee Family of Marblehead." *Essex Institute Historical Collections* 52:33–48, 145–60, 225–40 and 329–44 (1916).
Maas, John. "The Greatest Terror Imaginable: Cornwallis Brings His Campaign to Goochland, June 1781." *Goochland County Historical Society Magazine* 41:12–101 (2009).
Massey, Gregory Van. "The British Expedition to Wilmington, January-November, 1781." *The North Carolina Historical Review* 66:4, 387–411 (Oct. 1989).
Maguire, Robert. "The British Secret Service and the Attempt to Kidnap General Jacob Bayley of Newbury, Vermont, 1782." *Vermont History* 44:141–67 (Summer 1976).
McGroarty, William B. "Captain Cameron and Sergeant Champe." *William and Mary College Quarterly Historical Magazine*, 2nd Series, 19:1, 49–54 (Jan. 1939).
———. "Sergeant John Champe and Certain of His Contemporaries." *William and Mary College Quarterly Historical Magazine*. 2nd Series, 17:145–75 (April 1937).
Reuter, Frank T. "'Petty Spy' or Effective Diplomat: The Role of George Beckwith." *Journal of the Early Republic* 10:4, 471–92 (Winter 1990).
Richard-Morrow, Kevin. "The Attempt to Abduct General Phillip Schuyler and the Great Kidnap Plot of 1781." *The Burning*

Issues 14:1 (March 2006). (Official Newsletter of the Burning of the Valleys Military Association, Inc.)
Rowe, Gail S. "The Travail of John McKinly, First President of Delaware." *Delaware History* 17:21–36 (Spring-Summer 1976).
Scheer, George F. "The Sergeant Major's Strange Mission." *American Heritage* 8:6, 26–29 and 98 (Oct. 1957).
Toulmin, Llewellyn M. "Backcountry Warrior: Brig. Gen. Andrew Williamson, The 'Benedict Arnold of South Carolina' and America's First Major Double Agent-Part I." *Journal of Backcountry Studies* 7:1, 1–46 (Spring 2012).
"Traditions of the American War of Independence." *The United Service Journal and Naval and Military Magazine* 438–52 (Dec. 1834).
"Washington at Morristown." *Harper's New Monthly Magazine* 18:295–305 (Feb. 1859).
Watterson, John S. III. "The Ordeal of Governor Burk.," *North Carolina Historical Review* 44:2, 95–117 (April 1971).
Wyllie, John Cook. "New Documentary Light on Tarleton's Raid: Letters of Newman Brockenbrough and Peter Lyons." *The Virginia Magazine of History and Biography* 74, No. 4 (Oct. 1966), 452–61.

Online Sources

Bell, J. L. "Did Paul Revere's Ride Really Matter." April 21, 2014. The online *Journal of the American Revolution*, at www.allthingsliberty.com.
———. "Primary Sources on Richard Stockton." Sept. 8, 2008. In J. L. Bell's online website at boston1775.blogspot.com (for this and related articles, search for "Richard Stockton").
———. "Richard Stockton and the Creation of a Legend." Sept. 18, 2008. In J. L. Bell's online website at boston1775.blogspot.com (for this and related articles, search for "Richard Stockton").
———. "Richard Stockton's Release Date." July 28, 2009. In J. L. Bell's online website at boston1775.blogspot.com (for this and related articles, search for "Richard Stockton").
Braisted, Todd. "How George Washington Saved the Life of Abraham Van Buskirk's Son." Sept. 16, 2014. The online *Journal of the American Revolution*, at www.allthingsliberty.com.
Brooking, Greg. "The Arrest of Georgia's Royal Governor Sir James Wright." May 9, 2014. The online *Journal of the American Revolution*, at www.allthingsliberty.com.
Dictionary.com online dictionary. At www.dictionary.com.
Dictionary of Canadian Biography. University of Toronto, 2003, at www.biographi.ca/en/bio.
Huggins, Benjamin. "Raid Across the Ice: The British Operation to Capture Washington." Dec. 17, 2013. The online *Journal of the American Revolution*, at www.allthingsliberty.com.
Johnson Family of Newbury, Vermont Papers, 1775–1886 catalogue entry. Vermont Historical Society. At www.vermonthistory.org (hover over Research and click on Museum Collections; click on VHS Online Catalogue; search keyword "Johnson Family of Newbury, Vermont").
"Morristown" Pamphlet. Morristown National Historical Park. National Park Service, 2013.
The National Statuary Hall Collection. At www.aoc.gov/the-national-statuary-hall-collection and search for Richard Stockton.
"Old Streets of New York." At www.oldstreets.com.
On-Line Institute for Advanced Loyalist Studies. At www.royalprovincial.com. Operated by Todd Braisted.
Parker, Hershel. "Fanning's Bloody Sabbath as Traced by Alexander Gray." May 4, 2015. The online *Journal of the American Revolution*, at www.allthingsliberty.com.
Shattuck, Gary. "Plotting the 'Sacricide' of George Washington." July 25, 2014. The online *Journal of the American Revolution*, at www.allthingsliberty.com.
Sutherland, Stuart R. J. "Moody, James" in *Dictionary of Canadian Biography* 5, University of Toronto, 2003, at www.biographi.ca/en/bio/moody_james_5E.

Newspapers and Magazines

The American Museum or repository of ancient and modern fugitive pieces, &c. prose and poetical, 1789 (Philadelphia)
The Athenaeum. Journal of Literature, Science, and the Fine Arts, 1831 (London)
Boston Evening Post, 1782 (Boston)
Connecticut Courant, 1776–77 (Hartford)
Connecticut Gazette, 1777 and 1781 (New London)
Connecticut Journal, 1777 (New Haven)
Constitutional Gazette, 1776 and 1781 (New York)
Continental Journal, 1776 (Boston)
Essex Journal, 1775 (Newburyport, MA)
Independent Chronicle, 1777 (Boston)
Massachusetts Spy, 1777 (Worcester, MA)
The Mirror of Literature, Amusement, and Instruction, 1831 (London)

New England Chronicle, 1777 (Boston)
New England Magazine, 1833 (Boston)
New Jersey Gazette, 1777–80 (New Brunswick)
New Jersey Journal, 1780 (Elizabethtown)
New York Gazette, 1779 (New York)
Norwich Packet, 1777 (Norwich, CT)
Pennsylvania Evening Post, 1777 (Philadelphia)
Pennsylvania Ledger, 1778 (Philadelphia)
Pennsylvania Packet, 1777–82 (Philadelphia)
Providence Gazette, 1781 (Providence, RI)
Rivington's *Royal Gazette*, 1776–81 (New York)
Royal American Gazette, 1777 (New York)
Royal Georgia Gazette, 1781–82. (Savannah)
St. James's Chronicle or the British Evening Post, 1777 (London)
Scots Magazine, 1781 (Edinburgh)

Unpublished Sources—Original Sources

British National Archives (Kew, England): Army Correspondence
Muster Rolls of the 17th Light Dragoons
Fraunces Tavern (New York): Henry Russell Drowne Collection
Library of Congress, Manuscript Reading Room (Washington, D.C.):
British Intelligence Memorandum Book, MMC-2248
Friedrich Wilhelm Ludolf Gerhard Augustin, Baron von Steuben Papers, 1778–1783, Microfilm
George Washington Papers, Microfilm
Maine Historical Society (Portland, Maine): Collection 112, Box 1/11
Miscellaneous Loyalist Muster Rolls, 1778–1782
National Archives (Washington, D.C.):
Papers of the Continental Congress
Revolutionary War Pension Applications
Society of the Cincinnati (Washington, D.C.): Correspondence and Images
William L. Clements Library, University of Michigan (Ann Arbor): Henry Clinton Papers

Index

Abeel, James 169, 188n105
Adams, Abigail 42
Adams, John 20, 35, 42, 63, 191n167
Adams, Samuel 7
Afghanistan War 5
African Americans 50, 52, 66–67, 138–40, 155, 156
Alamance County 152
Albany, New York 136–43
Albany County Commissioners for Detecting and Defeating Conspiracies 137, 139, 142, 144
Albermarle County 120, 124
Alden, John 178
Alexander, William 18, 163, 172, 200n55
Alexandria, Virginia 8–9, 173n3
Allaire, Anthony 125–26
Allegiance 111
Allen, Ethan 29–31, 41–42, 49, 96, 146
Allen, Ira 147
Allen, Lieutenant 180n106
Allendale, New Jersey 27
Alston, Phillip 150
American Indians 50
American Legion 97, 102, 112, 189n143, 190n149
Anderson, Timothy 180n106
André, John 75, 97, 116, 131, 195n72
Appleby, Joseph 95–96
Aquidneck Island, Rhode Island 49–53
Arbuthnot, Marriott 115
Arlington, Massachusetts 7
Armstrong, Richard 91–92
Arnold, Benedict 3, 4, 50, 78, 96–103, 105, 112–17, 118, 142, 162, 189n143, 190n151
Asgill, Charles 67
Ashe, John 151
Augusta, Georgia 9

Bagaduce, Maine 108–09; *see also* Castine
Baldwin (spy) 99, 101–02
Balfour 165

Balfour, Andrew 154, 198n23
Balfour, Margaret 154–55, 199n23
Balfour, Nisbet 130–32, 194n72
Ballstown, New York 137, 142
Barber, John W. 85
Barrington, William 52–53
Barton, William 1, 48–53, 55, 56, 57, 60, 66, 80
Basking Ridge, New Jersey 36–40, 43, 47, 83–4, 118, 178
Baurmeister, Carl Leopold 107
Bayley, Jacob 144, 146, 147–48
Beckwith, George 75–77, 82, 87, 91–93, 95–96, 189n139
Beekman, Gerardus 161, 163
Bell, J.L. 25, 173n3
Bell, William 154, 199n23
Belvoir 120
Benbridge, Henry 44, 178n84
Bennett's Island, Battle of 45–46
Bennington, Vermont 143
Bergen, New Jersey 100–01
Bergen County, New Jersey 27, 30
Berkeley, West Virginia 173n6
Bernardsville, New Jersey 36
Bettys, Joseph 137, 142–43, 144
Birch, Samuel 26–27, 88–91, 93–94, 187n98
Black Hussars 88–89
Black Rock Harbor, Connecticut 80, 82
Bladen County 151
Blauvelt, Jacobus 30–31
Bleecker, John 137, 143
Boisbertrand, Lieutenant Colonel de 36–40
Bonnell, Isaac 80–81
Boone, Daniel 121–24, 125
Boone, Nathan 124
Bordentown, New Jersey 64
Boston, Massachusetts 3, 8, 35, 88, 108–09
Boudinot, Annis 23
Boudinot, Elias 23, 31–32, 179n98
Bowers, Lemuel 182n4

214 Index

Bowling Green 101, 160
Bradford, William 36–40
Braisted, Todd 22, 176n11, 178n83, 186n88
Brandywine, Battle of 61, 63, 120
Brantley, Benjamin 156
Brest, France 69, 71
Bristol, Rhode Island 51
British army 3, 7, 17, 21, 56–57, 59, 63, 66–67, 101, 103, 108, 153, 156, 158, 160; Arnold in 116–17; authorized Livingston's abduction 77; guides for 43, 47–48; Lee considered a deserter from 41–42; New York City, Long Island and New Jersey 20–32, 33, 40; raid against Morristown 87–90, 93–95, 186n88, 187n94; raids in Virginia 117–18; at Rhode Island 49–55; Schuyler raid 135–41; see also British army regiments
British army regiments: First Regiment of Foot Guards 11; Royal Welch Fusileers 118; 16th Light Dragoons, capture of Lee 36–42, 88; 17th Light Dragoon 26, 88–91, 186n88; 34th 136–41; 37th 75; 40th 163, 171, 200n56; 42nd (Black Watch) 73, 86; 64th 41; 71st 61; 74th 109–10; 82nd 149, 152
British navy 9, 13, 90, 121; Admiral Digby targeted 161, 163–64; against Jones 69–71; Chesapeake Bay 114–116; Prince William Henry joins 158–59; weak point at Rhode Island 50–54, 57, 59
Brittain, William 182n4
Broad Street 163, 200n55
Broadway (New York City) 58, 162, 105, 106, 160, 165, 180n113
Brockenbrough, Norman 120, 122–23
Brooklyn, New York 111, 157
Brown, Thomas 9
Brownson, Nathan 156–57
Bryant, John 154, 199n23
Buckingham Palace 157–58
Bucks County 43, 64, 75
Bullion's Tavern 178n73
Bunker Hill, Battle of 8–9, 88, 149
Burgoyne, John 77, 89, 96, 136, 166, 136
Burke, Edmund 122
Burke, Thomas 4, 150–53, 154
Burr, Aaron 21, 161
Burrows, Edwin: 28–29, 55, 177n41, 180n109
Burton, Benjamin 110
Bushy Creek, North Carolina 149
Buskirk, Abraham Van 4, 28, 30
Butler, John 150
Byrd, William 112

Cambridge, Massachusetts 84
Cameron, Captain 189–90n143

Campbell, Archibald 43–44, 156
Campbell, John 108–11
Canada: base for British secret service operations 134–48, 196n28; invaded 29, 42, 50; Tories move to after war 48, 156, 178n83
Cape Fear 149–50
Cape Henlopen 116
Carleton, Guy 67, 146, 148, 166
Carlisle, Pennsylvania 47, 179–80n98
Castine, Maine 108–11
Castle Hill 120, 122, 193n37
Champe, Jane 98
Champe, John 97, 98–103, 105–06, 189–90n143, 191n167
Champe, Colonel John (father) 98
Charleston, South Carolina 87, 127–28, 149, 128–32, 152, 155–56, 187n94
Charlottesville, Virginia 118, 120–21, 193n28, 193n34
Chatham, New Jersey 169
Chatham County 149–50
Chernow, Ron 19
Cherokee 125, 127, 156
Chesapeake Bay 114–16
Christ Church (Philadelphia) 56
Christina River 181n1
Clark, Abraham 23
Clarkson, Levinus 73
Clay, Joseph 9
Cleveland, Benjamin 124–27, 194n52
Cleveland, Robert 194n53
Clifton, Daniel 199n23
Clinton, George 79, 145, 105, 137, 139, 141, 143
Clinton, Henry 3, 45, 49, 57–60, 63, 66–67, 73–74, 79, 87, 94, 101–02, 103–08, 105, 110, 117, 128, 160, 162, 164–65, 167, 185, 187
Closen, Ludwig von 41, 178n73
Coates, William 64
Cockley, John 140, 196n28
Coenties Market (New York City) 163, 172, 200n55
Coffin, Mr. 49
Colfax, William 85
College of New Jersey 20, 161
Colleton County 128–29
Collier, Colonel 154
Collins, Colonel 199n23
Communipaw Bay 101
Conanicut Island, Rhode Island 49
Concord, Massachusetts 7–8, 43, 173n1–3
Condict, Silas 86
Connecticut 9, 11, 57, 70, 106, 116, 135, 145–46, 180n106; whaleboat war with Long Island 4, 80–82, 108
Connecticut Farms, New Jersey 90
Continental army 1, 3, 8, 14–15, 17–18, 29, 64–65, 78, 81, 84, 87, 96–97, 111, 113, 118, 120, 129, 145, 151, 153, 200n55; Barton

Index

named colonel of 53; first abduction 60; Champe deserted from 100–01, 102, 103; Lee named second-in-command and later terminated 35–36, 56; officers angry at Hayne's execution 131–32; Schuyler in 134–36; *see also* Continental army regiments

Continental army regiments: Webb's Additional 59, 106, 191*n*178; 1st New Jersey 161; 1st New York 137, 140, 195*n*11; 2nd Rhode Island 94; 11th Virginia 118; 12th 19; 13th 64

Continental Congress 9, 11, 14, 16, 35, 71, 75, 97, 111, 114, 116, 136, 150, 163; anti-kidnapping law passed 63–67; Asgill spared 67; Barton rewarded 53; Champe's family rewarded 103, 190*n*143; delegate captured 120; Hayne's hanging, retaliation for considered 132–33; kidnapping plan funded 104–05; Laurens captured 121; Lee kicked out 56; McKinly exchanged 62–63; Moody tries to steal papers of 79, 184*n*35; on prison conditions 31–33; retaliation threatened 42, 55; signers of the Declaration of Independence targeted 20–27; Witham Stockton appeals to 46–48

Cooch's Bridge, Delaware 181*n*1
Corlies, John 196*n*28
Cornwallis, Charles 26, 35–36, 43–45, 113, 179, 117–18, 121–24, 131–32, 133, 149, 151, 153, 160, 179*n*86
Covenhoven, John 21–26, 176*n*8
Coxe, Captain 150
Coxe's Mill, North Carolina 150
Craig, James Henry 149–53, 155
Cranbury, New Jersey 46
Cranes Mills, New Jersey 87, 90
Cuckoo Tavern 118, 193*n*28
Cumberland County 151, 198*n*23
Cunningham, William 29, 31
Cushing, Charles 6, 108
Cushing, Maine 110

Dark, Thomas 153
Davis, Myrick killed 156–57
Declaration of Independence 4, 20–27, 113
Deep River 127
Delaware River 21, 36, 41, 62, 65
Delaware 4, 11, 61–63, 74, 181*n*1
Derby, Connecticut 106, 145
Destouches, Chevalier 114–16
Diemar, Frederick 88, 187–88*n*103
Digby, Robert 158–60, 161–66, 171–72, 199*n*55
Dinkins, Henry 127
Dobbs Ferry, New York 95, 107
Drake 70
Draper, Lyman 125

Drowne, Solomon 18–19, 175*n*42
Dunham, Asher 45–47, 179*n*86
Dunmore, Earl of *see* Murray, John
Dunmore's War 123
Dutchess County 145
Duxbury, Massachusetts 109

East River 67, 106, 163, 200*n*55
East Windsor, Connecticut 53, 180*n*106
Elizabeth River 114
Elizabethtown, New Jersey 72–73, 87–93, 169, 186*n*86, 187*n*99, 188*n*125
Elkins, Jonathan, and Joseph 197*n*51
Elkton, Maryland 115, 181*n*1
Emmanuel, David 156–57
Eustis, William 19
L'Eveillé 114
Ewald, Johann 116–17

Fairfield, Connecticut 80, 185*n*51
Fanning, David 4, 149–53, 153–56, 198*n*23
Faragher, John Mack 124
Fayette County 123
Fell, John 27–33, 42, 75, 177*n*40
Fenno (Miss) 109
Ferguson, Israel 142
Few, Benjamin 128
First New York Continental Regiment 137, 140, 195–96*n*11
Fischer, David Hackett 173*n*1
Fisher, Andrew 61, 181*n*1
Five Nations (Indian tribes) 144
Flatbush, Brooklyn 81
Flavell, Julie 14
Florida 156
Ford, Gabriel 85
Ford, Jacob, Jr. 83–84, 185*n*65
Ford, Theodosia 84, 86
Ford Mansion 83–95, 185*n*65
Foreman, David 67
Fort Barton 56
Fort George 108–11
Fort Lee 35
Fort Mercer 62
Fort Mifflin 62
Fort Ninety-Six 126–27
Fort Schuyler 144
Fort Stanwix 144
Fort Ticonderoga 21, 29, 33, 96, 146
Fort Washington 28, 35
France/French 36–38, 41, 67, 69, 71, 79, 95, 101, 114–17, 132–33, 136, 157, 158, 160, 165, 191
Franklin, Benjamin 4, 11, 122
Franklin, William 4, 11, 43, 62–63, 67, 74, 183*n*13
Fraser, Francis 46–47
Fraser, Thomas 129

216 Index

Fredericksburg, Virginia 118
French and Indian War 28, 33, 136
French navy 101, 114–16
Frenchman's Bay 111
Fryer, Mary Beacock 140–41

Gage, Thomas 7, 173n3
Gaine, Hugh 93
Gansevoort, Peter 144–45
Gardiner's Bay 114
Gates, Ezra 148
Gates, Horatio 37, 47, 136
George III, King 10, 11–14, 33, 42, 54, 55, 157–60, 166
Georgia 9–11, 128, 156–57; see also Augusta; Savannah
Gerlach Don 196n15
Germain, George 71
German auxiliaries (Hessians) 26, 41–42, 48, 160, 163, 166, 181n1, 200n56
German regiments: Diemar's Black Hussars 88–89, 187–88n103; grenadiers, Landgrave and Knyphausen 200n56; jägers 117
Gerry, Elbridge 7, 20, 23, 173n1
Gibbons, Mary 17–19
Gibbs, Caleb 16, 84
Glen, Henry 139
Gloucester County 65
Glover, Isaac 80–81
Golson, Captain 150
Graham, Walter 52–53
Grand Duke 82
Grant, James 44
Graves, Mary 125
Gray, Alexander 154–55, 198n23
Great Britain 11–14, 33, 42, 69–71
Great Kidnap Caper of 1781 137, 142–48
Greene, Nathanael 16–19, 35, 118, 129–30, 131–33, 150, 153, 155–56, 157, 189, 194n72
Greenman, Jeremiah 94
Grey, Charles 169, 187n99
Grey, William de 13–14

Habersham, Joseph 10
Hackensack, New Jersey 93
Haddonfield, New Jersey 65, 181n124
Haldiman, Frederick 134–36, 141, 143, 147
Halfmoon, New York 145
Halifax, Canada 111
Halifax, North Carolina 151
Hamilton, Alexander 59–60, 63, 138
Hamilton, Dunbar (Earl of Selkirk) 69–70
Hammett, William 5, 65–66
Hammond, Andrew Snape 61–62
Hammond, Samuel 128
Hampshire County 103, 191n167
Hancock, John 7, 16, 22, 121
Hanover County 118

Hanover Square (New York City) 161, 163–64, 171, 199–200n55
Harcourt, William 1, 23, 36–41, 43–45, 55, 83, 109, 178n83, 179n86
Harden, George 145
Harden, William 128
Hardyston, New Jersey 76
Harnett, Cornelius 151
Harrison, Benjamin 20, 120
Hart, John 23, 26
Hart, Reverend Joshua 30
Harvard College 109
Hawley, David 81–82
Hay, Chris 178n83- 84, 192n189
Hayne Hall 128
Hayne, Isaac 5, 128–33, 194–95n72
Head of Elk, Maryland 115
Heath, William 18, 107, 191n78
Hemings, Martin 121
Hempstead, New York 89
Henderson, William 131
Hessians see German auxiliaries
Hickey, Thomas 16–19
Hildebrand, H. Harvey 44
Hillsborough, North Carolina 151–53
Hodgkins, Joseph 19
Holland 121
Hoops, Robert 77
Hoosick Falls, New York 137, 143
Horseneck, New Jersey 169
Howard, Matthew 137, 143
Howe, Henry 85–86
Howe, Richard 22
Howe, Robert 9, 174n11
Howe, William 20, 22–23, 26–28, 35, 42, 45, 47, 55–56, 59, 61–63, 176n8
Howland's Ferry, Rhode Island 56
Huddy, Josiah 67
Hudson, Christopher 121
Hudson River 36, 83, 89–91, 93–95, 96, 99, 101–02, 137, 139, 163–64; Humphreys's raid 106–08
Huggins, Benjamin 90–91
Hughes, Hugh 46
Hughes, Thomas 107
Humphreys, David 104, 105–08
Hunter, Andrew 155–56
Hunterdon County, New Jersey 26, 75

Iliff, John 32, 75
Indians 50, 123, 127, 139, 141, 156, 196n30
Iraq War 5, 55
Ireland 150
Iron Hill, Battle of 181n1
Isle aux Noix, Canada 147

Jacksonborough, South Carolina 128
Jamaica, New York 88, 90, 186n88

James River 112, 118, 124
James's Island 152
Jamestown, Rhode Island 49
Jamestown, Virginia 112
Jefferson, Thomas 4, 8, 112, 113, 117–21, 123, 193n37
Jersey (prison ship) 111, 157, 166
Jersey City, New Jersey 77
Jetson (a Tory kidnapper) 65
Jockey Hollow, New Jersey 84–85, 185n65
Johnson, Abigail (formerly Carleton) 146, 148
Johnson, John 134
Johnson, Thomas 4, 145–48
Jones, Daniel 29
Jones, John 108
Jones, John Paul 3, 59, 68, 69–71
Jones, Dr. Noble Wimberly 9
Jones, Thomas 80–82, 89, 93, 188n124
Jouett, Jack 118–21, 123
Jouett, John 123–24

Kennedy, Archibald 57, 106, 108, 160, 161, 180n113
Kentucky Territory 123–24, 191n167
Ketchum, Isaac 16, 19
King, Mr. 154
King's American Rangers 109, 145, 192n188
King's Ferry, New York 36
King's Militia Volunteers 80
King's Mountain, Battle of 125–26
Kingston, Massachusetts 109
Kinloch, Francis 120
Kirkcudbright, Scotland 69
Kirkebride, Joseph 64
Knox, Judge 181n19
Knyphausen, Wilhelm von 61, 74–76, 82–93, 106–08, 187–88n103
Krafft, John von 107
Kranish, Michael 102, 118, 193n34

Lafayette, Marquis de 96, 98, 115–17
Lake Champlain 135
Lake Champlain, Battle of 96, 142, 117
Lancaster, Pennsylvania 64
Lander, James 14
Laurens, Henry 48, 63–64, 121–22
Lawrence Brook 46
Lawrence Island, New Jersey 45
Lee, Arthur 12, 14
Lee, Charles 1, 3, 5, 8, 16, 24, 33–41, 48, 55, 55–56, 60, 80, 84, 83, 88, 118, 178n83, 180n113
Lee, Henry (Light Horse Harry) 98–103, 128, 131, 189–90n143
Lee, Jeremiah 7–8
Lee, Richard Henry 22–23, 114
Lee, William 12

Lee's Legion 98–103
Legrange, Jellis 142–43
Lenoir, William 125
Leslie, Alexander 152–53, 155–56
Lewis, Francis 26, 89
Lewis, Nicolas 124
Lewis, Thomas 156–57
Lexington and Concord, Battle of 7–8, 35, 109
Lexington, Massachusetts 7–8, 173n1, 173n3
Liberty Corner, New Jersey 178n73
Liberty Hall 72–73, 167, 182n4
Life Guard *see* Washington's Life Guard
Lindley's Mill, North Carolina 152
Lippincott, Richard 67
Little Egg Harbor 75
Livingston, Catherine 73
Livingston, William (governor) 4, 5, 21, 27, 32, 63, 72–79, 167, 182n4
Livingston, William, Jr. 74
Livingston family 136
Lloyd's Neck, Long Island 80–81
Lockwood, Samuel 81–82
London, England , 13–14, 16, 41–43, 50, 54–55, 67, 69–70, 121, 132–33, 161, 163, 166
Long (Captain) 109–10
Long Island 20, 26–27, 30, 48, 62, 80–82, 89–90, 92, 169, 108, 111, 166–67, 185n49–51
Long Island, Battle of 26, 28, 35, 88
Long Island Sound 80–82, 114–15
Longfellow, Henry Wadsworth 111
Lossing, Benson J. 85–86, 196n30
Loudoun County 98, 103, 173n6, 191n167
Louis XIV, King 67
Louisa County 118
Lovell, James 63
Lowery, Joseph 77
Lynch, Michael 16
Lynnhaven Bay 114–16
Lyons, Peter 122

Maas, John 193n28, 193n37
Mackenzie, Frederick 54
Madison, James 21
Maine 96, 117, 108–11, 192n88
Majendie, Henry 158, 161
Manhattan Island 3, 16–19, 57–60, 90, 94, 100, 105–08, 160–66, 171–72, 199–200n55
Manlove, Boaz 62
Marion, Francis 156
Marquard, Carl Levin 95
Martin, Isaac 76, 183n22
Martin, John 156
Martin, Josiah 9, 174n11
Martin, Thomas Byam 157–58
Maryland 115, 181n1; *see also* Elkton; Head of Elk

Index 217

218 Index

Massachusetts 7, 20, 23, 35, 43, 49, 64, 108–11, 173n3
Mater, Cyrenus 21, 26
Mathews, David 16–19, 32, 74, 104
Maxwell, Robert 77
Maxwell, William 61, 73
McCall, Hugh 156
McDougall, Alexander 103–06
McGroarty, William Buckner 189–90n143
McKean, Thomas 62–63
McKinly, John 4, 11, 61–63, 74
McLane, Louis 165, 200n61
McLoughlin, Thomas 129
McLeod, Kenneth 120–21, 193n33
McNab (British soldier) 109–10
McNair, Ralph 167
Meade, Richard Kidder 86
Mebane, Robert 152
Mee, John 32, 75
Meyers, John Walden 135–42, 195n5–6
Meyers's Independent Company 136
Middlesex County, New Jersey 46
Mifflin, Thomas 18
Mill Prison 197n51
Mill River 109
Millikin, William 154
Monhegan Island 110
Monmouth County 66–67
Monmouth Court House, Battle of 56, 88
Montgomery, Richard 42
Monticello 120–22, 193n34
Montreal, Canada 135, 147, 197n51
Moody, James 4, 75–79
Moody, John 78, 79
Moore County 155
Morgantown, West Virginia 191n167
Morris County, New Jersey 45, 83
Morris-Jumel Mansion 106
Morristown, New Jersey 4, 32, 36–37, 73–74, 82–94, 169, 185n64, 186n88, 188n124, 189n135
Morristown National Historical Park 185n65
Morven 21–26
Mount Independence, New York 146
Mount Vernon, Virginia 8–9, 173–4n6
Muhlenberg, John Peter 113–17
Murder's Creek, New York 106
Murray, Francis 64
Murray, John (Earl of Dunmore) 8–9, 173n6

Narragansett Bay 48–56
National Statuary Hall Collection 25–26
Nelson, Horatio 165
Nelson, Thomas 43
Neuse River 151
New Bern, North Carolina 9
New Brunswick, Canada 156

New Brunswick, New Jersey 35, 45, 73, 107
New Hampshire 148
New Jersey 2, 4–5, 6, 11, 17, 21–26, 27–32, 32, 35–41, 40, 42, 43–48, 49, 63, 64–67, 72–79, 82–94, 99, 145, 161, 163, 165, 167, 176, 177, 181, 185, 186, 199
New Jersey Volunteers 21–22, 26, 28–30, 32, 43–48, 75–76, 89, 176n5, 192n188
New Market, New Jersey 179n86
New Windsor, Connecticut 107
New York 4, 12, 14, 21, 26, 41, 46, 63, 79–80, 87, 105, 145, 134–44, 166
New York, New York 2, 3–4, 12, 14–19, 20–21, 26–33, 35, 41–42, 57–60, 63, 67, 72–79, 80–84, 87–94, 96–108, 111, 117, 145, 157, 160–66, 171–73, 180n113, 187n98, 188n124, 200n55–56, 201n1
Newark, Delaware 181n1
Newark Mountain Meeting (Newark), New Jersey 87, 91, 98, 186n86, 188n108
Newbury, Vermont 144–45, 147–48
Newport, Rhode Island 1, 48–50, 53–54, 66, 79–80, 114–16, 198n23
Newtown, New Jersey 77
Newtown, Pennsylvania 64
Nielson, John 46–47
Norfolk, Virginia 173n5
North Carolina 4, 9, 124–27, 149, 150–55
Nova Scotia, Canada 79, 156
Number One Broadway 57, 106, 160, 162, 165, 165, 180n113; *see also* Kennedy, Archibald

Oconee County 127
Ogden, Matthias 161–65, 171–72, 199n55, 200n58
O'Keefe, Sergeant 29, 31
Old Blazing Star Ferry 91–92
Olsen, Eric 185–86n70
Oneida Indians 139
Ontario, Canada 134
Orne, Azor 7
Overing, Henrietta 51, 53
Overing, Henry John 49
Overing, Mary 51, 53

Page, Jacob 197n51
Paine, Robert Treat 23
Paramus, New Jersey 27, 87, 91
Parker, Hershel 198n23
Parker, James 31–32
Parliament 12–13
Parsippany, New Jersey 73–74, 77, 182n4
Parsons, Samuel 57–60, 185n49
The Pastures 137–38
Pattison, James 90
Paulus Hook, New Jersey 28, 33, 77, 86–87, 89–91, 100–01, 169
Peacham, Vermont 146

Pearl Street 161
Pennington, New Jersey 36, 40, 45
Pennsylvania 11, 21, 36–37, 43, 46, 63–64, 67, 75, 79, 114
Penobscot Expedition 109
Penobscot River 109
Perth Amboy, New Jersey 21, 73, 91, 188n108
Peters, Thomas 179–80n98
Petersburg, Virginia 103, 118
Philadelphia, Pennsylvania 8, 21, 26, 33, 36, 46–47, 56, 61–65, 75, 79, 88, 97, 111, 114, 121, 132, 167, 179n94, 181n24, 192n190; see also Continental Congress
Phillips, William 117
Phips, David 111
Piecuch, Jim 133
Pintard, John 30, 177n40
Pintard, Lewis 29–32, 177n40
Plymouth, Massachusetts 109, 111
Point of Fork, Virginia 118
Portland, Maine 111
Portsmouth, England 158
Portsmouth, Virginia 112–17
Potter, Abel 53
Prescott, Richard 1, 5, 48–56, 57, 60, 66, 80, 180n106
Prince George 158–61
Prince William 160
Princeton, New Jersey 20, 23–25, 43, 45–46
Princeton University *see* College of New Jersey
Prisoners, in the Provost 29–32, 69–71
Pritchard, Azariah 144, 145–46, 147–48
Privy Council, New Jersey 65
Providence, Rhode Island 48, 56, 66
Provost, British jail, New York City 29–31, 177n40–41
Prudence Island, Rhode Island 51
Putnam, Israel 18, 46–47

Quebec, Canada 96, 135, 143, 146, 197n51
Quebec, Battle of 116–17, 161
Queen's Rangers 82–84, 86–92, 112, 118, 187n94
Quibbletown, New Jersey 179n86

Raeburn's Creek, South Carolina 149
Rahway, New Jersey 87, 90–93
Ramsey, Ambrose 150, 198n4
Randall, Willard Sterne 101
Randolph County 153, 155, 198n23
Ranger 69–70
Raritan River 37, 45
Raven 10
Rawdon, Francis (Earl of Moira) 130–33, 194n72
Read, George 62
Red Doe 149, 155–56

Reed, Joseph 64, 79, 97, 181n19
Reid, John 151
Rein, John 149
Rensselaer, Henry van 145
Revere, Paul 109, 173n3
Rhode Island 48–56, 57, 60, 66, 75, 93–94, 114, 132, 180n106
Rhode Island Historical Society 53
Richardson, Frank 11, 13
Richmond, Duke of 133
Richmond, New York 88, 92
Richmond, Virginia 112–13, 118, 123
Riddle, William 5, 126–27, 194n52
Riedesel, Ferderika Charlotte Louise von Massow 166, 167
Riedesel, Friedrich 166–67
Riley, James 145
Rivanna River 120
Robertson, James 28–32, 77
Robins, William 179n86
Robinson, Thomas 62
Rochambeau, General 114–15
Rochford, Earl of 12–14
Rocky River 151
Rodney, Caesar 62–63
Roebuck 61
Rogers, Robert 145–46
Rogers's Rangers 109, 140, 145
Rome, New York 144
Romney, Virginia 103
Romulus 115
Royal Navy *see* British navy
Rush, Dr. Benjamin 20, 21–26
Russell, John 66–67
Rutherford, Walter 31–32
Rutledge, John 128

Sabine, Lorenzo 142
Sag Harbor, New York 106
St. Augustine, Florida 156
St. Clair, Arthur 90, 92–94
Saint-Jean-sur-Richelieu, Canada 135
St. Johns, Canada 135, 139, 142–43, 146–47
St. Leger, Barry 135, 139–41, 143, 145–46
Salem, Massachusetts 141
Salisbury, North Carolina 125, 198n23
Sandy Hook, New Jersey 66–67, 108
Saratoga, New York 89
Saratoga, Battle of 89, 96, 116–17, 136, 144, 166, 186
Saratoga County 145, 196n28
Savage 174n6
Savannah, Georgia 9, 11, 156
Sayre, Stephen 11–14
Sayreville, New Jersey 45
Scarborough 10
Schenectady, New York 139
Schuyler, Catharine 138, 140–41, 196n28

Schuyler, Elizabeth 138
Schuyler, Margaret 141
Schuyler, Philip 4, 134–41, 143, 145
Schuyler Mansion 137–38, 142, 196n15
Scotland 69–71
Scott, Charles 18
Selkirk, Earl of 69–71
Selkirk, Lady 70–71
Shadwell Plantation 193n37
Sherwood, Justus 135, 142–45, 146–48
Shippen, Peggy 97
Shrewsbury, New Jersey 66
Silliman, Gold Selleck 80–82, 89, 185n51, 185n57
Silliman, Mary 80–82, 185n49, 185n51, 185n57
Silliman, William 81–82
Simcoe, John Graves 81, 82–84, 86–87, 91–92, 96, 112, 118, 169, 184–85n49, 186n86
Simsbury Mines, Connecticut 135
Skinner, Cortland 43–44, 48, 75, 89, 92, 169
Smith, Judge William 24, 74, 88, 92–93, 160
Smithtown, New York 106
Smyth, George 134–35, 141, 142–45, 146–48
Solebay 62
South 11, 118, 120–22, 124, 126–33, 149, 155–56, 187n94
South River 46
South Street Seaport 163
Spain 158, 161
Spencer, Joseph 57
Spies and spying 32, 57, 59, 94, 99, 106–07, 114–15, 144, 164–65, 180, 200n58
Staten Island, New York 45, 66–67, 72–73, 82, 86, 88–90, 92–93, 107, 165, 169, 183n22
Staunton, Virginia 123–24
Steuben, Baron von 113–15, 118
Stirling, Lord *see* Alexander, William
Stirling, Thomas 73–74, 86, 89, 91–93, 169, 186n86
Stockton, Charles Witham 109–11, 192n188
Stockton, Richard of 4, 20–26, 29, 45, 122, 176n8
Stockton, Richard Witham 24, 43–48, 109, 178n83, 178n84, 179n86, 179–80n98
Stone, William Leete 141, 145, 196n30
Stringer, Samuel 142
Stuart, Gilbert 53
Sullivan, Daniel 111
Sullivan, John 36, 40, 66, 111, 144
Sullivan's Island 152
Sussex County 75, 77, 183n22
Swan Tavern 120
Syren 9

Tarleton, Banastre 36–40, 44–45, 117–24
Tarrytown, New York 30

Tassel, Cornelius, and Peter Van 30
Tatom, A. 154
Thomaston, Maine 108
Thompson, William 63
Tilly, Le Gardeur de 114–15
Titus, Cornelius 66–67
Tiverton, Rhode Island 48, 56
Totowa, New Jersey 100
Tower of London 121–22
Trenton, New Jersey 77
Trenton, Battle of 41
Trinity Church (New York City) 27
Trinity Church (Newport) 53
Trumbull, John, Jr. 40
Tryon, William 16–19, 103–4
Tubbs, John 140, 196n28
Tuscarora Indians 139
Twiggs, John 156

Valley Forge, Pennsylvania 56, 64
Van Cortland family 136
Vanleer, Benjamin 65, 181n24
Van Rensselaer family 136
Van Schaik, Gosen 137
Van Schaik's Regiment 137
Varnum, James 132
Vergennes, Comte de 67
Vermont 4, 29, 41, 56, 134–35, 143–48
Vermont Historical Society 148
Victoria, Queen 166
Virginia 8–9, 12, 20, 43, 98–99, 103, 112–24, 126, 189–90n143, 191n167, 199n23
Virginia legislature 118–24
Virnejoux, Captain de 36–40

Wadsworth, Elizabeth 109–10
Wadsworth, Peleg 6, 108–11
Walker, John 120
Walker, Dr. Thomas 120, 122–23
Wall Street 161
Wallingford, Samuel 70
Ward, Artemis 35
Ward, Hans 140
Warren, James 23
Warren, Rhode Island 48
Warren County 75
Warwick Neck, Rhode Island 51–53, 180n104
Washington, George 1, 3, 5, 8–9, 14–19, 21–22, 27–28, 35, 43, 46–47, 53, 55–56, 57–60, 67, 64–65, 72–73, 78–79, 81, 82–94, 95–103, 113, 115, 132, 142, 147–48, 157–66, 167, 169, 171–72, 173–74n6, 175n42, 189–90n143, 191n167, 199n55, 200n58, 200n61–62
Washington, John Augustine 173n6
Washington, Lund 8, 173–74n6
Washington, Martha 8–9, 85–86, 173–74n6

Washington's Life Guard 16–19, 84–85, 95, 185n68
Waxhaws, South Carolina 118
Webster, James 22, 176n6
Welles, Roger 106
West Point, New York 78, 96–97, 106, 117, 142
West Virginia 173n6, 191n167
Westchester County, New York 30
Westover, Virginia 112
Weymouth, Nova Scotia 79
Wharton, Thomas 64
Wheeler, John w 126
White, Joseph 147–48
White, Mary 36–40
White, Philip 67
White Plains, New York 36, 95
White Plains, Battle of 88
Whitehaven, Great Britain 69
Whitestone, Long Island 26, 89
Widow White's Tavern 36–40, 55, 83
Wilfong, George 125
Wilkes, John 11–14
Wilkes County 124, 127, 194n52
Wilkesboro, North Carolina 194n52
Wilkinson, James 37–40, 57–60
William Henry, Prince 157–66, 171–72, 199–200n55, 200n61–62; see also William IV, King
William IV, King 161, 166, 200n61; see also William Henry, Prince
Williams, John 150
Williamsburg, Virginia 8
Williamson, Andrew 4, 127–28, 129–30, 194n54
Wilmington, Delaware 61
Wilmington, North Carolina 9, 149–53
Witherspoon, Reverend John 21
Wolcott, Erastus 180n106
Woodbridge, New Jersey 79, 87, 91–92
Wright, James seizure of 9–10

Yadkin River 125
York, Pennsylvania 47, 64
Yorktown, Virginia 138
Yorktown, Battle of 67, 117, 123, 133, 138, 147, 149, 151, 153, 157, 160

Zandt, Wynant van 30–31

www.ingramcontent.com/pod-product-compliance
Ingram Content Group UK Ltd.
Pitfield, Milton Keynes, MK11 3LW, UK
UKHW041952140426
5217IPUK00015B/766